GUIDE TO THE
Birds *of* Alaska

ROBERT H. ARMSTRONG

GUIDE TO THE
Birds *of* Alaska

4TH EDITION

ROBERT H. ARMSTRONG

Alaska Northwest Books®
Anchorage • Portland

Dedicated to the memory of M. E. "Pete" Isleib,
a good friend who was always willing to help.
Pete contributed so much to our knowledge of Alaska's birds.

Fourth Edition 1995
Updated 2000
Eighth Printing 2007

Library of Congress Cataloging-in-Publication Data
Armstrong, Robert H., 1936-
    Guide to the birds of Alaska / by Robert H. Armstrong. — 4th ed.
        p.   cm.
    Includes bibliographical references and index.
    ISBN-10 0-88240-462-8   ISBN-13 978-0-88240-462-2
    1. Birds—Alaska—Identification.   I. Title.
QL684.A4A75 1995
598.29798—dc20   95-5431
                                                              CIP

Managing Editor: Ellen Harkins Wheat
Editor: Don Graydon
Production Editor: Kris Fulsaas
Designers: Cameron Mason, Alice Merrill (front cover)
Map: Vikki Leib

Photographs: Photographs by the author except as noted in Photo Credits.
Front Cover: *Bald Eagle.* End Papers: *Wing feathers, Chestnut-backed Chickadee.* Title Page: *Bald Eagle.* Back Cover: *Tufted Puffin* (D. Menke); *Black Oystercatcher; Gray Jay.*

Alaska Northwest Books®
An imprint of Graphic Arts Center Publishing Company
P.O. Box 10306, Portland, OR 97296-0306
503/226-2402; www.gacpc.com

Printed in China

CONTENTS

FOREWORD

Watching birds is fun! Being able to identify the birds you are watching increases this pleasure. And watching birds in Alaska has its special excitement, both for resident observers and visitors.

This photographic book on Alaska's birds is designed to enhance your enjoyment of birds by helping you to identify them, understand their habits, and know where to find them.

Seeing birds that have adapted to the harsh environments of the boreal forest, tundra, and sea ice of the North, and that cannot be seen farther south, is one exciting aspect of observing birds in Alaska. Even those bird species that visit more southern climes during migration and winter often look and behave quite differently when on their northern breeding grounds. Not only may their plumage be strikingly different from in winter, but they may occupy entirely different habitats (e.g., many sandpipers and other shorebirds nest in Alaska's mountains, far from seashores and marshes) and they may be singing and executing various courtship antics that they perform only on their northern breeding grounds.

In addition to the northern-adapted species, two other groups of geographically restricted birds add particular zest to bird watching in Alaska. The first is a group of endemics that apparently differentiated, historically, in the Bering/Chukchi sea area ("Beringia") in isolated glacial refugia. These birds still have their centers of abundance in this relatively inaccessible region, and many have not extended their ranges much beyond the Aleutian Islands or southcoastal Alaska. Hence, it is necessary to visit Alaska (or Siberia) to see many of these geographically restricted species (e.g., Red-faced Cormorant; Emperor Goose; Red-legged Kittiwake; Aleutian Tern; Parakeet, Least, and Whiskered auklets; and McKay's Bunting).

The second group is sometimes referred to as the "Asiatics," birds that have their origins in Asia and most of which can be seen in North America only in Alaska. Some are regular breeders (Bar-tailed Godwit, Bluethroat, Arctic Warbler, White Wagtail, and Yellow Wagtail), but most are migrants or are casual or accidental visitants. The occurrence of these Asiatics is facilitated by the nearness of Siberia, with some species passing across parts of Alaska—especially the western Aleutian Islands and the islands of the Bering Sea—during migration. A few even straggle occasionally as far as mainland Alaska (e.g., Spot-billed Duck, Common Crane, Common Ringed Plover, Eurasian Dotterel, Wood Sandpiper, Terek Sandpiper, Great Knot, Sharp-tailed Sandpiper, Eurasian Hoopoe, Eurasian Wryneck, Common House-Martin, Eyebrowed Thrush, Dusky Thrush, Fieldfare, Brambling, Eurasian Bullfinch, etc.).

One of the most exciting aspects of watching birds in Alaska is that there is so much yet to be learned about them. We are still at the frontier of knowledge about so many aspects of Alaska's bird life that any observant bird-watcher has a good chance of contributing new and valuable information about them: range extensions; dates of migration, eggs, young, fledglings; clutch and brood

Arctic Tern

sizes; food habits; flight speeds and distances; habitat requirements during nesting, migration, winter; behavior relative to others of their own species, to different species, and under various kinds of stress, including that caused by man; behavioral means of adapting to the rigors of northern life; ad infinitum.

Watching birds is indeed fun, whether you watch casually or seriously. Whether your enjoyment comes from watching birds through a window of your home as they sing or feed; from adding new kinds of birds to your life list; from seeing birds with different plumages, habits, and behavior patterns; from studying the natural history or ecology of a species; or from matching wits with game birds during the hunting season, you will be glad to have this Alaska bird guide, with its beautiful photographs, close at hand.

Brina Kessel
Professor of Zoology and Curator
Terrestrial Vertebrates Collection
University of Alaska Fairbanks

ACKNOWLEDGMENTS

To the many fine ornithologists and birders who have published information on Alaska's birds and answered my many questions, I am especially grateful. Without their publications and help, this book would not have been possible.

Those who have been most helpful by providing information outside of publications include Ed Bailey, Bob Day, Dan Gibson, Frank Glass, Richard Gordon, Pete Isleib, Brina Kessel, Jim King, Richard MacIntosh, Don McKnight, Doug Murphy, Bruce Paige, Dennis Paulson, John Pitcher, Dan Timm, Thede Tobish, Jr., and George West.

The publications by Brina Kessel and Dan Gibson at the University of Alaska Fairbanks have been invaluable. Richard Gordon of Juneau reviewed the entire manuscript and helped me a great deal.

Information on the status and distribution charts is based on Gabrielson and Lincoln (1959), Gibson and Kessel (1992), Johnson and Herter (1989), Kessel (1989), and Kessel and Gibson (1978); seasonal bird sightings as reported by Gibson (1978-1986), Gibson, Tobish, and Isleib (1987-1989), Tobish and Isleib (1989-1992), and Tobish (1993-1999); plus several published checklists and the knowledge of individuals familiar with specific areas. The species of birds occurring in Alaska are based on Gibson (1999).

Many voice descriptions used in this book are from The Audubon Society Field Guide to North American Birds—Western Region (1977), text by Miklos D. F. Udvardy, and reprinted here by permission of Alfred A. Knopf.

Sandhill Crane

A NOTE ON ALASKA'S BIOGEOGRAPHIC REGIONS

To understand and visualize the distribution of birds found throughout Alaska, the state has been subdivided into six biogeographic regions based on Kessel and Gibson (1978). Each region has a characteristic flora, geography, and climate that influences the species, numbers, and origins of birds found there. These regions, briefly defined below, are outlined on the map on pages 8 and 9, and are referred to throughout this book.

Southeastern—Sitka spruce-hemlock coastal forest predominates. A number of species, both seabirds and others, reach either their northern or southern distribution extremes in this region. Interior Canada's birds enter this region via mainland river systems.

Southcoastal—Sitka spruce-hemlock coastal forest predominates, but its composition is less richly developed than in southeastern Alaska. This region includes the northernmost open water for overwintering waterfowl and shorebirds as well as major migration stopover sites for Pacific Coast migrants and for some trans-Pacific migrants.

Southwestern—Tundra and marine influences predominate. Some bird species breed only in this region (Red-legged Kittiwake and Whiskered Auklet). A number of Old World species are regular migrants and visitants as well as occasional breeders in this region. Albatrosses and shearwaters breed in the southern hemisphere and visit this region's offshore waters—some species in the millions during summer.

Central—Taiga habitats, especially white spruce, predominate; alpine tundra occurs above 750 meters in foothills and mountain systems. Interior Canada's bird species reach the northwestern extremity of their range within this region.

Western—Tundra and marine influences predominate. Pack ice covers much of the sea surface in winter. Some bird species (Black Turnstone, Bristle-thighed Curlew, and McKay's Bunting) nest only in this region, and most Old World species that have become well-established breeders in Alaska have done so here.

Northern—Tundra and marine influences predominate; the ocean surface, except for leads, is frozen 9 to 10 months a year and the ice pack is never far from shore. Most birds (Old World and Aleutian species) enter this region from the west and from the east via the Canadian Arctic. Taiga birds reach the region only casually or rarely via the drainage systems of the Brooks Range.

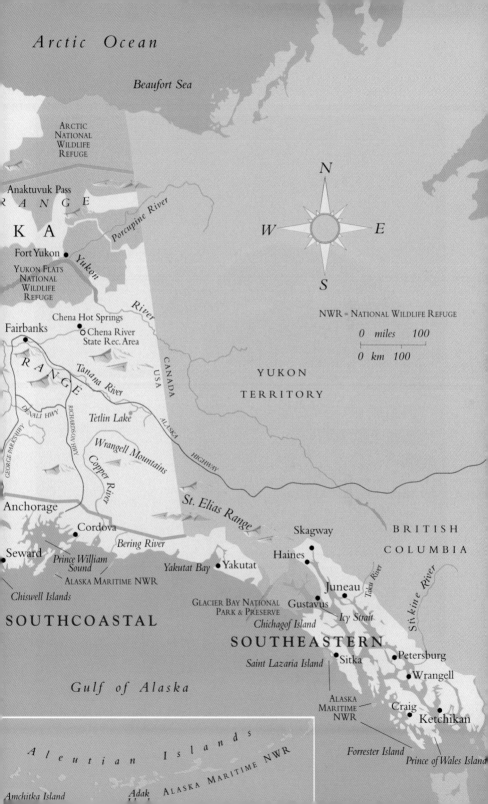

Great Blue Heron

INTRODUCTION

Alaska is a wonderful place for birds. The state attracts birds from all over the world to breed in its vast and varied habitats and to feed on its abundant fish, invertebrates, seeds, and berries. Alaska helps protect its birds with more than 130 million acres of national wildlife refuges and parklands, about three-fourths of the total for the entire United States. Alaska is also a great place for birders, who can see these creatures in habitats as natural and as beautiful as the birds themselves.

As the human population grows and development continues, Alaska's birds and the places they use will come under increasing pressure. Their future depends in part on our educated awareness of the richness of Alaskan birdlife. I hope this book contributes to this awareness and to an enhanced appreciation of Alaska's birds.

The Features of this Revised Edition

This fully updated and revised *Guide to the Birds of Alaska* provides information on all 457 species of birds known to occur in the state. The book features many changes from previous editions to make it even more useful in the field. Physically, the book has been fully redesigned and is more compact for ease of carrying. Within the pages of the book, you'll find photos along with key identification and location information for the 298 species that appear regularly in Alaska. For the other 159 species that are "casuals" and "accidentals"— birds that have been spotted in very small numbers, but not every year— a list is provided at the back of the book, which includes their principal identifying features, known as field marks.

For almost every species of Alaska's birds, this version of the book offers more field mark information, while information not essential for field identification has been minimized. For the species that are easily confused with look-alikes, information on similar species has been added. There is expanded photo coverage for many hard-to-identify birds. The status and distribution charts showing the seasonal occurrence of each bird in Alaska's six biogeographic regions have been updated with new information.

In compiling the most useful field marks for each species, I have drawn important information from many of the books and articles listed in the reading list at the back of the book. Readers who want more details on particular birds or bird families can consult these specialized publications, in which several pages are sometimes devoted to a single species.

Some Explanation About the Species Descriptions

The 298 species pictured in this book are organized into 47 families, with each family introduced by a brief discussion of its main characteristics. Becoming familiar with family characteristics can save a great deal of time as you try to identify birds in the field.

For each different bird within a family, you'll find a species description that includes one or more photos; a list of principal field marks; key details, when useful in identification, on behavior, similar species, voice, and habitat; and a status and distribution chart.

Photographs have been selected to show field marks, not simply a pretty pose. Many species descriptions include more than one photo to depict differences in appearance by sex, age, color phase, or subspecies. Comparing the photographs to the listed field marks can help you visualize these important features.

Field marks are essential for bird identification. I have listed the most obvious, and a few of the not so obvious, features characteristic of each species in Alaska. For the most part, these field marks point out key features of the bird's plumage and body parts and are not meant to fully describe the bird; the photographs should serve as the basic general description. Each field-marks category begins with a measurement in inches; this is the approximate average length of the bird, measured from bill tip to tail tip. Wingspan, measured in feet, is also included for some soaring birds.

For many species, the listing of field marks is divided into such subcategories as male, female, breeding, nonbreeding, juvenile, and so forth. These subcategories are included only if a bird of a particular sex or at a certain age or time of year looks different enough from other members of its species to make identification difficult. Field marks that are useful at all times, regardless of sex or age, are listed in the subcategory of "all plumages."

Behavior can be an important identifying characteristic of a bird species. In cases where a bird acts in some way that sets it apart from other species, the category of behavior is included.

Similar species are those birds that look enough like the species under consideration that identification might be difficult. I have listed only those species that a birder with some experience might be likely to confuse with the species being discussed. For the beginning birder who thinks all sandpipers or all gulls look alike, please have patience. The number of look-alikes will diminish as you learn the main differences.

Voice descriptions are included only when they aid identification. For some species, learning the voice is essential to positive identification. Written descriptions of a bird's voice are helpful, but they often vary and can be difficult to interpret. I encourage readers to learn bird voices through field study and by listening to recordings. Many birds can be identified by voice alone.

Vocalizations are usually divided into songs and calls. Most songs are given by adult males when on territory during nesting season, in late spring, and in early summer, but they may also be given during spring migration. Calls can be given by either sex throughout the year and may be used in a variety of situations, such as to express alarm or to maintain contact with others in the flock.

Habitat in which a species usually occurs is included for each bird. The habitat information for many species is divided into subcategories that describe the species' Alaskan habitat during breeding, migration, or winter.

Times of migration and breeding vary among species and can be influenced by weather, but follow a general pattern. The annual migration of birds into

Alaska begins in early March and peaks during May, with a few species arriving in early June. Nesting for most of Alaska's year-round resident birds begins in April, while most migrants begin nesting in late May and during June and continue to raise their young into July or August. Fall migration begins for many species in July and August, with a peak in August and September. A few species do not leave the state until late November. By December, only residents and a few hardy migrant birds remain.

Under habitat, references to inshore waters mean all marine waters within three nautical miles of the outer coast and islands of Alaska; all waters of the inside passages of southeastern Alaska are inshore waters. Offshore waters encompass all marine waters beyond three nautical miles of the state's outer coast and islands.

A **status and distribution chart** is provided for each bird species because knowing the seasonal occurrence of a particular bird in a region and the bird's relative abundance can be helpful in narrowing the choices leading to identification. The charts use the six biogeographic areas of Alaska recognized by Kessel and Gibson (1978): Southeastern, Southcoastal, Southwestern, Central, Western, and Northern. A note of caution: Each region is quite large, and bird's are seldom evenly distributed. A bird that is common in Anchorage may be rare in Cordova, although both cities are in the southcoastal region where the bird may be listed as uncommon. A number of checklists and bird-finding guides for selected areas of Alaska can be helpful when used with this book. These resources are included in the reading list.

The periods covered by each season in the status and distribution charts generally follow the time frames used by the Audubon Society in its seasonal reports published in *American Birds*. They are: spring (Sp), March through May; summer (S), June and July; fall (F), August through November; and winter (W), December through February, although winter in some parts of Alaska may begin in October and linger into May. Most migrant bird species do not arrive in the state to breed until May.

Key to Status and Distribution Charts

C = Common
U = Uncommon
R = Rare
+ = Casual or accidental
- = Not known to occur
★ = Known or probable breeder

Region	Sp	S	F	W
Southeastern ★	U	U	U	U
Southcoastal ★	C	C	C	U
Southwestern ★	C	C	C	U
Central	-	-	+	-
Western ★	C	C	C	-
Northern	R	C	C	-

Chart terms based on Isleib and Kessel, *Birds of the North Gulf Coast—Prince William Sound Region, Alaska* (1973).

CHECKLIST OF ALASKA'S BIRDS

This checklist includes all birds found in Alaska, and readers may wish to use the list to record species they have seen. Birds are listed by family, in the same order in which they appear in the main text of the book.

Birds that do not occur in Alaska every year are indicated by an asterisk; these birds are classed as casuals or accidentals, and they are also listed at the back of the book, along with their field marks.

LOONS
- ❏ Red-throated Loon
- ❏ Arctic Loon
- ❏ Pacific Loon
- ❏ Common Loon
- ❏ Yellow-billed Loon

GREBES
- ❏ Pied-billed Grebe
- ❏ Horned Grebe
- ❏ Red-necked Grebe
- ❏ Eared Grebe*
- ❏ Western Grebe

ALBATROSSES
- ❏ Short-tailed Albatross
- ❏ Black-footed Albatross
- ❏ Laysan Albatross

FULMARS, PETRELS, SHEARWATERS
- ❏ Northern Fulmar
- ❏ Mottled Petrel
- ❏ Cook's Petrel*
- ❏ Buller's Shearwater
- ❏ Sooty Shearwater
- ❏ Short-tailed Shearwater

STORM-PETRELS
- ❏ Fork-tailed Storm-Petrel
- ❏ Leach's Storm-Petrel

PELICANS
- ❏ American White Pelican*

CORMORANTS
- ❏ Double-crested Cormorant
- ❏ Brandt's Cormorant
- ❏ Pelagic Cormorant
- ❏ Red-faced Cormorant

FRIGATEBIRDS
- ❏ Magnificent Frigatebird*

BITTERNS, HERONS
- ❏ American Bittern
- ❏ Yellow Bittern*
- ❏ Great Blue Heron
- ❏ Great Egret*
- ❏ Chinese Egret*
- ❏ Chinese Pond Heron*
- ❏ Cattle Egret*
- ❏ Green Heron*
- ❏ Black-crowned Night-Heron*

SWANS, GEESE, DUCKS
- ❏ Tundra Swan
- ❏ Whooper Swan
- ❏ Trumpeter Swan
- ❏ Bean Goose
- ❏ Greater White-fronted Goose
- ❏ Lesser White-fronted Goose*
- ❏ Snow Goose
- ❏ Ross's Goose*
- ❏ Emperor Goose
- ❏ Brant

- ❏ Canada Goose
- ❏ Wood Duck*
- ❏ Green-winged Teal
- ❏ Baikal Teal*
- ❏ Falcated Teal*
- ❏ American Black Duck*
- ❏ Mallard
- ❏ Spot-billed Duck*
- ❏ Northern Pintail
- ❏ Garganey
- ❏ Blue-winged Teal
- ❏ Cinnamon Teal
- ❏ Northern Shoveler
- ❏ Gadwall
- ❏ Eurasian Wigeon
- ❏ American Wigeon
- ❏ Common Pochard
- ❏ Canvasback
- ❏ Redhead
- ❏ Ring-necked Duck
- ❏ Tufted Duck
- ❏ Greater Scaup
- ❏ Lesser Scaup
- ❏ Common Eider
- ❏ King Eider
- ❏ Spectacled Eider
- ❏ Steller's Eider
- ❏ Harlequin Duck
- ❏ Oldsquaw
- ❏ Black Scoter
- ❏ Surf Scoter
- ❏ White-winged Scoter
- ❏ Common Goldeneye
- ❏ Barrow's Goldeneye
- ❏ Bufflehead
- ❏ Smew
- ❏ Hooded Merganser

- ❑ Common Merganser
- ❑ Red-breasted Merganser
- ❑ Ruddy Duck

AMERICAN VULTURES
- ❑ Turkey Vulture*

HAWKS, EAGLES
- ❑ Osprey
- ❑ Bald Eagle
- ❑ White-tailed Eagle*
- ❑ Steller's Sea-Eagle*
- ❑ Northern Harrier
- ❑ Sharp-shinned Hawk
- ❑ Northern Goshawk
- ❑ Swainson's Hawk
- ❑ Red-tailed Hawk
- ❑ Rough-legged Hawk
- ❑ Golden Eagle

FALCONS
- ❑ Eurasian Kestrel*
- ❑ American Kestrel
- ❑ Merlin
- ❑ Eurasian Hobby*
- ❑ Peregrine Falcon
- ❑ Gyrfalcon

GROUSE, PTARMIGAN
- ❑ Spruce Grouse
- ❑ Blue Grouse
- ❑ Willow Ptarmigan
- ❑ Rock Ptarmigan
- ❑ White-tailed Ptarmigan
- ❑ Ruffed Grouse
- ❑ Sharp-tailed Grouse

RAILS, COOTS
- ❑ Virginia Rail*
- ❑ Sora
- ❑ Eurasian Coot*
- ❑ American Coot

CRANES
- ❑ Sandhill Crane
- ❑ Common Crane*

PLOVERS
- ❑ Black-bellied Plover
- ❑ American Golden-Plover
- ❑ Pacific Golden-Plover
- ❑ Mongolian Plover
- ❑ Snowy Plover*
- ❑ Common Ringed Plover
- ❑ Semipalmated Plover
- ❑ Little Ringed Plover*
- ❑ Killdeer
- ❑ Eurasian Dotterel

OYSTERCATCHERS
- ❑ Black Oystercatcher

STILTS, AVOCETS
- ❑ Black-winged Stilt*
- ❑ American Avocet*

PRATINCOLES
- ❑ Oriental Pratincole*

SANDPIPERS
- ❑ Common Greenshank
- ❑ Greater Yellowlegs
- ❑ Lesser Yellowlegs
- ❑ Marsh Sandpiper*
- ❑ Spotted Redshank*
- ❑ Wood Sandpiper
- ❑ Green Sandpiper*
- ❑ Solitary Sandpiper
- ❑ Wandering Tattler
- ❑ Gray-tailed Tattler
- ❑ Common Sandpiper
- ❑ Spotted Sandpiper
- ❑ Terek Sandpiper*
- ❑ Upland Sandpiper
- ❑ Little Curlew*
- ❑ Eskimo Curlew*
- ❑ Whimbrel
- ❑ Bristle-thighed Curlew
- ❑ Far Eastern Curlew*
- ❑ Black-tailed Godwit*
- ❑ Hudsonian Godwit

- ❑ Bar-tailed Godwit
- ❑ Marbled Godwit
- ❑ Ruddy Turnstone
- ❑ Black Turnstone
- ❑ Surfbird
- ❑ Great Knot*
- ❑ Red Knot
- ❑ Sanderling
- ❑ Semipalmated Sandpiper
- ❑ Western Sandpiper
- ❑ Red-necked Stint
- ❑ Little Stint*
- ❑ Temminck's Stint*
- ❑ Long-toed Stint
- ❑ Least Sandpiper
- ❑ White-rumped Sandpiper
- ❑ Baird's Sandpiper
- ❑ Pectoral Sandpiper
- ❑ Sharp-tailed Sandpiper
- ❑ Purple Sandpiper*
- ❑ Rock Sandpiper
- ❑ Dunlin
- ❑ Curlew Sandpiper*
- ❑ Stilt Sandpiper
- ❑ Spoonbill Sandpiper*
- ❑ Broad-billed Sandpiper*
- ❑ Buff-breasted Sandpiper
- ❑ Ruff
- ❑ Short-billed Dowitcher
- ❑ Long-billed Dowitcher
- ❑ Jack Snipe*
- ❑ Common Snipe
- ❑ Pin-tailed Snipe*
- ❑ Wilson's Phalarope*
- ❑ Red-necked Phalarope
- ❑ Red Phalarope

JAEGERS, GULLS, TERNS
- ❑ Pomarine Jaeger
- ❑ Parasitic Jaeger
- ❑ Long-tailed Jaeger
- ❑ South Polar Skua*
- ❑ Franklin's Gull*
- ❑ Black-headed Gull
- ❑ Bonaparte's Gull

❏ Heermann's Gull*
❏ Black-tailed Gull*
❏ Mew Gull
❏ Ring-billed Gull
❏ California Gull
❏ Herring Gull
❏ Thayer's Gull
❏ Slaty-backed Gull
❏ Lesser Black-backed
  Gull*
❏ Western Gull*
❏ Great Black-backed
  Gull*
❏ Glaucous-winged Gull
❏ Glaucous Gull
❏ Black-legged Kittiwake
❏ Red-legged Kittiwake
❏ Ross's Gull
❏ Sabine's Gull
❏ Ivory Gull
❏ Caspian Tern
❏ Common Tern
❏ Arctic Tern
❏ Forster's Tern*
❏ Aleutian Tern
❏ Sooty Tern*
❏ White-winged Tern*
❏ Black Tern*

ALCIDS
❏ Dovekie
❏ Common Murre
❏ Thick-billed Murre
❏ Black Guillemot
❏ Pigeon Guillemot
❏ Long-billed Murrelet*
❏ Marbled Murrelet
❏ Kittlitz's Murrelet
❏ Ancient Murrelet
❏ Cassin's Auklet
❏ Parakeet Auklet
❏ Least Auklet
❏ Whiskered Auklet
❏ Crested Auklet
❏ Rhinoceros Auklet
❏ Tufted Puffin
❏ Horned Puffin

PIGEONS, DOVES
❏ Rock Dove
❏ Band-tailed Pigeon
❏ Oriental Turtle-Dove*
❏ White-winged Dove*
❏ Mourning Dove

CUCKOOS
❏ Common Cuckoo*
❏ Oriental Cuckoo*
❏ Yellow-billed Cuckoo*

TYPICAL OWLS
❏ Oriental Scops-Owl*
❏ Western Screech-Owl
❏ Great Horned Owl
❏ Snowy Owl
❏ Northern Hawk Owl
❏ Northern Pygmy-Owl
❏ Barred Owl
❏ Great Gray Owl
❏ Long-eared Owl*
❏ Short-eared Owl
❏ Boreal Owl
❏ Northern Saw-whet
  Owl

GOATSUCKERS
❏ Lesser Nighthawk*
❏ Common Nighthawk
❏ Whip-poor-will*
❏ Jungle Nightjar*

SWIFTS
❏ Black Swift
❏ Chimney Swift*
❏ Vaux's Swift
❏ White-throated
  Needletail*
❏ Common Swift*
❏ Fork-tailed Swift*

HUMMINGBIRDS
❏ Ruby-throated
  Hummingbird*
❏ Anna's Hummingbird
❏ Costa's Hummingbird*
❏ Rufous Hummingbird

HOOPOES
❏ Eurasian Hoopoe*

KINGFISHERS
❏ Belted Kingfisher

WOODPECKERS
❏ Eurasian Wryneck*
❏ Yellow-bellied
  Sapsucker*
❏ Red-breasted Sapsucker
❏ Great Spotted
  Woodpecker*
❏ Downy Woodpecker
❏ Hairy Woodpecker
❏ Three-toed Woodpecker
❏ Black-backed
  Woodpecker
❏ Northern Flicker

**TYRANT
FLYCATCHERS**
❏ Olive-sided Flycatcher
❏ Western Wood-Pewee
❏ Yellow-bellied
  Flycatcher*
❏ Alder Flycatcher
❏ Willow Flycatcher*
❏ Least Flycatcher
❏ Hammond's Flycatcher
❏ Dusky Flycatcher*
❏ Pacific-slope Flycatcher
❏ Eastern Phoebe*
❏ Say's Phoebe
❏ Great Crested
  Flycatcher*
❏ Tropical Kingbird*
❏ Western Kingbird*
❏ Eastern Kingbird

LARKS
❏ Sky Lark
❏ Horned Lark

SWALLOWS
❏ Purple Martin*
❏ Tree Swallow
❏ Violet-green Swallow

❏ Northern Rough-
   winged Swallow
❏ Bank Swallow
❏ Cliff Swallow
❏ Barn Swallow
❏ Common House-
   Martin*

**JAYS, MAGPIES,
CROWS**
❏ Gray Jay
❏ Steller's Jay
❏ Clark's Nutcracker*
❏ Black-billed Magpie
❏ American Crow
❏ Northwestern Crow
❏ Common Raven

CHICKADEES
❏ Black-capped Chickadee
❏ Mountain Chickadee*
❏ Gray-headed Chickadee
❏ Boreal Chickadee
❏ Chestnut-backed
   Chickadee

NUTHATCHES
❏ Red-breasted Nuthatch

CREEPERS
❏ Brown Creeper

WRENS
❏ Winter Wren

DIPPERS
❏ American Dipper

**OLD WORLD
WARBLERS**
❏ Middendorff's
   Grasshopper-Warbler*
❏ Lanceolated Warbler*
❏ Wood Warbler*
❏ Dusky Warbler*
❏ Arctic Warbler

KINGLETS
❏ Golden-crowned
   Kinglet
❏ Ruby-crowned Kinglet

**OLD WORLD
FLYCATCHERS**
❏ Narcissus Flycatcher*
❏ Red-breasted Flycatcher*
❏ Siberian Flycatcher*
❏ Gray-spotted Flycatcher*
❏ Asian Brown Flycatcher*

THRUSHES
❏ Siberian Rubythroat
❏ Bluethroat
❏ Siberian Blue Robin*
❏ Red-flanked Bluetail*
❏ Northern Wheatear
❏ Stonechat*
❏ Mountain Bluebird
❏ Townsend's Solitaire
❏ Veery*
❏ Gray-cheeked Thrush
❏ Swainson's Thrush
❏ Hermit Thrush
❏ Eyebrowed Thrush
❏ Dusky Thrush*
❏ Fieldfare*
❏ American Robin
❏ Varied Thrush

MIMIC THRUSHES
❏ Gray Catbird*
❏ Northern Mockingbird*
❏ Brown Thrasher*

ACCENTORS
❏ Siberian Accentor*

WAGTAILS, PIPITS
❏ Yellow Wagtail
❏ Gray Wagtail*
❏ White Wagtail
❏ Black-backed Wagtail
❏ Tree Pipit*
❏ Olive-backed Pipit*
❏ Pechora Pipit*

❏ Red-throated Pipit
❏ American Pipit

WAXWINGS
❏ Bohemian Waxwing
❏ Cedar Waxwing

SHRIKES
❏ Brown Shrike*
❏ Northern Shrike

STARLINGS
❏ European Starling

VIREOS
❏ Cassin's Vireo*
❏ Warbling Vireo
❏ Philadelphia Vireo*
❏ Red-eyed Vireo

WOOD WARBLERS
❏ Tennessee Warbler
❏ Orange-crowned Warbler
❏ Yellow Warbler
❏ Chestnut-sided Warbler*
❏ Magnolia Warbler
❏ Cape May Warbler*
❏ Yellow-rumped Warbler
❏ Townsend's Warbler
❏ Black-throated Green
   Warbler*
❏ Prairie Warbler*
❏ Palm Warbler*
❏ Blackpoll Warbler
❏ Black-and-white
   Warbler*
❏ American Redstart
❏ Ovenbird*
❏ Northern Waterthrush
❏ Mourning Warbler*
❏ MacGillivray's Warbler
❏ Common Yellowthroat
❏ Wilson's Warbler
❏ Canada Warbler*

TANAGERS
❏ Scarlet Tanager*
❏ Western Tanager

GROSBEAKS

- ❏ Rose-breasted
  Grosbeak*
- ❏ Black-headed
  Grosbeak*
- ❏ Blue Grosbeak*
- ❏ Indigo Bunting*

SPARROWS,
BUNTINGS

- ❏ Spotted Towhee*
- ❏ American Tree Sparrow
- ❏ Chipping Sparrow
- ❏ Clay-colored Sparrow*
- ❏ Brewer's Sparrow*
- ❏ Lark Sparrow*
- ❏ Savannah Sparrow
- ❏ Fox Sparrow
- ❏ Song Sparrow
- ❏ Lincoln's Sparrow
- ❏ Swamp Sparrow*
- ❏ White-throated
  Sparrow*
- ❏ Golden-crowned
  Sparrow
- ❏ White-crowned Sparrow
- ❏ Harris's Sparrow

- ❏ Dark-eyed Junco
- ❏ Lapland Longspur
- ❏ Smith's Longspur
- ❏ Pine Bunting*
- ❏ Little Bunting*
- ❏ Rustic Bunting
- ❏ Yellow-throated
  Bunting*
- ❏ Yellow-breasted
  Bunting*
- ❏ Gray Bunting*
- ❏ Pallas's Bunting*
- ❏ Reed Bunting*
- ❏ Snow Bunting
- ❏ McKay's Bunting

BLACKBIRDS

- ❏ Bobolink*
- ❏ Red-winged Blackbird
- ❏ Western Meadowlark*
- ❏ Yellow-headed
  Blackbird*
- ❏ Rusty Blackbird
- ❏ Brewer's Blackbird*
- ❏ Common Grackle*
- ❏ Brown-headed Cowbird

FINCHES

- ❏ Brambling
- ❏ Gray-crowned Rosy
  Finch
- ❏ Pine Grosbeak
- ❏ Common Rosefinch*
- ❏ Purple Finch*
- ❏ Cassin's Finch*
- ❏ House Finch*
- ❏ Red Crossbill
- ❏ White-winged Crossbill
- ❏ Common Redpoll
- ❏ Hoary Redpoll
- ❏ Eurasian Siskin*
- ❏ Pine Siskin
- ❏ American Goldfinch*
- ❏ Oriental Greenfinch*
- ❏ Eurasian Bullfinch*
- ❏ Evening Grosbeak*
- ❏ Hawfinch*

OLD WORLD
SPARROWS

- ❏ House Sparrow*

BIRD FAMILIES

LOONS
Family *Gaviidae*

Loons are goose-sized swimming birds with sharply pointed bills. They usually swim low in the water. To become airborne, loons must run across the surface of the water. In flight the head and neck are held lower than the body, giving the birds a hunchbacked appearance. They fly with rapid wingbeats in a beeline, with feet projecting well beyond the tail. Loons feed mostly on fish, which they chase underwater and grab with their bills. The wailing, yodeling calls of loons are a characteristic sound of Alaska's wilderness. Very young loons are often carried on the parents' back.

Red-throated Loon
Gavia stellata

Region	Sp	S	F	W
Southeastern ★	C	U	C	U
Southcoastal ★	C	C	C	U
Southwestern ★	C	C	C	U
Central ★	U	U	U	-
Western ★	C	C	C	-
Northern ★	C	C	C	-

Field marks. 25½". *Breeding:* Pale gray head, red throat patch, black-and-white stripes on back part of head and neck, white-flecked brownish back. *Winter:* Head is paler gray and contrasts little with white throat.

Behavior. Carries head and slender bill slightly uptilted.

Similar species. In summer, other loons have black-and-white checkered pattern on back. In winter, other loons are darker on top of head and back of neck. Grebes are more slender and have a longer neck.

Voice. In flight a rapid repeated *kwuk* or *quack*. A variety of calls in summer including wails, shrieks, and mews; also a series of vibrating guttural sounds mixed with low wails.

Habitat. *Breeding:* Lakes, usually smaller and shallower than those used by other loons. Nests on shores and islands; flies to larger lakes and salt water to feed. *Migration and winter:* Inshore marine waters.

Red-throated Loon, breeding

Red-throated Loon, winter

Arctic Loon
Gavia arctica

Region	Sp	S	F	W
Southeastern	-	-	-	-
Southcoastal	-	-	-	-
Southwestern	+	-	-	-
Central	-	-	-	-
Western ★	R	R	R	-
Northern	-	+	-	-

Field marks. 28". See Pacific Loon. *Breeding:* White patch on rear flanks (visible just above waterline when swimming), green sheen on throat (difficult to see), smoky gray on back of neck. *Winter:* White patch on rear flanks.

Similar species. Very difficult to distinguish from the Pacific Loon, but Pacific Loon lacks white flank patch. In summer, Pacific Loon is lighter (pearl gray) on the head and back of the neck; most Pacific Loons have a purple or violet sheen on their throat (difficult to see). In winter, many Pacific Loons have a dark "chin-strap."

Habitat. Apparently very similar to Pacific Loon's; both species occur on the Seward Peninsula near Wales and Nome. Nests only at Wales.

Arctic Loon, breeding

Pacific Loon
Gavia pacifica

Field marks. 26". *Breeding:* Gray crown and back of neck; the throat looks black and is bordered with white stripes; patches of bold white checkers on black back. *Winter:* Dark color of cap reaches just below the eye in a relatively straight dark line.

Similar species. See Arctic Loon. Common Loon in winter has considerable white around the eyes and an irregular border between the cap and throat colors.

Voice. A barking *caw-wow* and a variety of wailing and howling notes.

Habitat. *Breeding:* Lakes on tundra or in coniferous forests. Nests on projecting points or small islands. *Migration and winter:* Inshore and offshore marine waters.

Region	Sp	S	F	W
Southeastern	C	R	C	C
Southcoastal ★	C	U	C	C
Southwestern ★	C	C	C	U
Central ★	C	C	C	-
Western ★	C	C	C	-
Northern ★	C	C	C	-

Pacific Loon, winter

Pacific Loon, breeding

Common Loon
Gavia immer

Field marks. 32". *Breeding:* All black head, broken white collar. *Winter:* Heavy straight bill, white around the eyes.

Similar species. Yellow-billed Loon has yellowish upturned bill; in winter Yellow-billed has a dark smudge behind the ears.

Voice. Distinctive loud, resonant yodeling call on breeding grounds.

Habitat. *Breeding:* Lakes in coniferous forests; heath in the Aleutian Islands. Nests on a mound of vegetation near water, often on small islands, sometimes on top of old muskrat houses. Prefers secluded lakes away from human activity. Highly territorial; usually only a single pair is found on the smaller lakes. *Winter:* Inshore marine waters.

Region	Sp	S	F	W
Southeastern ★	C	U	C	U
Southcoastal ★	C	U	C	U
Southwestern ★	U	U	U	U
Central ★	C	C	C	-
Western ★	U	U	U	-
Northern ★	R	R	R	-

Common Loon, winter

Common Loon, breeding

Yellow-billed Loon
Gavia adamsii

Field marks. 35". *All plumages:* Large yellowish, chisel-shaped, slightly upturned bill. *Winter:* Dark smudge behind the ears.

Behavior. Holds head and bill upward.

Similar species. Common Loon lacks yellowish bill. Common Loon in winter has darker face and lacks dark smudge behind the ears.

Voice. Similar to Common Loon.

Habitat. *Breeding:* Medium to large, deep tundra lakes. May visit inshore marine waters to feed. Nests in vegetation on small islands or on shore. *Migration and winter:* Inshore and offshore marine waters.

Region	Sp	S	F	W
Southeastern	U	R	R	U
Southcoastal	U	R	R	U
Southwestern	R	-	R	R
Central	+	-	+	
Western ★	U	U	U	-
Northern ★	U	U	U	-

Yellow-billed Loon, breeding

Yellow-billed Loon, winter

GREBES
Family *Podicipedidae*

Grebes are thin-necked diving birds. Compared with loons, grebes are smaller, have a longer neck in proportion to body size, and rarely fly. Their legs are set well back on the body. They have flat lobes on their toes and a virtually nonexistent tail. When alarmed they often swim with only bill and eyes exposed. Young grebes, except for the Western Grebe, have a striped head. The very young are carried on the parents' back. Grebes feed on fish and a variety of other aquatic organisms.

Pied-billed Grebe
Podilymbus podiceps

Field marks. 13". *All plumages:* Short, almost chickenlike pale bill; only grebe that is mostly brown, white under tail. *Breeding:* Black band across whitish bill; black throat.
Similar species. Other grebes have slender bills.
Voice. A low, hollow, yelping *eeow-eeow-eeow-keeowm-kowmkowm*.
Habitat. Inshore marine waters, lakes and ponds, marshy areas with vegetation.

Region	Sp	S	F	W
Southeastern ★	+	+	R	R
Southcoastal ★	+	+	+	+
Southwestern	-	-	-	-
Central	-	-	-	-
Western	-	-	-	-
Northern	-	-	-	-

Pied-billed Grebe, winter

Pied-billed Grebe, breeding

Horned Grebe
Podiceps auritus

Field marks. 13½". *Breeding:* Broad, buff-colored ear tufts conspicuous against black head, red neck. *Winter:* Clear white cheeks, throat, and breast; short neck, short slender bill.

Similar species. Red-necked Grebe in winter has less white on cheeks and a gray neck; has a longer neck and longer yellowish bill,

Voice. When breeding, makes loud croaks, barks, and shrieks as well as various clucking, mewing, and gurgling sounds.

Habitat. *Breeding:* Freshwater ponds, sloughs, and lakes, usually in areas containing emergent vegetation. Nests are floating platforms of vegetation and mud anchored to growing vegetation in shallow lakes. *Migration and winter:* Inshore marine waters.

Region	Sp	S	F	W
Southeastern	C	R	C	U
Southcoastal ★	C	U	C	C
Southwestern ★	C	U	C	C
Central ★	C	C	C	-
Western ★	R	R	R	-
Northern ★	+	+	-	-

Horned Grebe, winter

Horned Grebe, breeding

Red-necked Grebe
Podiceps grisegena

Field marks. 20". *Breeding:* Black crown, conspicuous white cheeks and throat, chestnut-red neck; only grebe with narrow, white wing patch on both front and rear edge of each wing. *Winter:* Long yellowish bill, long gray neck; immature grebe has only a little white on cheeks; adult has white crescent bordering lower part of gray cheek.

Similar species. Horned Grebe in winter has obvious white cheeks and throat, short neck. Western Grebe has strong contrast of black and white on head and neck.

Voice. When breeding, a sharp *kack* and wailing courtship call.

Habitat. *Breeding:* Freshwater lakes, marshes, and slow-moving rivers. Nests float and are placed in vegetation along margins of shallow lakes. *Winter:* Inshore marine waters.

Region	Sp	S	F	W
Southeastern	C	R	C	U
Southcoastal ★	C	U	C	U
Southwestern ★	U	R	U	U
Central ★	C	C	C	-
Western ★	U	U	U	-
Northern ★	+	+	-	-

Red-necked Grebe, winter

Red-necked Grebe, breeding

Western Grebe
Aechmophorus occidentalis

Field marks. 26". Long slender neck and bill; the black on top of head, back of neck, and back contrasts sharply with white throat, front of neck, and breast.

Similar species. In winter, Red-necked Grebe is smaller, without contrasting black and white; loons are larger, with a shorter neck.

Habitat. Inshore marine waters mostly in the southern part of southeastern Alaska from mid-September through early May.

Region	Sp	S	F	W
Southeastern	U	R	U	U
Southcoastal	-	-	+	+
Southwestern	-	-	+	+
Central	-	-	+	-
Western	-	-	-	-
Northern	-	-	-	-

Western Grebe

ALBATROSSES
Family *Diomedeidae*

Albatrosses are goose-sized seabirds that frequent the Gulf of Alaska, the North Pacific, and the southern Bering Sea. They have long, narrow, bowed wings and fly low over the water with scarcely a wingbeat on windy days. The bill is strongly hooked at the tip and has tubular nostrils near the base. After nesting on the northwestern Hawaiian Islands and elsewhere, albatrosses visit Alaskan waters in summer, feeding well away from shore on fish and squid and on waste from fishing boats.

Short-tailed Albatross
Phoebastria albatrus

Region	Sp	S	F	W
Southeastern	+	-	-	-
Southcoastal	-	-	+	+
Southwestern	R	R	R	-
Central	-	-	-	-
Western	-	-	-	-
Northern	-	-	-	-

Field marks. 35". *Adult:* White body, head tinged with yellow, top half of wing near body is white. *Immature:* Chocolate brown body and wings, conspicuous pink bill and feet. Intermediate plumages between brown juveniles and full adults can be confusing; however, these subadults retain a blackish hoodlike area on the top of their head and develop white on their upperwings rather early.

Similar species. Older Black-footed Albatrosses become paler and may resemble an intermediate plumage of the Short-tailed, but the older Black-footed lacks the black hood and white on upperwings.

Habitat. Mostly offshore marine waters. On Endangered Species List.

Short-tailed Albatross, adult

Short-tailed Albatross, immature

Black-footed Albatross
Phoebastria nigripes

Field marks. 32". Wingspan 7 feet. Dark body, feet, and bill. In flight, the white shafts of feathers near the wing tip may be visible. Older birds may have varying amounts of white on their undersides and rump and considerable white on their head.
Behavior. Follows ships, sometimes for hours.
Similar species. Older birds may be confused with an intermediate-plumaged Short-tailed Albatross, but the older Black-footed lacks the black hood and white on upper-wings.
Habitat. Mostly offshore marine waters. Most often seen from vessels crossing the Gulf of Alaska and near the Aleutian Islands.

Region	Sp	S	F	W
Southeastern	C	C	C	-
Southcoastal	C	C	C	R
Southwestern	C	C	C	R
Central	-	-	-	-
Western	R	R	R	-
Northern	-	-	-	-

Black-footed Albatross

Laysan Albatross
Phoebastria immutabilis

Field marks. 32". Wingspan 6 ½ feet. White body; black back, upper wing, and tail. From below shows dark patches on otherwise white underwings. This albatross has no distinctive immature and adult plumages (its species name, *immutabilis,* means unchangeable).
Similar species. Adult Short-tailed Albatross has pink bill, yellow-tinged head, and white back.
Habitat. Inshore and offshore marine waters. The western and central Aleutian Islands are the best areas to find this species.

Region	Sp	S	F	W
Southeastern	R	+	-	-
Southcoastal	R	R	R	-
Southwestern	U	U	U	R
Central	-	-	-	-
Western	R	R	R	-
Northern	-	-	-	-

Laysan Albatross

Laysan Albatross, from below

FULMARS, PETRELS, SHEARWATERS
Family *Procellariidae*

Fulmars, petrels, and shearwaters are gull-sized seabirds that resemble gulls but have longer, more slender wings and tubular nostrils. Sailing over the open sea with occasional rapid wingbeats, they are often seen skimming low over the waves on stiff, bowed wings. They feed at, or just under, the ocean surface on small fish, squid, and crustaceans. The Northern Fulmar is the only member of this family that breeds in Alaska.

Northern Fulmar
Fulmarus glacialis

Field marks. 18". Stubby large yellowish bill, stocky build, thick neck. Light phase is white with gray back and wings. Dark phase is dark gray overall. Varying other plumages occur, including almost pure white and, when molting, a mottled look.

Behavior. Holds bill pointed downward both on water and in flight. Stiff-winged flight. Follows ships and concentrates near canneries to feed on refuse.

Similar species. Gulls are more slender, flap wings steadier, and have a more slender bill. Shearwaters also have a more slender appearance with narrow, more tapered wings, and hold bill nearly horizontal.

Habitat. Inshore and offshore marine waters. Nests in colonies on sea cliffs on some Alaskan islands, including the Semidi, Aleutian, and Pribilof islands.

Region	Sp	S	F	W
Southeastern	U	U	U	U
Southcoastal	C	C	C	U
Southwestern ★	C	C	C	U
Central	-	-	-	-
Western ★	U	C	U	R
Northern	-	R	R	-

Northern Fulmar, light phase

Northern Fulmar, dark phase

Mottled Petrel
Pterodroma inexpectata

Field marks. 14". White throat; white upper breast and tail separated by a dark gray band that is visible in flight from underneath. Black forward edge of underwing. Dark around eye. Short dark bill.

Behavior. Sometimes flies in great loops.

Habitat. Mostly offshore marine waters; occasionally inland marine waters in summer. Usually seen singly or in small groups on the open North Pacific.

Region	Sp	S	F	W
Southeastern	U	U	U	-
Southcoastal	U	U	U	-
Southwestern	U	U	U	-
Central	-	-	-	-
Western	-	R	-	-
Northern	-	-	-	-

Mottled Petrel

Sooty Shearwater
Puffinus griseus

Field marks. 17". Appears all dark at a distance. Most have whitish wing linings, though some are dark. Dark bill and feet.

Behavior. Dives and swims underwater. Forms huge flocks; millions may occur in Alaska's offshore waters.

Similar species. Short-tailed Shearwater may look identical under most conditions. Under good light, the Short-tailed may show a whitish throat (dark in Sooty), rounded forehead (sloping in Sooty), plain gray in underwings (whitish in Sooty), and a shorter bill and tail.

Habitat. Inshore and offshore marine waters. Approaches the coastline more often than other shearwaters.

Region	Sp	S	F	W
Southeastern	C	C	C	-
Southcoastal	C	C	C	-
Southwestern	C	C	C	+
Central	-	-	-	-
Western	-	-	-	-
Northern	-	-	-	-

Sooty Shearwater, in flight

Sooty Shearwater

Short-tailed Shearwater
Puffinus tenuirostris

Field marks. 14". Appears all dark at a distance. Throat is often whitish. Plain gray wing linings.
Behavior. Similar to Sooty Shearwater. Also may occur in the millions.
Similar species. See Sooty Shearwater.
Habitat. Inshore and offshore marine waters. Most abundant near the Aleutian Islands and in the Bering Sea. Only shearwater likely to be found in far northern waters.

Region	Sp	S	F	W
Southeastern	R	R	R	-
Southcoastal	U	C	U	+
Southwestern	C	C	C	+
Central	-	-	+	-
Western	C	C	C	-
Northern	-	U	U	-

Short-tailed Shearwater, in flight

Buller's Shearwater
Puffinus bulleri

Field marks. 16". In flight has light gray upperparts with a dark M mark on wings. From below it has white underparts and wings.
Behavior. Slow wingbeats and buoyant flight.
Habitat. Offshore marine waters.

Region	Sp	S	F	W
Southeastern	R	R	R	-
Southcoastal	R	R	R	-
Southwestern	-	-	-	-
Central	-	-	-	-
Western	-	-	-	-
Northern	-	-	-	-

Buller's Shearwater, in flight

STORM-PETRELS
Family *Hydrobatidae*

Storm-petrels are small, blackbird-sized birds of the open sea with tubular nostrils and a forked or notched tail. While larger seabirds soar above the waves, the little storm-petrels flutter about between the wave crests. They are often seen hovering over or diving onto the ocean surface in search of their food—small fishes, shrimp, squid, and other marine animals and even oil from wounded whales or seals.

Fork-tailed Storm-Petrel
Oceanodroma furcata

Field marks. 8½". Pearl gray color on body and head, dark ear patch, wing linings blue-gray with blackish areas.

Similar species. Leach's Storm-Petrels are dark brown overall. Phalaropes, which fly steadily and are often seen in flocks, are the only other small, pale birds likely to be seen at sea.

Habitat. Inshore and offshore marine waters. Nests in colonies on offshore islands. Breeding pairs dig burrows in the soil or, more commonly, occupy rock crevices. Breeding locations include St. Lazaria and Forrester islands of southeastern Alaska; the Aleutian Islands; the Barren and Chiswell islands of southcoastal Alaska; and the Semidi and Shumagin islands off the Alaska Peninsula. This species is commonly seen near shore, especially in fall.

Region	Sp	S	F	W
Southeastern ★	C	C	C	R
Southcoastal ★	C	C	C	R
Southwestern ★	C	C	C	R
Central	-	-	+	-
Western	-	U	U	-
Northern	-	-	-	-

Fork-tailed Storm-Petrel

Leach's Storm-Petrel
Oceanodroma leucorhoa

Field marks. 8". Dark brown overall with white rump.
Similar species. Fork-tailed Storm-Petrel is pale overall.
Habitat. Inshore and offshore marine waters. Nests on islands in colonies, with each nest placed at the end of a shallow burrow. Breeds on the Aleutian, Semidi, and Shumagin islands; in the Sandman Reefs, south of the Alaska Peninsula; and on St. Lazaria and Forrester islands of southeastern Alaska. Feeds nocturnally near its breeding grounds, hence it is rarely seen near shore.

Region	Sp	S	F	W
Southeastern ★	U	C	C	-
Southcoastal ★	R	R	R	-
Southwestern ★	U	C	C	-
Central	-	-	-	-
Western	-	+	-	-
Northern	-	-	-	-

Leach's Storm-Petrel

CORMORANTS
Family *Phalacrocoracidae*

Cormorants are large, dark, water birds with slender bills. All 4 toes on each foot are connected by webs, unlike ducks and loons, which have webbing between 3 toes. Cormorants hold their bill up at an angle and are longer tailed and broader winged than loons. Unlike ducks their feathers are not completely waterproof, so they often go to shore and hold their wings out to dry. They feed mostly on small fish. Adults in breeding plumage look much like nonbreeding adults, but may develop small rows of white feathers about the head and neck, white flank patches, crests, and more vivid coloration about the face, eyes, and throat.

Double-crested Cormorant
Phalacrocorax auritus

Field marks. 33". *Adult:* Orange-yellow throat pouch, black bill. *Immature:* Brown above, varying amounts of white on underparts, some yellow on bill.

Behavior. Bulky neck is kinked in flight. Often flies higher than other cormorants.

Similar species. Brandt's Cormorant has a shorter tail, slender neck and bill. Pelagic and Red-faced Cormorants are much smaller and thinner-necked and fly with their neck straight out.

Habitat. Lakes, rivers, inshore marine waters. Nests in a variety of locations, including cliff ledges, trees near fresh or salt water, or on the ground on small islands. Only cormorant to be seen on freshwater and in shallow estuaries.

Region	Sp	S	F	W
Southeastern ★	U	U	U	U
Southcoastal ★	C	C	C	U
Southwestern ★	C	C	C	U
Central	-	+	-	-
Western ★	-	+	+	-
Northern	-	-	-	-

Double-crested Cormorant, breeding

Double-crested Cormorant, immature

Brandt's Cormorant
Phalacrocorax penicillatus

Region	Sp	S	F	W
Southeastern ★	+	R	+	+
Southcoastal ★	-	R	-	-
Southwestern	-	-	-	-
Central	-	-	-	-
Western	-	-	-	-
Northern	-	-	-	-

Field marks. 34". *Breeding:* Bright blue throat pouch, fine white plumes on sides of neck and back, large head. *Immature:* Dark brown with pale V-shaped area on the upper breast, which may extend to belly; large head.

Behavior. Flies with neck straight or only slightly crooked.

Similar species. Other cormorants have a longer tail. Pelagic and Red-faced show large white flank patches when breeding.

Habitat. Inshore marine waters, rocky islands.

Brandt's Cormorant, breeding

Brandt's Cormorant, immature

Pelagic Cormorant
Phalacrocorax pelagicus

Field marks. 25½". *Breeding:* Ruby red throat and face, small dark bill, fore and aft crests on head, white flank patches. *Immature:* All dark, small dark bill, long tail.
Behavior. Flies with neck straight out.
Similar species. Red-faced Cormorant also has white flank patches and fore and aft crests in breeding plumage, but Red-faced is larger than the Pelagic and has a thicker pale bill.
Habitat. Inshore marine waters, sea cliffs, rocky islands. Nests in colonies on small islands and narrow cliff ledges near the sea.

Region	Sp	S	F	W
Southeastern ★	C	U	C	C
Southcoastal ★	C	C	C	C
Southwestern ★	C	C	C	C
Central	-	-	-	-
Western ★	C	C	C	+
Northern	-	R	+	-

Pelagic Cormorant, immature

Pelagic Cormorant, breeding

Red-faced Cormorant
Phalacrocorax urile

Region	Sp	S	F	W
Southeastern	-	-	-	+
Southcoastal ★	C	C	C	C
Southwestern ★	C	C	C	C
Central	-	-	-	-
Western	-	+	-	-
Northern	-	-	-	-

Field marks. 29". *Breeding:* Bright red face patch and blue throat, white flank patches, pale bill. *Immature:* Pale bill, dark brown overall.

Behavior. Flies with neck straight out.

Similar species. See Pelagic Cormorant. Red-faced has more facial skin and color that can be seen at a distance, whereas Pelagic looks all dark. Pelagic has a thinner, darker bill.

Habitat. Inshore marine waters. Nests in colonies on ledges of sea cliffs, small piles of rocks, and small shelves on volcanic cinder cones. In North America this bird appears only in Alaska. Can be seen on Gull Island tour from Homer, from ferries that venture into the Gulf of Alaska, and on the Pribilof Islands.

Red-faced Cormorant, breeding

Red-faced Cormorant, adults and juveniles

BITTERNS, HERONS
Family *Ardeidae*

Bitterns and herons are long-legged birds that stalk the shallows of lakes, marshes, and coastal waters searching for small fish, their chief food. Most species have a long neck and a rather long, straight, pointed bill. They are often seen waiting patiently and motionless until a fish appears; then they take the fish with a rapid thrusting or jabbing motion of their neck and head.

American Bittern
Botaurus lentiginosus

Region	Sp	S	F	W
Southeastern ★	R	R	R	-
Southcoastal	-	-	-	-
Southwestern	-	-	-	-
Central	-	-	-	-
Western	-	-	-	-
Northern	-	-	-	-

Field marks. 23"-28". Heavily striped with white and warm brown. In flight, very pointed at front end; appear all brown, with darker wing feathers.

Behavior. A skulker in heavy marsh vegetation, may remain motionless with head and bill up, very difficult to see.

Voice. When breeding, its call sounds somewhat like an old-fashioned pump in combination with an iron stake being hammered into the ground: *pump-er-lunk*.

Habitat. Freshwater lakes and marshes with heavy aquatic vegetation. Nests consist of platforms of dead stalks in heavy vegetation. Found mostly along major mainland river systems of southeastern Alaska.

American Bittern

Great Blue Heron
Ardea herodias

Field marks. 47". Wingspan 6 feet. Blue-gray body, somewhat streaked; long neck.

Similar species. Sandhill Crane is plain gray and streakless. Crane flies with neck outstretched; heron's neck is doubled back with head against shoulders.

Voice. A hoarse *croak,* often uttered in flight.

Habitat. Tidal sloughs, saltwater inlets and beaches, lower reaches of salmon spawning streams, shallow lakes, freshwater ponds and marshes. Nests in colonies in upperparts of tall trees and more rarely in bushes or on the ground. Perches in trees.

Region	Sp	S	F	W
Southeastern ★	U	U	U	U
Southcoastal ★	U	U	U	U
Southwestern	-	-	-	-
Central	-	+	+	+
Western	-	-	-	-
Northern	-	+	-	-

Great Blue Heron

SWANS, GEESE, DUCKS
Family *Anatidae*

Most members of this family have a bill with toothlike ridges that interlock when the bill is closed. These ridges strain water from such foods as plants, seeds, and aquatic invertebrates. This family of waterfowl is best described in the following groups.

SWANS
Swans are the largest waterfowl in which the adults have an all-white plumage and very long neck. The usual family seen in fall or winter includes 2 white parents and 3 to 5 gray young. The young assume pure white adult plumage early in their second year. Both sexes are identical in plumage. Three species occur in Alaska.

GEESE
Geese are smaller than swans and larger and longer necked than ducks. They walk better than ducks and feed more frequently on land and in very shallow water. Both sexes are identical in plumage. Seven species occur in Alaska.

DUCKS
The sexes of ducks are usually easily identified in winter and spring, with the males being the more colorful. After nesting, ducks undergo what is called an eclipse molt, causing males to look much like females, a similarity that causes some confusion in identification. Molting does not change the distinctive speculum—the brightly colored wing patch—of surface-feeding ducks, providing a handy way to identify these ducks in flight. The photos of ducks in this book are of winter-spring plumages.

Surface-feeding ducks: Includes birds from Green-winged Teal through American Wigeon on the checklist of Alaska's birds (see front of book). Surface-feeding, or dabbling, ducks have feet set in the middle of their body; they walk well, often nesting far from the water in meadows or woodlands. They feed while walking or by tipping tail up in the water. Most have the brightly colored wing patch called a speculum. These ducks leap from the water when taking flight. Fourteen species occur in Alaska.

Diving ducks: Includes birds from Common Pochard through Bufflehead on the checklist of Alaska's birds (see front of book). They have feet set far back on their body and must balance in an awkward fashion when walking. They feed underwater and can dive to depths of a hundred feet or more in search of food. These ducks patter across the water in a long takeoff run before becoming airborne. Nineteen species occur in Alaska.

Mergansers: Fish-eating ducks with slender bills equipped with sharp projections especially adapted for catching and holding small fish. Most mergansers have a distinctive crest. Four species occur in Alaska.

Stiff-tailed ducks: Represented in Alaska by 1 species, the Ruddy Duck. They have stiff, elongated tail feathers and unusually large feet. They are nearly helpless on land and feed almost exclusively underwater.

Tundra Swan
Cygnus columbianus

Field marks. 52". Wingspan 6 to 7 feet. *Adult:* Bright yellow spot on black bill just in front of eye; this mark is sometimes absent or too small to see.

Similar species. If yellow spot on bill is not visible, may be difficult to distinguish from the Trumpeter Swan. The calls are different.

Voice. A high-pitched, often quavering *oo-oo-oo* accentuated in the middle.

Habitat. *Summer:* Tundra. Nests usually on dry upland sites sometimes many yards from water, and occasionally on small islands. *Migration:* Salt water, wetlands, lakes, rivers.

Region	Sp	S	F	W
Southeastern	U	-	C	R
Southcoastal	C	R	C	R
Southwestern ★	C	C	C	R
Central ★	C	U	C	-
Western ★	C	C	C	-
Northern ★	U	U	U	-

Tundra Swan, adult

Whooper Swan
Cygnus cygnus

Field marks. 52". Wingspan 6 to 7 feet. *Adult:* Extensive yellow saddle covering half or more of the upper bill. Otherwise very similar to the Trumpeter Swan.

Similar species. Adult Tundra and Trumpeter swans lack the extensive yellow saddle. Immatures of the 3 species are very similar looking.

Voice. Named for the low-pitched *whoop-whoop* usually given in flight.

Habitat. Mostly found in western and central Aleutian Islands, where a few dozen winter, and more rarely in the Pribilof Islands before early May.

Region	Sp	S	F	W
Southeastern	-	-	-	-
Southcoastal	-	-	+	-
Southwestern ★	R	R	R	U
Central	-	-	-	-
Western	R	R	-	-
Northern	-	-	-	-

Whooper Swan, adult

Trumpeter Swan
Cygnus buccinator

Field marks. 65". Wingspan 6 to 8
feet. *Adult:* All-black bill; obvious
pink area where upper and lower
mandibles meet may be visible at
close range.
Similar species. Difficult to distinguish from the Tundra Swan unless
yellow spot at base of the Tundra's
bill is visible or they call.
Voice. A low-pitched hornlike *ko-
hoh.*
Habitat. Forest wetlands, lakes,
marshes, rivers with dense vegetation. Nests in water by making a
platform 6 to 12 feet in diameter
from surrounding vegetation.

Region	Sp	S	F	W
Southeastern ★	U	R	U	R
Southcoastal ★	U	U	U	U
Southwestern	-	-	-	+
Central ★	U	U	U	-
Western ★	-	+	-	-
Northern ★	-	R	-	-

Trumpeter Swan, adult

Bean Goose
Anser fabalis

Field marks. 28"-36". *Adult:* Black
bill with irregularly shaped orange
ring around the middle. *Immature:*
Usually has an all-dark bill.
Similar species. Adult Greater
White-fronted Goose has white on
face and black bars on belly; imma-
ture has a pink bill. The calls are dif-
ferent.
Voice. A low-pitched *ong-angk.*
Habitat. This Eurasian goose found
mostly in the western and central
Aleutian Islands during spring.
Note. Now considered casual by
Gibson (1999).

Region	Sp	S	F	W
Southeastern	-	-	-	-
Southcoastal	-	-	-	-
Southwestern	R	+	-	-
Central	-	-	-	-
Western	+	-	-	-
Northern	-	-	-	-

Bean Goose, adult

Greater White-fronted Goose
Anser albifrons

Field marks. 28½". Brown with white under the tail. *Adult:* White patch on front of face, heavy spotting or barring underneath. *Immature:* Pink bill, orange legs and feet.

Similar species. Bean Goose lacks white face patch and underneath barring; adult has yellow across middle of bill and immature has a dark bill. Calls are different.

Voice. High-pitched ringing *gli-gli* or *gla-gla-gla* that is rather melodious.

Habitat. *Breeding:* Nests on flats or slight hummocks, often bordering a stream or lake. *Migration:* Coastal saltwater grass flats and inland open grassy fields.

Region	Sp	S	F	W
Southeastern	U	+	U	+
Southcoastal ★	C	R	C	+
Southwestern ★	C	C	C	+
Central ★	C	U	C	-
Western ★	C	C	C	-
Northern ★	C	C	C	-

Greater White-fronted Goose, adult

Greater White-fronted Goose,
immature

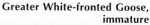

Snow Goose
Chen caerulescens

Field marks. 28". *Adult:* Pure white with black wing tips, pink bill with black "lips." *Immature:* Pale gray above, whitish below. *Blue phase:* Very rare in Alaska; slate gray body, with white head and neck.

Similar species. Ross's Goose (casual) looks like a small Snow Goose, but bill is much smaller and lacks the distinct black "lips." Immature Greater White-fronted Goose has pink bill and orange legs and feet.

Voice. Most vociferous of all waterfowl, call is a high-pitched yelp similar to bark of small dog.

Habitat. *Breeding:* Low, grassy tundra. Nests in grassy areas on the tundra. *Migration:* May occur along almost all coastal areas of Alaska, except the Aleutian Islands, and in several locations in the interior, including the Yukon and Tanana river valleys.

Region	Sp	S	F	W
Southeastern	U	-	U	+
Southcoastal	C	+	C	-
Southwestern	C	-	C	-
Central	C	+	C	-
Western ★	C	R	C	-
Northern ★	C	U	C	-

Snow Goose, adult

Snow Goose, blue phase

Snow Goose, immature

Emperor Goose
Chen canagica

Field marks. 27". *Adult:* White head and hindneck, black throat and chin, blue-gray body scaled with black and white, white tail, orange legs and feet. *Immature:* Overall dark plumage changes gradually to white feathers of adult throughout the fall.
Similar species. Blue-phase Snow Goose (very rare in Alaska) has black "lips" and lacks the scaly appearance of the Emperor.
Voice. Loud musical notes, *cla-ha, cla-ha, cla-ha.*
Habitat. *Breeding:* Low, wet tundra near the coast, often near lakes and ponds. Nests near water in grassy marsh habitat on an island or bank or in a large tussock. *Winter:* Salt-water beaches.

Region	Sp	S	F	W
Southeastern	+	-	-	+
Southcoastal	R	+	R	U
Southwestern ★	C	U	C	C
Central	-	-	-	-
Western ★	C	C	C	-
Northern	-	R	-	-

Emperor Goose, adult

Brant
Branta bernicla

Field marks. 26". *Adult:* Dark head, neck, and belly; narrow barred white patches on sides of neck. *In flight:* Looks dark, with conspicuous white posterior.
Similar species. Canada Goose has white cheeks.
Voice. Low croaking sound very unlike the calls of other geese.
Habitat. *Breeding:* Lowland, coastal tundra, usually just above high tide line. Perhaps half the population nests on the Yukon-Kuskokwim delta on low, grassy flats dissected by numerous tidal streams. The rest nest farther north in coastal Alaska, Siberia, and Canada. *Migration:* Saltwater bays and estuaries.

Region	Sp	S	F	W
Southeastern	U	R	R	R
Southcoastal	C	R	R	+
Southwestern	C	R	C	R
Central	+	-	+	-
Western ★	C	C	C	-
Northern ★	C	C	C	-

Brant, adult

Canada Goose
Branta canadensis

Field marks. 22"-35". Black head and neck, white cheeks. White rump conspicuous in flight.
Similar species. Brant has white on sides of neck but not on face.
Voice. Larger subspecies have the familiar honk; smaller subspecies have a higher pitched call.

Region	Sp	S	F	W
Southeastern ★	C	C	C	C
Southcoastal ★	C	C	C	U
Southwestern ★	U	R	C	+
Central ★	C	C	C	-
Western ★	C	C	C	-
Northern ★	C	C	C	-

Canada Goose

The following 6 subspecies of Canada Goose occur in Alaska.

Vancouver Canada Goose *(B. c. fulva):* Dark goose, weighing up to 16 pounds. Nests from British Columbia through southeastern Alaska and perhaps to Prince William Sound. Nests are widely scattered and tend to be well hidden in the woods. Winters primarily within its breeding range in flocks of up to 500, thus is essentially nonmigratory. This goose is probably most often seen at the tideflats near the Juneau airport; some individuals are present there almost all year.

Dusky Canada Goose *(B. c. occidentalis):* Superficially similar to but slightly smaller than Vancouver Canada Goose. Mostly nests in one great colony in grasslands of Copper River Delta and migrates to Willamette River Valley in Oregon.

Canada Geese

Lesser Canada Goose *(B. c. parvipes):* Medium-sized goose distributed in summer from Cook Inlet north through forested valleys of the Interior. Most often seen at Potter Marsh near Anchorage and at Minto Flats near Fairbanks. Also seen at Creamer's Field near Fairbanks in spring. Major areas of concentration before migration, known as staging areas, are islands in the Yukon River and Cook Inlet. Some Lessers migrate to the eastern portion of the Arctic slope for molting, where they mix with the Taverner's Canada Goose. Winters mostly in Pacific Coast states.

Taverner's Canada Goose *(B. c. taverneri):* Medium-sized goose that breeds mostly on the tundra along Alaska's coastal areas north of the Alaska Peninsula and then east along the Beaufort Sea coast into the Arctic National Wildlife Refuge. Up to 73,500 Taverner's Canada Geese have been counted staging for their fall migration in the Cold Bay area. Winters mostly in Washington, Oregon, and California.

Aleutian Canada Goose *(B. c. leucopareia):* Small goose with a broad white ring at the base of the neck. Rarest of all Canada Geese. Formerly nested over most of the Aleutian Islands, but foxes introduced by fur farmers exterminated this subspecies on all islands except Buldir in the western Aleutians and Chagulak in the eastcentral Aleutians. Closed hunting areas in California and Oregon, release of captive reared birds, and a decline in number of foxes in the Aleutians are allowing an increase in this rare bird. Winters in western Oregon and in northwestern and central California. Movements of this subspecies within Alaska are not well known. The Aleutian Canada Goose can be easily confused with the more abundant Cackling Canada Goose, which can have a white neck-ring.

Cackling Canada Goose *(B. c. minima):* Smallest of all Canada Geese; not much larger than a Mallard. Nests in a loose colony along 100 miles of coastline between mouths of the Kuskokwim and Yukon rivers. Winters mostly in California.

Green-winged Teal
Anas crecca

Field marks. 14". *Male:* Green patch behind eye, rust-colored head, vertical white stripe before wing, creamy buff patches under tail. *In flight:* Both male and female show a bright green speculum (wing patch). Males of a subspecies of Green-winged Teal that breeds in the western and central Aleutians, *A. c. nimia,* and the Eurasian subspecies *A. c. crecca,* also seen in Alaska, have a horizontal white stripe above the wings and lack the vertical white stripe on side of body. They also have a light line above their green face patch.

Similar species. Female Baikal Teal (accidental) has a distinctive white spot at base of bill. Female Blue-winged Teal has a blue forewing, conspicuous in flight.

Voice. Male: A high *dreep.* Female: A low *quack.*

Habitat. *Breeding:* Freshwater ponds, marshes, and shallows of lakes surrounded by woods. Nests on the ground in long grass, usually near water. *Migration and winter:* Brackish intertidal areas near the mouths of streams.

Region	Sp	S	F	W
Southeastern ★	C	U	C	U
Southcoastal ★	C	C	C	R
Southwestern ★	C	C	C	U
Central ★	C	C	C	+
Western ★	C	C	C	-
Northern ★	U	U	U	-

Green-winged Teal, male

Green-winged Teal, female

Green-winged Teal, Aleutian subspecies

Mallard
Anas platyrhynchos

Region	Sp	S	F	W
Southeastern ★	C	C	C	C
Southcoastal ★	C	C	C	C
Southwestern ★	C	C	C	C
Central ★		C	C	R
Western ★	C	C	C	-
Northern ★	R	R	R	-

Field marks. 20½"-28". *Male:* Green head, narrow white collar, dark brown chest. *Female:* Orange bill marked with black. *In flight:* Blue speculum bordered fore and aft with white are good identifying marks for both male and female.

Similar species. American Black Duck (accidental) may be confused with female Mallard. Head is conspicuously paler than body; speculum darker blue than Mallard, with a narrower white border. Sexes alike.

Voice. Female: *Quack.* Male: Quiet *reeb* or low *kwek.*

Habitat. Marshes, sloughs, lakes, rivers, and most flooded land. Forages on land, especially upper tideland habitats. Seems to prefer fresh to salt water but will frequent estuarine areas, especially in winter. Nests on the ground, sometimes far from water and on rare occasions in trees.

Mallard, male

Mallard, female

Northern Pintail
Anas acuta

Field marks. Male 25"-29"; female 20½"-22½". *Male:* Brown head, long slender neck with white stripe, long pointed tail. *Female:* Lacks eye stripe that characterizes most other surface-feeding ducks; blue-gray bill, long slender neck. *In flight:* Green speculum on male and brown speculum on female, with a white trailing edge.

Voice. Male: A high pitched *dreep-up.* Female: A low *quack.*

Habitat. *Breeding:* Marshy, low country with shallow freshwater lakes; brackish estuaries and sluggish streams with marshy borders. Nests on the ground usually near freshwater in tall grass, occasionally some distance from water. *Migration and winter:* Salt water and brackish waters along the coast.

Region	Sp	S	F	W
Southeastern ★	C	U	C	U
Southcoastal ★	C	C	C	U
Southwestern ★	C	C	C	U
Central ★		C	C	+
Western ★		C	C	-
Northern ★		C	C	-

Northern Pintail, female

Northern Pintail, male

Garganey
Anas querquedula

Field marks. 15". *Male:* Broad white stripe over eye, reddish purple head, long pointed feathers on back. *Female:* Pale spot at base of bill, dark line through eye, light and dark stripes on face.

Similar species. Other female teal are very similar looking but usually lack the light and dark stripes on the face.

Habitat. This Asiatic species has occurred most often as a spring and fall migrant in the western and central Aleutian Islands.

Region	Sp	S	F	W
Southeastern	-	-	-	-
Southcoastal	-	-	+	-
Southwestern	R	+	R	-
Central	-	-	-	-
Western	-	-	-	-
Northern	-	-	-	-

Garganey, male

Garganey, female

Blue-winged Teal
Anas discors

Field marks. 15". *Male:* White crescent in front of eye, white flank patch just before tail. *Female:* Dark line through eye, pale spot at base of bill. *In flight:* Both sexes have a blue forewing.

Similar species. Female Cinnamon Teal and Northern Shoveler also have a blue forewing, but Northern Shoveler has a large distinctive bill, and female Cinnamon Teal has a less distinct facial pattern and larger bill than the female Blue-winged Teal. Female Garganey has light and dark stripes on face.

Voice. Female: A high *quack*. Male: When courting, a high whistled note.

Habitat. Shallow muddy ponds, lakeshores, and sloughs overgrown with aquatic vegetation.

Region	Sp	S	F	W
Southeastern ★	U	R	U	-
Southcoastal ★	R	R	R	+
Southwestern	+	-	+	-
Central ★	U	R	U	-
Western	-	-	-	-
Northern	-	+	-	-

Blue-winged Teal, male

Blue-winged Teal, female

Cinnamon Teal
Anas cyanoptera

Field marks. 16". *Both sexes:* In flight, have blue forewing patch. *Male:* Cinnamon red head and underparts. *Female:* Rather plain face without distinct markings, reddish brown plumage.

Similar species. Female Blue-winged Teal has more distinct dark line through eye and slightly shorter, slenderer bill.

Habitat. Intertidal wetlands, lakes.

Region	Sp	S	F	W
Southeastern	R	R	+	-
Southcoastal	+	+	-	-
Southwestern	-	-	-	-
Central	+	+	-	-
Western	-	-	-	-
Northern	-	-	-	-

Cinnamon Teal, male

Cinnamon Teal, female

Northern Shoveler
Anas clypeata

Field marks. 18½". *Both sexes:* Long broad bill, light blue forewing patch. *Male:* In flight, can be recognized at long distances by white breast contrasting markedly with dark head and belly.

Similar species. In flight, the female Blue-winged Teal has a blue forewing patch, but this teal is smaller, with a much smaller bill.

Habitat. *Breeding:* Shallow, often muddy, freshwater marshes, sloughs, and lakes. Nests on ground, often but not necessarily close to water. *Migration and winter:* Coastal saltwater mudflats and shallow freshwater areas.

Region	Sp	S	F	W
Southeastern ★	U	R	U	R
Southcoastal ★	C	C	C	+
Southwestern	R	R	R	+
Central ★	C	C	C	+
Western ★	U	U	U	-
Northern ★	R	R	R	-

Northern Shoveler, female

Northern Shoveler, male

Gadwall
Anas strepera

Field marks. 18½"-23". *Male:* Gray with black posterior. *Female:* Slender gray bill with orange sides, dark tail feathers. *In flight:* Only surface-feeding duck with small white patch on hind wing.

Similar species. Female Mallard has a slightly larger bill that is dull orange and brown, a more sloping forehead, and gray tail feathers. Female Falcated Teal (casual) has a dark speculum and all-dark bill.

Voice. Male: Low *rreb* notes and a high whistle. Female: Low flat *quack*.

Habitat. Sedge-grass marshes. Nests in heavy vegetation often several yards from water.

Region	Sp	S	F	W
Southeastern ★	U	R	U	R
Southcoastal ★	C	U	C	U
Southwestern ★	U	U	U	U
Central	R	R	R	-
Western ★	+	+	+	-
Northern	+	+	-	-

Gadwall, female

Gadwall, male

Eurasian Wigeon
Anas penelope

Region	Sp	S	F	W
Southeastern	R	+	+	+
Southcoastal	R	+	+	+
Southwestern	U	R	U	R
Central	R	+	-	-
Western	R	R	+	-
Northern	-	+	-	-

Field marks. 18". *Male:* Red-brown head topped with cream; gray back and sides. *Female:* Reddish-tinged head. *Both sexes:* Blue-gray bill with dark tip. *In flight:* Conspicuous white forewing patches.

Similar species. Male American Wigeon has a white crown, and brown head with green area behind eye. Female American Wigeon has a gray head.

Voice. Male: High-pitched 2-noted whistle. Female: A whirring call.

Habitat. Most sightings have been of only one or a few birds, and greatest numbers are seen in the Aleutian Islands. Habits are similar to those of the American Wigeon and, when present, Eurasian Wigeons are almost always found with American Wigeons.

Eurasian Wigeon, female

Eurasian Wigeon, male

American Wigeon
Anas americana

Field marks. 20". *Male:* White crown, green area behind eye. *Female:* Reddish body with contrasting gray head. *Both sexes:* Blue-gray bill with dark tip. *In flight:* Conspicuous white forewing patches.

Similar species. Male Eurasian Wigeon has a red-brown head topped with cream and lacks the green area on face. Female Eurasian Wigeon has a reddish-tinged head.

Voice. Male: High-pitched 3-note whistle, like a flock of rubber ducks. Female: A low *quack*.

Habitat. *Breeding:* Freshwater marshes, sloughs, ponds, marshy edges of lakes. Nests on the ground, sometimes a considerable distance from water. *Migration and winter:* Shallow coastal bays.

Region	Sp	S	F	W
Southeastern ★	C	U	C	U
Southcoastal ★	C	C	C	U
Southwestern ★	C	C	C	R
Central ★		C	C	C	+
Western ★		C	C	C	-
Northern ★		U	U	U	-

American Wigeon, female

American Wigeon, male

Common Pochard
Aythya ferina

Field marks. 18". *Both sexes:* Dark bill with pale blue band in the middle. *Male:* Chestnut head and neck, silvery gray upperparts. *Female:* Thin buff-colored line behind the eye, grayish tinge on back.

Similar species. Redhead has more rounded head and lacks the dark gray at the base of the bill. Male Redhead is darker on back and sides and has a yellow iris (reddish in Common Pochard). Canvasback has a solid black bill and more sloping forehead.

Habitat. This Eurasian species seen most often in western and central Aleutian Islands and in the Pribilof Islands.

Region	Sp	S	F	W
Southeastern	-	-	-	-
Southcoastal	+	-	-	-
Southwestern	R	R	+	-
Central	-	-	-	-
Western	-	+	-	-
Northern	-	-	-	-

Common Pochard, male

Common Pochard, female

Canvasback
Aythya valisineria

Field marks. *22".* *Both sexes:* Long black bill, sloping forehead. *Male:* White back, sides, and inner half of wing; chestnut head and neck. *Female:* Light brown head and neck, grayish back.

Similar species. Male Redhead has rounded head, bluish bill, and gray back. Male Greater and Lesser scaups have rounded black heads, bluish bills, grayer backs, and in flight show dark wings with white on trailing edge.

Habitat. *Breeding:* Marshes, sloughs, and deepwater lakes with vegetated shorelines. Nests in marsh vegetation near open waters with sufficient depth for diving and abundant bottom vegetation. *Migration:* Saltwater bays, large lakes, rivers.

Region	Sp	S	F	W
Southeastern	U	+	U	+
Southcoastal ★	U	U	U	+
Southwestern	R	+	R	R
Central ★	U	U	U	-
Western ★	R	R	R	-
Northern	+	+	-	-

Canvasback, male

Canvasback, female

Redhead
Aythya americana

Region	Sp	S	F	W
Southeastern ★	R	+	R	+
Southcoastal ★	R	R	R	+
Southwestern	+	+	+	-
Central ★	U	R	U	-
Western ★	+	+	+	-
Northern	+	+	-	-

Field marks. 20". *Male:* Round red-brown head, pale blue bill with black tip, gray back, black breast and tail. *Female:* Brownish with a light patch about the base of bill, pale blue bill with black tip.

Similar species. Canvasback has sloping forehead and all-black bill. Male Ring-necked Duck has black head and back; female has triangular or pointed head, gray bill with white ring and black tip. Male Common Pochard has sloping forehead and silvery gray upperparts. Female scaup has obvious white patch at base of bill; male scaup has black glossy head.

Voice. Male: Loud catlike *meow* when courting. Female: Rather silent.

Habitat. *Breeding:* Freshwater marshes and lakes. Most breed in eastcentral Alaska in area of Tetlin Lakes and Yukon Flats. Nests in emergent vegetation over standing water or on a mass of plant material surrounded by water. *Migration:* Saltwater bays, river deltas, freshwater lakes and marshes.

Redhead, female (left) and male

Ring-necked Duck
Aythya collaris

Field marks. 16". *Both sexes:* Triangular or rather pointed head shape, white ring around bill. *Male:* Black back, white vertical blaze behind black breast.

Similar species. Tufted Duck has rounder head and lacks white bill ring. Male scaup has gray back and no white ring around bill; female scaup has rounded head with larger white patch at base of bill and no bill ring.

Habitat. Mostly freshwater; sometimes found in saltwater bays during migration. Breeds in eastcentral Alaska in such places as Tetlin Lakes and the Yukon Flats and more rarely in southcoastal and southeastern Alaska.

Region	Sp	S	F	W
Southeastern ★	U	R	U	R
Southcoastal ★	R	R	R	R
Southwestern	+	+	+	+
Central ★	U	U	U	-
Western	-	+	-	-
Northern	+	+	-	-

Ring-necked Duck, female

Ring-necked Duck, male

Tufted Duck
Aythya fuligula

Field marks. 17". *Both sexes:* Tuft of feathers on back of head (not always visible), gray bill with black tip. *Male:* Black back and head contrasts sharply with white sides. *Female:* Back darker than sides.

Similar species. Ring-necked Duck has a rather pointed head and a white ring around bill. Male Ring-necked Duck has white vertical blaze behind breast. Female scaup has white patch at base of bill and less contrast between back and sides.

Habitat. This Eurasian species occurs mostly in western and central Aleutian Islands, where it has been found year-round.

Region	Sp	S	F	W
Southeastern	-	-	+	-
Southcoastal	+	+	+	+
Southwestern	R	R	R	R
Central	-	-	-	-
Western	+	+	-	-
Northern	-	-	+	-

Tufted Duck, female

Tufted Duck, male

Greater Scaup
Aythya marila

Field marks. 19". *Both sexes:* Smoothly rounded head. *In flight:* White stripe on wing extends nearly to wing tip. *Male:* Black breast and rump, gray back. *Female:* Large white area at base of bill.

Similar species. Lesser Scaup has a more "puffy" head that comes almost to a point on top; in flight, the white wing stripe of Lesser Scaup extends only about half the length of the wing. Female Lesser Scaup has a smaller white patch at base of bill.

Voice. Female: A low *arr.* Male: When courting, a soft, cooing whistle.

Habitat. *Breeding:* Tundra or low forest closely adjacent to tundra; freshwater lakes and ponds. Nests near water in dense vegetation. *Winter:* Coastal saltwater bays.

Region	Sp	S	F	W
Southeastern	C	R	C	C
Southcoastal ★	C	C	C	C
Southwestern ★	C	C	C	C
Central ★	C	C	C	+
Western ★	C	C	C	-
Northern ★	U	U	U	-

Greater Scaup

Greater Scaup, female (left) and male

Lesser Scaup
Aythya affinis

Field marks. 16". *Both sexes:* "Puffy" head that rises to a peak toward the rear of the crown. *In flight:* White stripe on trailing edge of wing extends about half the length of the wing. *Male:* Black breast and rump, gray back. *Female:* Small white area at base of bill.

Similar species. Greater Scaup has more rounded head, and white wing stripe extends more toward wing tip. Female Greater Scaup has larger area of white at base of bill.

Voice. Similar to Greater Scaup.

Habitat. *Breeding:* Interior lakes and ponds, especially in the upper Yukon River Valley and its tributaries. Nests in dry grassy areas near lakeshores. *Winter:* Saltwater bays, but in smaller numbers than Greater Scaup.

Region	Sp	S	F	W
Southeastern ★	C	R	C	R
Southcoastal ★	R	+	R	R
Southwestern	+	-	-	+
Central ★	C	C	C	+
Western ★	R	R	R	-
Northern	+	+	-	-

Lesser Scaup, male

Lesser Scaup, female

Lesser Scaup

Common Eider
Somateria mollissima

Region	Sp	S	F	W
Southeastern ★	R	R	R	R
Southcoastal ★	U	U	U	U
Southwestern ★	C	C	C	C
Central	-	-	-	-
Western ★	C	C	C	R
Northern ★	C	C	C	-

Field marks. 25". *Both sexes:* Sloping forehead with feathers not extending as far onto bill as at the sides; largest wild duck in North America. *Male:* White back and breast, black crown and sides. *Female:* Brown with barring.

Behavior. Flocks fly in long lines, often low over the water, and thousands may pass on peak migration days along the Arctic coast. When on water they typically point their bill toward the water.

Similar species. Though both species have a rich color, female King Eider has richer color (reddish brown) and has crescent-shaped rather than straight bars on sides; feathering on forehead extends farther forward than on sides of bill; tends to hold bill parallel to water. Male Spectacled Eider has black breast, female has feathering to nostrils, and both sexes have huge pale spectacles around their eyes.

Habitat. *Breeding:* Low-lying rocky marine shores with numerous islands. Nests on the ground, often in areas sheltered by rocks. *Winter:* Inshore marine waters.

Common Eider, female

Common Eider, male

King Eider
Somateria spectabilis

Field marks. 22". *Male:* At a distance appears white in front and black behind, and is the only duck with this appearance; white shoulder patches separated from white neck by black back; head has orange knoblike frontal shield outlined in black. *Female:* Reddish brown with crescent-shaped markings on sides.

Behavior. Tends to hold bill parallel to water.

Similar species. Female Common Eider has straight bars on sides and tends to point bill toward the water.

Habitat. *Breeding:* Ponds and lakes on Arctic tundra or lakes and streams not far from the coast. Breeds in small numbers along the Arctic coast from Point Hope to Demarcation Point. Nests on the ground near lakes or islands in lakes and sometimes on almost bare hillsides. *Migration and winter:* Inshore marine waters.

Region	Sp	S	F	W
Southeastern	R	+	-	R
Southcoastal	U	+	U	U
Southwestern	C	R	C	C
Central	-	-	-	+
Western ★	C	U	C	R
Northern ★	C	U	C	-

King Eider, female

King Eider, male

Spectacled Eider
Somateria fischeri

Field marks. 21". *Both sexes:* Huge pale spectacles around the eyes. *Male:* Black breast. *Female:* Feathering down to nostrils.
Similar species. Male Common Eider has a white breast. Female Common and King eiders lack the pale spectacles and show less feathering on bill.
Habitat. *Breeding:* Lowland tundra with small ponds. Nests in fairly high grass near ponds. *Winter:* Open areas among the ice in the central Bering Sea.

Region	Sp	S	F	W
Southeastern	+	-	-	-
Southcoastal	-	-	-	+
Southwestern	+	+	+	R
Central	-	-	-	-
Western ★	C	C	C	C
Northern ★	U	U	U	-

Spectacled Eider, male (left) and female

Steller's Eider
Polysticta stelleri

Field marks. 18". *Male:* White head, black back, white shoulders; in flight, shows chestnut-colored breast and belly. *Female:* Dark brown with mottling instead of barring; in flight, shows blue speculum bordered by white stripe, similar to Mallard. *Both sexes:* Small size with no feathering on bill.
Similar species. Other female eiders are larger and paler, show barring, and have feathers that extend onto the bill. Other eiders lack the blue speculum.
Habitat. *Breeding:* Lowland tundra adjacent to the coast. Nests on slight rises near tidewater; also in flat mossy tundra. *Winter:* Inshore marine waters around Kodiak Island, the south side of the Alaska Peninsula, and the eastern Aleutian Islands.

Region	Sp	S	F	W
Southeastern	+	-	+	R
Southcoastal	C	+	U	C
Southwestern	C	U	C	C
Central	-	-	-	-
Western ★	U	U	U	-
Northern ★	U	U	U	-

Steller's Eider, male

Steller's Eider, female

Harlequin Duck
Histrionicus histrionicus

Field marks. 17". *Male:* Mostly slate blue with white spots and stripes and chestnut-colored flanks; in flight, white stripes on back are evident. *Female:* Dusky brown with two or three white spots on side of head.

Similar species. Female scoters have larger bill, and facial markings are less distinct. Female Bufflehead has elongated white mark on head rather than a spot.

Voice. Male: High squealing notes. Female: A harsh *croak*.

Habitat. *Breeding:* Cold, rapidly flowing streams, often but not always surrounded by forest. Nests on the ground, close to water and in areas protected by dense vegetation. *Winter:* Inshore marine waters, rocky shores, and reefs; often perches on rocks for preening and sleeping.

Region	Sp	S	F	W
Southeastern ★	C	C	C	C
Southcoastal ★	C	C	C	C
Southwestern ★	C	C	C	C
Central ★	U	U	U	+
Western ★	U	U	U	+
Northern ★	-	R	-	-

Harlequin Duck, female (left) and male

Oldsquaw
Clangula hyemalis

Field marks. 16"–22". *Male:* Long pointed tail; in winter, considerable white on head and body; in summer, dark brown with white patch on head, white on sides and underneath. *Female:* Head white with dark patches, dark above. *In flight:* Both sexes show unpatterned dark wings.

Voice. A noisy duck with a variety of calls; some sound like *ow-owly, owly, owly.*

Habitat. *Breeding:* Arctic tundra near lakes or ponds and along the coast. Nests on the ground, often under low shrubs. *Winter:* Inshore marine waters.

Region	Sp	S	F	W
Southeastern ★	C	R	C	C
Southcoastal ★	C	U	C	C
Southwestern ★	C	U	C	C
Central ★	C	U	C	-
Western ★	C	C	C	C
Northern ★	C	C	C	-

Oldsquaw, winter, male

Oldsquaw, summer, male

Oldsquaw, winter, female

Black Scoter
Melanitta nigra

Field marks. 19". *Male:* Solid black, with base of bill bright yellow-orange. *Female:* Dark brown, with darker cap and pale cheeks and throat. *Both sexes:* Shorter, more ducklike bill than other scoters; undersides of wings quite pale in flight.
Similar species. Other scoters have larger bills.
Voice. More vocal than other scoters; male gives a peculiar whistling note, *coar-loo.*
Habitat. *Breeding:* Lakes, ponds, or rivers in tundra or woodlands. Nests on the ground near water. *Winter:* Inshore marine waters.

Region	Sp	S	F	W
Southeastern	U	R	U	U
Southcoastal	C	U	C	C
Southwestern ★	C	C	C	C
Central ★	R	R	R	-
Western ★	C	C	C	-
Northern	-	R	R	-

Black Scoter, female (left) and male

Surf Scoter
Melanitta perspicillata

Field marks. 20". *Male:* Solid black with white patches on forehead and back of head, brightly colored bill. *Female:* Dark brown body, pale spots on side of head.
Similar species. Female White-winged Scoter has white speculum.
Habitat. *Breeding:* Not well known but probably like other scoters, which use freshwater ponds, lakes, and rivers with shrubby cover or woodland nearby. *Winter:* Inshore marine waters.

Region	Sp	S	F	W
Southeastern	C	C	C	C
Southcoastal	C	C	C	C
Southwestern	C	U	C	C
Central ★	C	C	C	-
Western ★	C	C	C	-
Northern ★	U	U	U	-

Surf Scoter, female (left) and male

White-winged Scoter
Melanitta fusca

Field marks. 21". Largest scoter. Identified in flight, and often on water, by white wing patches. *Male:* White crescent around eye. *Female:* Dark brown body, pale spots on side of head.

Similar species. Female Surf Scoter lacks white patch on wing; base of bill is unfeathered, whereas in the female White-winged, feathering extends almost to the nostrils.

Habitat. *Breeding:* Most definite breeding records are near streams and lakes of the Interior, chiefly in the upper Tanana River Valley and on the Yukon Flats. Nests on the ground under shrubs and trees sometimes several hundred yards from water. *Winter:* Inshore marine waters.

Region	Sp	S	F	W
Southeastern	C	C	C	C
Southcoastal ★	C	C	C	C
Southwestern	C	C	C	C
Central ★	C	C	C	-
Western ★	U	U	U	-
Northern ★	U	U	U	-

**White-winged Scoter,
male (left) and female**

Common Goldeneye
Bucephala clangula

Field marks. 18". *Male:* Glossy, greenish head with round white spot behind bill; white sides. *Female:* Yellow tip on dark bill, brown puffy head, gray body. *In flight:* Both sexes show large white patch on inner wing.

Similar species. Male Barrow's Goldeneye has a large white crescent at base of bill and shows less white on sides. Female Barrow's Goldeneye has a nearly all-yellow bill in winter and spring and has a darker body.

Habitat. *Breeding:* Ponds and lakes with adjacent stands of trees. Nests in a tree cavity. *Winter:* Inshore marine waters.

Region	Sp	S	F	W
Southeastern ★	C	R	C	C
Southcoastal ★	C	R	C	C
Southwestern ★	C	U	C	U
Central ★	C	C	C	+
Western ★	U	R	U	-
Northern	+	+	-	-

**Common Goldeneye,
female (left) and male**

Barrow's Goldeneye
Bucephala islandica

Field marks. 18". *Male:* Glossy purplish head with a large white crescent at base of bill, black and white sides. *Female:* Nearly all-yellow bill in winter and spring, brown puffy head, gray body. *In flight:* Both sexes show large white patch on inner wing.

Similar species. Male Common Goldeneye has greenish head with round spot behind bill; shows more white on sides. Female Common Goldeneye has dark bill with yellow tip and lighter body. In flight, both sexes of Common Goldeneye show more white on wings.

Habitat. *Breeding:* Lakes and ponds, usually in wooded country. Nests in tree cavities, or if these are not available, may nest in holes among rocks or cliffs. *Winter:* Inshore marine waters and lakes and rivers if open water present.

Region	Sp	S	F	W
Southeastern ★	C	U	C	C
Southcoastal ★	C	C	C	C
Southwestern ★	C	U	C	C
Central ★	C	C	C	-
Western	-	-	-	-
Northern	-	-	-	-

Barrow's Goldeneye,
female (left) and male

Bufflehead
Bucephala albeola

Field marks. 14". *Male:* Small size, large white patch on head behind eye, black back, white sides. *Female:* Small size, puffy brown head with oval white spot behind each eye. *Both sexes:* In flight, show white speculum.

Similar species. Female Harlequin Duck has 2 or 3 roundish white spots on head. Male Common Goldeneye has round white spot at base of bill.

Habitat. *Breeding:* Ponds and lakes in or near open woodland. Nests in cavities in trees, often in holes made by woodpeckers. *Winter:* Inshore marine waters; freshwater if open.

Region	Sp	S	F	W
Southeastern	C	+	C	C
Southcoastal ★	C	R	C	C
Southwestern ★	C	U	C	C
Central ★	C	C	C	+
Western ★	R	R	R	-
Northern	-	+	-	-

Bufflehead, female

Bufflehead, male

Smew
Mergellus albellus

Field marks. 16". *Male:* Small merganser, mostly white with narrow
black markings on head and body
and black eye patch. *Female:* White
throat and lower face, brown head,
gray body.
Habitat. This Asiatic species found
mostly in the western and central
Aleutian Islands.

Region	Sp	S	F	W
Southeastern	-	-	-	-
Southcoastal	-	-	+	+
Southwestern	R	+	R	R
Central	-	-	-	-
Western	-	-	-	-
Northern	-	-	-	-

Smew, female

Smew, male

Hooded Merganser
Lophodytes cucullatus

Field marks. 18". *Male:* White head patch appears narrow when crest is down and very conspicuous when erect; black above with dark, reddish sides and white breast. *Female:* Puffy brown crest, dark back. *Both sexes:* In flight, shows a more slender head and longer neck than other small ducks.

Similar species. Other female mergansers are larger, with more wispy crests and reddish brown heads. Female Wood Duck (casual) has an obvious patch of white around its eye.

Habitat. *Breeding:* Wooded streams and, to a lesser degree, wooded shorelines of lakes. Nests in tree cavities or on top of snags. In Alaska, nests along the valleys of larger mainland rivers in southeastern Alaska where cottonwoods occur. *Migration and winter:* Freshwater ponds and streams and occasionally saltwater bays.

Region	Sp	S	F	W
Southeastern ★	U	U	U	U
Southcoastal ★	R	R	R	R
Southwestern	+	+	+	+
Central	R	R	R	+
Western	-	-	-	-
Northern	-	-	-	-

Hooded Merganser, female

Hooded Merganser, male

Common Merganser
Mergus merganser

Field marks. 22"-27". *Male:* Long, slender red bill; black head and back; white breast and sides. *Female:* Slender red bill; gray body with a sharply set-off brown head with ragged crest. *Both sexes:* In flight, appears very pointed in front and has especially rapid, shallow wingbeats.

Similar species. Female Red-breasted Merganser has a reddish brown head that blends into the light throat (head color is more sharply cut off in female Common Merganser). Male Red-breasted Merganser has crested head and reddish breast.

Habitat. *Breeding:* Forested areas where ponds are associated with upper portions of rivers and clear freshwater lakes. Nests in hollow trees, in crevices of cliffs, and on the ground under cover. *Migration and winter:* Prefers freshwater, but if not available, then saltwater bays and inlets.

Region	Sp	S	F	W
Southeastern ★	C	C	C	C
Southcoastal ★	C	C	C	C
Southwestern ★	C	C	C	C
Central ★	R	R	R	R
Western	R	R	R	-
Northern	-	+	-	-

Common Merganser, female (left) and male

Red-breasted Merganser
Mergus serrator

Field marks. 23". *Male:* Greenish black crested head, red eyes, reddish breast, gray sides. *Female:* Reddish brown head with ragged crest; head color blends into lighter throat.

Similar species. Female Common Merganser head color is sharply cut off from light throat. Male Common Merganser lacks head crest; has dark eyes, white breast and sides.

Habitat. *Breeding:* Lakes, ponds, rivers, often near seacoast. Occasionally may nest along the coast or on coastal islands. Nests on the ground under overhanging branches of trees among tree roots or in a pile of driftwood. *Migration and winter:* Inshore marine waters.

Region	Sp	S	F	W
Southeastern ★	C	U	C	C
Southcoastal ★	C	C	C	C
Southwestern ★	C	C	C	C
Central ★	R	R	R	R
Western ★	C	C	C	+
Northern ★	R	R	R	-

Red-breasted Merganser, male

Red-breasted Merganser, female

Ruddy Duck
Oxyura jamaicensis

Field marks. 15". *Both sexes:* Small diving duck with long tail, often held up at an angle; chunky and short-necked, with long bill. *Breeding male:* Cinnamon red body, black cap, white cheeks, and bright sky-blue bill. *Winter male:* Brown bill and cap, whitish cheeks, grayish body. *Female:* Brown, pale cheeks crossed with dark line.

Similar species. Female Black Scoter is larger and has a proportionately smaller bill.

Habitat. *Breeding:* Interior lakes; broods have been sighted at Tetlin Lakes and Minto Lakes in central Alaska. *Migration and winter:* Inshore marine waters; lakes.

Note. Now considered casual by Gibson (1999).

Region	Sp	S	F	W
Southeastern	+	+	+	+
Southcoastal	+	-	+	-
Southwestern	-	-	+	-
Central ★	R	R	R	-
Western	+	-	-	-
Northern	-	-	-	-

Ruddy Duck, male

Ruddy Duck, winter male

Ruddy Duck, female

HAWKS, EAGLES
Family *Accipitridae*

The birds of this family have hooked beaks and sharp, curved talons for catching and holding their prey. The family includes ospreys, which have a spiny structure on the soles of the feet to aid in holding live fish, their main food supply. Eagles are large, with very long wings, fairly short tails, and large heads and bills. Harriers are medium-sized hawks with long wings, slim bodies, and long tails. Hawks of the genus *Accipiter* have very short, rounded wings and long tails; they fly with short wingbeats, then sail briefly. Hawks of the genus *Buteo* are medium-sized hawks with broad wings, short broad tails, and stout bodies. As birds of prey, members of this family catch and eat a wide variety of other animals, including fish, small mammals (such as rabbits, squirrels, and lemmings), and other birds (such as ptarmigan and ducks).

Osprey
Pandion haliaetus

Field marks. 20"-25". Wingspan 4½ to 6 feet. White head, dark eye stripe; dark brown above, entirely white below. *In flight:* Arched wings with wrist at the highest point, black mark at wrist. *Adult female:* Dark marking on breast and forehead.

Similar species. Immature Bald Eagle looks similar in some plumages, but is splotchier and lacks the arched wings in flight.

Voice. High, whistled *k-yewk, k-yewk, k-yewk.*

Habitat. Near lakes, rivers, and seacoasts. Nests near water in trees or on cliffs. Occurs more frequently in Bristol Bay than elsewhere.

Region	Sp	S	F	W
Southeastern ★	R	R	R	-
Southcoastal ★	R	R	R	-
Southwestern ★	R	R	R	-
Central ★	R	R	R	-
Western ★	R	R	R	-
Northern	-	+	-	-

Osprey

Bald Eagle
Haliaeetus leucocephalus

Field marks. 30"-43". Wingspan 6 ½ to 8 feet. *Adult:* White head and tail, yellow bill. *Immature:* Black bill; overall dark brown body, but plumages highly variable with white spotting and marbling.

Similar species. Immature Golden Eagle has a white tail with distinct dark terminal band and well-defined white patches at base of primary feathers.

Voice. A series of squeaky chitters and screams.

Habitat. Coniferous forests, deciduous woodlands, rivers and streams, beaches and tidal flats, rocky shores and reefs, alpine ridges. Nests in old-growth timber along the coast and larger mainland rivers. In treeless areas, nests on cliffs or on the ground.

Region	Sp	S	F	W
Southeastern ★	C	C	C	C
Southcoastal ★	C	C	C	C
Southwestern ★	C	C	C	C
Central ★	U	U	U	R
Western ★	R	R	R	-
Northern	-	+	+	-

Bald Eagle, immature

Bald Eagle, adult

Northern Harrier
Circus cyaneus

Field marks. 20". Wingspan 3½ to 4½ feet. *Both sexes:* Conspicuous white rump patch, slender body, long narrow tail. *Adult male:* Mostly gray, turning whitish on spotted belly. *Adult female:* Brown above, buff below. *Immature:* Similar to adult female but richer brown above and rich reddish brown below.

Similar species. Short-eared Owl, which hunts in similar habitat, lacks white rump patch and flies with deeper wing strokes with down-turned wing tips (harrier flies with shallow strokes, then glides with wings held in a shallow V).

Habitat. Open country, especially tidal marshes and freshwater marshes; open mountain ridges of the Interior. Nests on the ground in wet marshy areas.

Region	Sp	S	F	W
Southeastern ★	C	R	U	R
Southcoastal ★	C	U	C	R
Southwestern ★	U	U	U	R
Central ★	U	U	U	+
Western ★	U	U	U	-
Northern ★	R	R	R	-

Northern Harrier, female

Northern Harrier, male

Sharp-shinned Hawk
Accipiter striatus

Field marks. 12". Wingspan 2 feet. Small, with short, rounded wings and long tail crossed with 4 dark bands. *Adult:* Blue-gray back; rusty, barred breast; tail tip notched or square-cut. *Immature:* Brown back often spotted with white; cream-colored underparts with streaks on breast and barring on flanks.

Similar species. Northern Goshawk is much larger, with a light stripe over its eye.

Habitat. Coastal and interior coniferous forests, shrubs, mixed deciduous/coniferous woodlands, forest edges. Nests in conifers, usually 20 to 60 feet from the ground.

Region	Sp	S	F	W
Southeastern ★	C	U	C	U
Southcoastal ★	C	U	C	U
Southwestern	-	-	-	-
Central ★	C	C	C	+
Western ★	R	R	R	-
Northern	-	-	+	-

Sharp-shinned Hawk, adult

Sharp-shinned Hawk, immature

Northern Goshawk
Accipiter gentilis

Field marks. 23". Wingspan 3½ to 4 feet. Long tail, short rounded wings. *Adult:* Blue-gray back, light stripe over eye, whitish underparts with gray barring. *Immature:* Pale stripe above eye; brown above, white with bold brown streaks below.

Similar species. Sharp-shinned Hawk much smaller and lacks the white eye stripe. Other large brown hawks, such as Red-tailed Hawk, also lack the white eye stripe.

Habitat. Coastal and boreal forests, forest edges. Nests in heavy timber, usually 30 to 40 feet up in a conifer.

Region	Sp	S	F	W
Southeastern ★	U	U	U	U
Southcoastal ★	U	U	U	U
Southwestern ★	U	U	U	U
Central ★	U	U	U	U
Western	R	R	R	-
Northern	-	+	-	-

Northern Goshawk, immature

Northern Goshawk, adult

Swainson's Hawk
Buteo swainsoni

Field marks. 22". Wingspan 4 to 4½ feet. Long wings with pointed tips that extend beyond tail when bird is perched; holds wings up at a slight angle when soaring; light undertail with narrow, dark bands (looks all dark at a distance). *Light-phase adult:* Dark brown back and breast; white throat and belly. *Light-phase immature:* White below with dark streaks all over. *Dark-phase adult and immature:* All dark, including wings; light undertail.

Similar species. Red-tailed and Rough-legged hawks have paler flight feathers.

Habitat. Open forests of the Interior. Nest locations are not well known in Alaska. Elsewhere they commonly nest in trees, usually deciduous, and sometimes on cliffs.

Region	Sp	S	F	W
Southeastern	+	+	+	+
Southcoastal	+	-	+	+
Southwestern	-	-	-	-
Central ★	R	R	R	-
Western	-	-	-	-
Northern	-	-	-	-

Swainson's Hawk, light-phase adult

Swainson's Hawk, light-phase immature

Swainson's Hawk, dark-phase adult

Red-tailed Hawk
Buteo jamaicensis

Field marks. 19"-25". Wingspan 4
to 4 ½ feet. Large hawk with broad
wings and broad, relatively short,
rounded tail. Plumage is highly variable in color but usually has a dark
head. Dark belt of streaks across
abdomen in most. Breast and belly
varies from mostly white to reddish
or dark brown to black. In coastal
Alaska the adult has reddish color
on upper side of tail. In eastern
Alaska a form occurs—Harlan's
Hawk—that is usually blackish
(occasionally light) underneath,
with a whitish mottled tail.

Similar species. Swainson's Hawk
has dark flight feathers and lacks the
dark belly band. Rough-legged
Hawk has a large, dark patch near
crook in wing and white at base of
the tail.

Habitat. Coniferous forests and deciduous woodlands with open areas for
hunting. Nests in trees or on cliffs.

Region	Sp	S	F	W
Southeastern ★	U	U	U	+
Southcoastal ★	U	R	U	+
Southwestern	-	-	-	-
Central ★	C	C	C	-
Western	-	+	-	-
Northern	+	-	-	-

Red-tailed Hawk, adult

Red-tailed Hawk, immature

Rough-legged Hawk
Buteo lagopus

Field marks. 19"-24". Wingspan 4
to 4½ feet. Large, with whitish tail
and dark terminal band; long,
rounded wings, usually with dark
patch near crook; head usually pale.
Plumage variable; most common is
dark back, light breast and lower
belly, with some dark streaking, and
a solid, wide band of black across
lower breast and upper belly. Some
are all dark but in flight show light
undersides of primary feathers and
light-and-dark tail.

Similar species. Swainson's Hawk
has dark flight feathers and darker
head. Red-tailed Hawk is broader-
winged and usually has a darker
head.

Habitat. Upland tundra with cliffs
and rocky outcrops. Nests on cliffs
or trees.

Region	Sp	S	F	W
Southeastern	R	+	R	+
Southcoastal	R	+	R	+
Southwestern ★	U	C	U	+
Central ★		C	U	C	+
Western ★	U	C	U	-
Northern ★		C	C	C	-

Rough-legged Hawk, light phase

Rough-legged Hawk, dark phase

Golden Eagle
Aquila chrysaetos

Field marks. 30"–41". Wingspan 6 ⅓ to 7 ⅔ feet. *Adult:* Golden back of neck, all dark brown plumage including tail. *Immature:* Broad white band at base of tail, white area on underside of spread wings only at base of primary feathers (toward the tip). *Subadult in flight:* Loses most of the white in wings but retains some white at base of tail.

Similar species. Immature Bald Eagle usually has a blotchier underwing pattern, less distinct white on tail.

Habitat. Upland tundra, mountain ridges. Nests on cliffs and in the tops of trees.

Region	Sp	S	F	W
Southeastern ★	R	R	R	R
Southcoastal ★	R	R	R	R
Southwestern ★	U	U	U	R
Central ★	C	C	C	+
Western ★	U	U	U	+
Northern ★	U	U	U	-

Golden Eagle, adult

Golden Eagle, immature

FALCONS
Family *Falconidae*

Falcons are fast-flying birds of prey that are characterized by long, pointed wings and medium-to-long, slender tails. Their wings are designed for speed, unlike the broad wings of the hawk and eagle, which are designed for soaring. Like hawks and eagles, falcons have a hooked beak and sharp, curved talons, but their bill is toothed and notched, a characteristic absent in the hawk and eagle family. Also characteristic of the family is a black mark on the side of the head. Falcons prey primarily on other birds, but some falcons, especially the smaller species, will take insects and small rodents.

American Kestrel
Falco sparverius

Field marks. 9"-12". Wingspan 1¾ to 2 feet. *Both sexes:* Reddish color in tail and on back, black-and-white face pattern (2 black marks on cheeks). *Male:* Blue-gray wings. *Immature:* Resembles adult, but with more streaking underneath.

Behavior. Habitually hovers with wings beating rapidly; when perched, occasionally flicks tail.

Habitat. Forest edges and openings. Nests in tree cavities.

Region	Sp	S	F	W
Southeastern	C	+	C	+
Southcoastal ★	R	+	R	+
Southwestern	-	-	+	-
Central ★	C	C	C	-
Western ★	+	+	+	-
Northern	+	+	+	-

American Kestrel

Merlin
Falco columbarius

Region	Sp	S	F	W
Southeastern ★	U	R	U	R
Southcoastal ★	U	R	U	R
Southwestern ★	U	U	U	+
Central ★	U	U	U	+
Western ★	R	R	R	-
Northern	R	R	-	-

Field marks. 12". Wingspan 2 feet. *Adult male:* Blue-gray above, tan or buff with brown streaking below; tail is dark, with gray bands and white tip. *Adult female and immature:* Similar to adult male, but dark brown above.

Similar species. American Kestrel has reddish back and tail and a more striking facial pattern. Peregrine Falcon has a distinctive black patch on each cheek. Immature Sharp-shinned Hawk has short, rounded wings.

Habitat. Open coastal and interior forests, particularly near tidal marshes and interior muskegs. Nests on cliff ledges, in tree hollows, or on the ground, sometimes in Black-billed Magpie nests.

Merlin, adult male

Merlin, immature

Peregrine Falcon
Falco peregrinus

Field marks. 15"-21". Wingspan 3 ¼ to 3 ¾ feet. *Adult:* Black head with a broad-to-narrow black patch on each cheek (known as a malar stripe), slate-colored back, barred underparts. *Immature:* Dark patch on each cheek; brown to bluish brown above, heavy streaking on white underparts. Arctic-breeding birds are lighter-colored than birds of the Aleutian Islands and southcoastal areas.

Similar species. Other falcons lack the Peregrine's distinctive black patch on each cheek.

Habitat. Open country, especially shores and marshes frequented by waterfowl and shorebirds; cliffs (on islands, along the coast, and in the mountains). Nests on cliff ledges.

Region	Sp	S	F	W
Southeastern ★	U	U	U	R
Southcoastal ★	U	R	U	R
Southwestern ★	C	U	C	U
Central ★	R	R	R	-
Western ★	R	R	R	-
Northern ★	R	R	R	-

Peregrine Falcon, immature

Peregrine Falcon, adult

Gyrfalcon
Falco rusticolus

Region	Sp	S	F	W
Southeastern	R	-	R	R
Southcoastal ★	R	R	R	R
Southwestern ★	U	U	U	U
Central ★	U	U	U	R
Western ★	U	U	U	U
Northern ★	U	U	U	-

Field marks. 20"-25". Wingspan 4 feet. Largest falcon; long narrow tail, broad wings. Much variation in color exists, from mostly white to black. Gray phases are most common in Alaska.

Similar species. Peregrine Falcon has shorter wings and tail and very pronounced black patch on each cheek. Northern Goshawk has rounded wings and light stripe over eye.

Habitat. Open country. Nests on cliff ledges.

Gyrfalcon, gray phase

GROUSE, PTARMIGAN
Family *Phasianidae*

Grouse and ptarmigan are chickenlike birds that are distinguished by the presence of feathers over the nostrils, lower legs, and, in ptarmigan, the entire foot. The males of most species have a colorful patch of skin above each eye. During courtship, males of some species perform elaborate dances, and others make unusual booming sounds. Grouse and ptarmigan forage for food on the ground, or in trees when the ground is snow-covered. Foods include berries, flowers and leaves of herbaceous plants, conifer needles, buds and twigs of trees, seeds, catkins, and various insects. The Willow Ptarmigan is Alaska's official state bird.

Spruce Grouse
Falcipennis canadensis

Region	Sp	S	F	W
Southeastern ★	R	R	R	R
Southcoastal ★	U	U	U	U
Southwestern ★	R	R	R	R
Central ★	C	C	C	C
Western ★	R	R	R	R
Northern	-	-	-	-

Field marks. 16". *Male:* Sharply defined black throat and upper breast, red comb over eye; rusty orange band at tip of black tail is characteristic, though this band is missing in birds found in southern southeastern Alaska, which instead have a row of conspicuous white spots at base of black tail. *Female:* Rusty brown and thickly barred underneath; short, fan-shaped tail, with narrow, buff-colored band at tip.

Similar species. Ruffed Grouse is spotted rather than barred, has dark band near tip of tail, and a ruff of black feathers on side of neck. Female Blue Grouse is not barred underneath and has black tail with gray tip.

Voice. Similar to the hooting series of the Blue Grouse, but even lower in pitch. In display, flies up with a loud clap of wings.

Habitat. Mixed woodlands of spruce/paper birch, black spruce bogs, and, in lower southeastern Alaska, Sitka spruce and hemlock forests. Nests on the ground at the base of a tree or under a log.

Spruce Grouse, male

Spruce Grouse, female

Blue Grouse
Dendragapus obscurus

Field marks. 15½"-21". *Both sexes:* Black tail with pale gray tip. *Male:* Slate-colored; bare yellow skin on side of neck surrounded by white feathers; red to yellow comb over eye. *Female:* Brown without barring on breast and belly.

Similar species. Spruce Grouse is heavily barred underneath. Ruffed Grouse has brown or gray tail with black band near tip.

Voice. Male in courtship gives a booming or hooting sound like *whoop, whoop, whoop* that increases in volume and tempo toward the end of a series. Locating one is difficult due to ventriloquial quality of the voice and grouse's habit of changing the direction of hooting every few minutes.

Habitat. Coniferous forests, muskegs, and subalpine meadows. Nests on the ground, often near a tree, log, or rock.

Region	Sp	S	F	W
Southeastern ★	C	C	C	C
Southcoastal	+	-	-	-
Southwestern	-	-	-	-
Central	-	-	-	-
Western	-	-	-	-
Northern	-	-	-	-

Blue Grouse, female

Blue Grouse, male

Willow Ptarmigan
Lagopus lagopus

Region	Sp	S	F	W
Southeastern ★	U	U	U	U
Southcoastal ★	U	U	U	U
Southwestern ★	C	C	C	C
Central ★	C	C	C	C
Western ★	C	C	C	C
Northern ★	C	C	C	C

Field marks. 16". *Both sexes, all plumages:* White wings and black or dark brown tail feathers tipped with white (wings and tail may be concealed). *Breeding male:* Reddish brown head and neck, white body; by midsummer, mostly reddish brown with white wings and belly. *Female in spring and summer:* Brownish with yellowish barring on underparts; white wings (may be concealed). *Both sexes in winter:* All-white plumage without black eye bar.

Similar species. Rock Ptarmigan males and some females have a black bar through eye in winter; in summer they are brown, not reddish; have a slightly smaller bill. White-tailed Ptarmigan is smaller, has a white tail, and lacks reddish brown color of the male Willow Ptarmigan.

Voice. Male has a deep, raucous call that sounds much like *go back go back.*

Habitat. Willow shrub thickets, tundra, muskeg. Nests on the ground, usually in wetter places with more luxuriant vegetation than the other 2 species of ptarmigan.

Willow Ptarmigan, breeding male

Willow Ptarmigan, summer female

Willow Ptarmigan, winter

Rock Ptarmigan
Lagopus mutus

Region	Sp	S	F	W
Southeastern ★	C	C	C	C
Southcoastal ★	C	C	C	C
Southwestern ★	C	C	C	C
Central ★	C	C	C	C
Western ★	U	U	U	U
Northern ★	U	U	U	U

Field marks. 14". *Both sexes, all plumages:* White wings and black or dark brown tail feathers tipped with white (wings and tail may be concealed). *Winter:* All white; males and some females have a black bar through eye. *Summer:* Brown, with gray flecking (males) or yellow barring (females).

Similar species. Willow Ptarmigan lacks black eye bar in winter; in spring and summer, males have reddish brown head and neck; female Willows difficult to distinguish, but have heavier, broader bill. White-tailed Ptarmigan is smaller, lacks black in tail, and has no black eye bar in winter.

Voice. Courting male: A growling *kurr kurr.*

Habitat. Upland and coastal tundra, particularly rocky mountain ridges; shrub thickets. Nests on the ground, usually under shrubs.

Rock Ptarmigan, summer female

Rock Ptarmigan, winter

White-tailed Ptarmigan
Lagopus leucurus

Field marks. 13". *Both sexes, all plumages:* Smallest ptarmigan; all-white tail. *Breeding male:* Brown and white barring above, white belly. *Breeding female:* Barred above and below with black and yellow.

Similar species. Other ptarmigan are larger and have black in tail (this field mark is sometimes difficult to see; most obvious in flight). Rock Ptarmigan males and some females have black eye bar in winter. Willow Ptarmigan males have a reddish brown head and neck when breeding.

Voice. Cackling notes, clucks, and soft hoots.

Habitat. Upland tundra, particularly high mountain ridges; shrub thickets. Nests on the ground on mossy mountain ledges, or against big boulders to catch the sun's warmth.

Region	Sp	S	F	W
Southeastern ★	U	U	U	U
Southcoastal ★	U	U	U	U
Southwestern	-	-	-	-
Central ★	U	U	U	U
Western	-	-	-	-
Northern	-	-	-	-

White-tailed Ptarmigan, winter

White-tailed Ptarmigan, summer

Ruffed Grouse
Bonasa umbellus

Region	Sp	S	F	W
Southeastern ★	R	R	R	R
Southcoastal	-	-	-	-
Southwestern	-	-	-	-
Central ★	C	C	C	C
Western	-	-	-	-
Northern	-	-	-	-

Field marks. 17 ½". Dark band near tip of tail, ruff of black feathers on side of neck, barred flanks, spotted on upper sides. Two color phases: reddish brown phase, with brown back and tail; gray phase, with gray tail (gray phase most common in Alaska).

Similar species. Blue Grouse is not barred on flanks and has black tail with gray tip. Female Spruce Grouse has dark barring on entire undersides and a narrow buff-colored band on tip of tail; male has sharply defined black throat and upper breast. Sharp-tailed Grouse has short, pointed tail with white outer tail feathers and V-marked underparts.

Voice. Male makes a drumming sound that suggests the starting of a motor in the distance. This sound is produced by quick forward and upward strokes of the wings while standing erect.

Habitat. Deciduous woodlands: stands of aspen and birch mostly on drier south-facing slopes, willow and alder thickets along streams and rivers. Nests on the ground under dense cover, usually near the base of a tree.

Ruffed Grouse

Sharp-tailed Grouse
Tympanuchus phasianellus

Field marks. 15"-20". *Both sexes:* Short, pointed tail with white outer tail feathers, V-marked underparts, white spots on wings. Displaying male has a purple neck patch and yellow comb over eye.

Similar species. Ruffed and Spruce grouse lack the V-marked underparts, white spots on wings, and pointed tail.

Voice. Male in courtship follows a routine of feet drumming and circling, accompanied by tail rasping and popping sounds generated by his bulging air sacs.

Habitat. Muskegs in interior coniferous forests, willow and stunted spruce thickets, forest edges in areas more open than those preferred by the forest grouse. Nests on the ground in brush or grass.

Region	Sp	S	F	W
Southeastern	-	-	-	-
Southcoastal	-	-	-	-
Southwestern	-	-	-	-
Central ★	U	U	U	U
Western	-	-	-	-
Northern	-	-	-	-

Sharp-tailed Grouse

RAILS, COOTS
Family *Rallidae*

Rails and coots are small to medium-sized marsh and water birds, with short tails and wings, and large feet. Rails are secretive—often heard but seldom seen. Coots are ducklike birds except for their smaller head and chicken-like bill. These birds eat a variety of foods, including aquatic plants and insects. Only 1 rail, the Sora, and 1 coot, the American Coot, are routinely found in Alaska.

Sora
Porzana carolina

Field marks. 8½". *Adult:* Black face patch and bright yellow bill; striped brown back, gray neck and breast, barred sides. *Immature:* Lacks black face patch; buff brown breast, barred flanks.

Similar species. Virginia Rail (accidental) has a long, thin bill.

Voice. A rising whistled *ner-wee?* Also a squeal followed by a descending series of whistled notes, suggesting a whinny: *kweee-wi-wi-wi* . . .

Habitat. Freshwater marshes and ponds. Nests in a basket of woven marsh grass attached to vegetation over water or on the ground near marsh or pond. Found mostly along mainland rivers of southeastern Alaska.

Region	Sp	S	F	W
Southeastern ★	R	R	R	-
Southcoastal	-	+	+	-
Southwestern	-	-	-	-
Central	+	R	-	-
Western	-	-	-	-
Northern	-	-	-	-

Sora, adult

American Coot
Fulica americana

Field marks. 15". *Adult:* All-blackish plumage with a white bill and white undertail feathers. Has lobed rather than webbed feet. *Immature:* Similar to adult, but with duller bill and paler plumage.

Similar species. Eurasian Coot (accidental) has dark undertail feathers and more white on forehead.

Voice. Low croaking notes and a higher cackle. Also various "laughing" notes, such as *ka-ha-ha*.

Habitat. Lakes, ponds, marshes; intertidal ponds and sloughs. Floating nests of vegetation are attached to surrounding plants.

Region	Sp	S	F	W
Southeastern	+	+	R	R
Southcoastal	+	+	+	-
Southwestern	-	-	+	-
Central ★	R	R	R	-
Western	-	+	-	-
Northern	-	+	-	-

American Coot, adult

CRANES
Family *Gruidae*

Cranes are among the tallest birds in the world. They are large, long-legged, long-necked wading birds. During migration, groups of flying cranes will form long lines or Vs high overhead, necks outstretched, as they give their loud, trumpetlike calls. On the ground, groups of cranes may be seen "dancing" with each other. This unusual behavior can consist of bows, jumps, wing flaps, and sometimes stick tosses. Sandhill Cranes eat a variety of foods, including roots, seeds, berries, lemmings, earthworms, insects, and small birds.

Sandhill Crane
Grus canadensis

Field marks. 34"–48". Wingspan 6 to 7 feet. *Adult:* Long, straight neck; gray plumage; bold red crown. *Juvenile:* Reddish brown plumage without the red crown. *In flight:* Flies with neck extended and wings jerking upward with each beat.

Similar species. Great Blue Heron is solitary, relatively silent, and flies with neck retracted. Seldom seen in same habitat.

Voice. Loud, trumpetlike calls that sound somewhat like a cross between a French horn and a squeaky barn door.

Habitat. *Breeding:* Lowland tundra marshes. Nests on the ground in grassy marshes. *Migration:* Tidal flats, muskegs.

Region	Sp	S	F	W
Southeastern ★	U	R	U	+
Southcoastal ★	U	R	U	+
Southwestern ★	C	C	C	-
Central ★	C	U	C	-
Western ★	C	C	C	-
Northern ★	U	U	U	-

Sandhill Crane

PLOVERS
Family *Charadriidae*

Plovers are plump-bodied shorebirds with a thick pigeonlike bill, short legs, and large eyes. They characteristically run short distances, stop, and then tip down to feed. They feed mostly on insects when on land and on insects and small mollusks and crustaceans when along salt water.

Black-bellied Plover
Pluvialis squatarola

Field marks. 12". *Breeding male:* Solid black lower face, throat, breast, and upper belly; pure white lower belly and undertail; upperparts marbled with white. *Breeding female:* Similar to male, but some brown on upperparts and mottled white on underparts. *Nonbreeding:* Gray upperparts with pale feather edges, dull white line above eye, white underparts. *Juvenile:* Upperparts spotted white to golden yellow, streaked breast and belly. *In flight:* Conspicuous white wing stripe, white tail and rump, black at base of underwing shows in all plumages.

Similar species. American and Pacific golden-plovers are distinctly smaller and have upperparts marbled with golden yellow; breeding males are entirely black underneath. In-flight golden-plovers appear all dark with uniformly dark wings, rump, and tail.

Voice. Noisy; common call is plaintive, whistled *whee-e-ee,* with the second note lower-pitched.

Habitat. *Breeding:* Tundra, usually drier ridges within wet tundra areas. Nests on ground in tundra. *Migration:* Tidal flats; saltwater and freshwater shores.

Region	Sp	S	F	W
Southeastern	C	-	C	-
Southcoastal	C	U	C	+
Southwestern	C	-	C	-
Central	R	R	R	-
Western ★	C	U	C	-
Northern ★	U	U	U	-

Black-bellied Plover, breeding male

Black-bellied Plover, juvenile

American Golden-Plover
Pluvialis dominica

Field marks. 10". *All plumages:*
Wing tips typically project well
beyond tail tip. *Breeding adult:*
Upperparts marbled with golden
yellow. *Breeding male:* Narrow white
stripe on head and neck extends
only to breast; undersides entirely
black. *Nonbreeding adult, and juvenile:*
Dark crown and contrasting white
eyebrow. *In flight:* Appears all dark,
with uniformly dark wings, rump,
and tail.

Similar species. Pacific Golden-
Plover typically has wing tips that
extend to or slightly beyond tail tip.
Breeding male Pacific Golden-
Plover has a narrower white side
stripe that extends to the flanks and
white undertail. Nonbreeding adult
Pacific Golden-Plover typically has
more yellowing overall and a buff
yellow eyebrow. Juvenile Pacific
Golden-Plover may have more gold
on upper breast and a buff yellow
eyebrow. (Note: The features of
nonbreeding birds and especially
juveniles overlap, and thus the
Pacific Golden-Plover cannot always
be told apart from the American
Golden-Plover.) Breeding Black-
bellied Plover is marbled with white
on upperparts. Nonbreeding Black-
bellied Plover shows less contrast
between crown and eyebrow. In
flight, Black-bellied Plover shows
conspicuous white wing stripe, tail,
and rump, and black at base of
underwing.

Voice. A whistled *queedle.*

Habitat. *Breeding:* Tundra on drier
hillsides. Nests on tundra in moss.
Migration: Tidal flats, usually the
drier upper portions, and tundra.

Region	Sp	S	F	W
Southeastern	U	-	U	+
Southcoastal	C	+	C	-
Southwestern	C	-	C	-
Central ★	C	C	C	-
Western ★	C	C	C	-
Northern ★	C	C	C	-

American Golden-Plover, breeding male

American Golden-Plover, juvenile

Pacific Golden-Plover
Pluvialis fulva

Field marks. 9½". *All plumages:* Wing tips typically extend to or slightly beyond tail tip. *Breeding adult:* Upper parts marbled with golden yellow. *Breeding male:* White stripe on side extends to flanks; much white underneath tail. *Nonbreeding adult, and juvenile:* Buff yellow eyebrow.

Similar species. In American Golden-Plover, the wing tips typically extend well beyond tail tip. Breeding male American Golden-Plover's white side stripe extends only to breast and is wider; black undertail. Winter adult and juvenile American have less yellowing and a white eyebrow. (Note: Overlap occurs.) See Black-bellied Plover.

Habitat. *Breeding:* Lower elevations, often quite moist, on the Seward Peninsula in western Alaska. *Migration:* Tidal flats, usually the drier upper portions, and tundra.

Region	Sp	S	F	W
Southeastern	+	-	R	-
Southcoastal	R	-	U	-
Southwestern	-	-	-	-
Central	-	-	-	-
Western ★	U	U	U	-
Northern	+	+	+	-

Pacific Golden-Plover, nonbreeding

Pacific Golden-Plover, breeding male

Mongolian Plover
Charadrius mongolus

Field marks. 7½". *Breeding:* Conspicuous rusty breast band and rust-colored crown and collar. *Non-breeding and juvenile:* Brown, usually incomplete, breast band; dark legs.

Region	Sp	S	F	W
Southeastern	-	-	-	-
Southcoastal	-	+	-	-
Southwestern ★	R	+	R	-
Central	-	+	-	-
Western ★	R	+	+	-
Northern	-	+	+	-

Similar species. Other banded plovers have black or darker brown breast bands and light legs. Juvenile Semipalmated Plover has white collar on hindneck (lacking in non-breeding and juvenile Mongolian). Snowy Plover (accidental) also has white collar on hindneck.

Voice. A short trill.

Habitat. Most often seen in spring in western Aleutian Islands and on St. Lawrence Island. Has been recorded nesting on the mainland coast of western Alaska. Asiatic bird.

Mongolian Plover, juvenile

Mongolian Plover, adult

Common Ringed Plover
Charadrius hiaticula

Field marks. 7 ½". *Breeding:* Usually
broad black breast band, large white
spot behind eye, white forehead
patch pointed toward eye.

Similar species. Semipalmated Plover
has narrow breast band; smaller, less
defined spot (or no spot) behind
eye; white forehead patch rounded
toward eye.

Voice. Soft and mellow, a liquid
musical *too-i* and *queep*; unlike the
sharper *chu-wi* call of the Semipalmated Plover.

Habitat. This Asiatic species has
occurred as a spring migrant and
breeder on St. Lawrence Island in
the Bering Sea and as a casual
migrant in the Aleutian Islands.

Region	Sp	S	F	W
Southeastern	-	-	-	-
Southcoastal	-	-	-	-
Southwestern	+	-	+	-
Central	-	-	-	-
Western ★	R	R	-	-
Northern	-	-	-	-

Common Ringed Plover, breeding

Semipalmated Plover
Charadrius semipalmatus

Field marks. 7". *Breeding:* Single black breast band; legs and base of bill orange. *Juvenile:* Brown breast band, black bill.

Similar species. Common Ringed Plover has broader black breast band and a large white spot behind eye; call is softer and more mellow. Juvenile Mongolian Plover lacks white collar on hindneck. Little Ringed Plover (casual) has yellow eye ring, full white line separating crown from black band across forehead and face, black bill, and no white wing stripe. Killdeer has 2 black breast bands.

Voice. A plaintive *chu-wi*.

Habitat. *Breeding:* Gravelly or sandy beaches of lakes, ponds, rivers, and glacial moraines. Nests on the ground in sand, gravel, or moss. *Migration:* Lakes, ponds, rivers, glacial moraines, and tidal flats.

Region	Sp	S	F	W
Southeastern ★	C	C	C	-
Southcoastal ★	C	C	C	-
Southwestern ★	C	C	C	-
Central ★		C	C	C	-
Western ★		C	C	C	-
Northern ★		U	U	U	-

Semipalmated Plover, juvenile

Semipalmated Plover, breeding

Killdeer
Charadrius vociferus

Field marks. 10". Two black breast bands, reddish base of tail. In flight, tail looks longer than in other shorebirds.

Similar species. Other banded plovers have only 1 band. (Note: Very young Killdeer has single breast band.)

Voice. A raucous cry of *kill-dee, kill-dee.*

Habitat. Marshes, tidal sloughs, lakeshores, rivers, ponds, grasslands. Nests on gravel shores or in fields or pastures.

Region	Sp	S	F	W
Southeastern ★	U	U	U	R
Southcoastal ★	R	R	R	+
Southwestern	+	+	-	-
Central ★	R	R	R	-
Western	+	+	-	-
Northern	+	+	-	-

Killdeer, breeding

Eurasian Dotterel
Charadrius morinellus

Field marks. 8½". *Breeding:* Obvious white eyebrow and breast band; chestnut belly. *Juvenile:* Obvious buff-colored eyebrow and faint breast band.

Similar species. Juvenile Golden-Plover lacks breast band and has much fainter eyebrows that do not extend to back of head.

Voice. A musical twitter or trill.

Habitat. This Asiatic shorebird breeds in small numbers on alpine tundra in western Alaska; rarely seen at sea level.

Region	Sp	S	F	W
Southeastern	-	-	-	-
Southcoastal	-	-	+	-
Southwestern	-	-	+	-
Central	-	+	-	-
Western ★	R	R	-	-
Northern ★	-	+	-	-

Eurasian Dotterel, breeding

Eurasian Dotterel, juvenile

OYSTERCATCHERS
Family *Haematopodidae*

The oystercatcher family contains large, chunky, short-legged shorebirds with long, red bills that are flattened laterally. The oystercatcher, with its chisel-like bill tip, pries shellfish off rocks and also inserts its bill between the 2 shells of a mollusk to sever the strong adductor muscle. The oystercatcher's food includes mussels, clams, chitons, limpets, and barnacles. It also probes in the sand and mud for marine worms and other invertebrates.

Black Oystercatcher
Haematopus bachmani

Field marks. 17". *Adult:* Crow-sized; dark brown with black head and neck (looks all black at a distance), bright red bill, pinkish legs and feet. *Juvenile:* All brownish; dull orange bill with brown tip.

Voice. A loud, whistled *wheee-whee-whee-whee.*

Habitat. Rocky shores, reefs, and islands. Nests in beach gravel, often near grass line.

Region	Sp	S	F	W
Southeastern ★	C	C	C	R
Southcoastal ★	C	C	C	U
Southwestern ★	C	C	C	C
Central	-	-	-	-
Western	-	-	-	-
Northern	-	-	-	-

Black Oystercatcher

SANDPIPERS
Family *Scolopacidae*

Members of the Sandpiper family vary considerably in size, shape, and color. The bill is more slender than the plover's and is soft and rather flexible. Unlike plovers, sandpipers typically move slowly and continuously when foraging—probing or picking from the surface. These shorebirds typically inhabit lakeshores, intertidal areas, or other moist places. They usually lay 4 eggs in a shallow depression in the ground. Before and after the breeding season, most are gregarious and can be seen in large flocks, often several species together. Many sandpipers travel long distances to reach Alaska. Some even winter in South America as far south as Patagonia, more than 8,000 miles from their summer home in Alaska. Sandpipers feed mostly on insects, crustaceans, mollusks, and worms.

Common Greenshank
Tringa nebularia

Field marks. 12". Greenish legs, blackish area on shoulder of folded wing. In flight, white rump and lower back.

Similar species. Greater Yellowlegs has bright yellow legs and in flight shows white rump with no white on lower back. Marsh Sandpiper (accidental) is smaller and has proportionately longer legs, slimmer bill, whiter face in nonbreeding plumage; in flight, toes project farther beyond tip of tail (entire length versus about two-thirds of its length in Common Greenshank).

Habitat. This Asiatic shorebird is seen mostly in western Aleutian Islands.

Region	Sp	S	F	W
Southeastern	-	-	-	-
Southcoastal	-	-	-	-
Southwestern	R	+	+	-
Central	-	-	-	-
Western	+	+	-	-
Northern	-	-	-	-

Common Greenshank, breeding

Common Greenshank

Greater Yellowlegs
Tringa melanoleuca

Field marks. 14". *All plumages:* Long, bright yellow legs; long, slightly upturned bill. *In flight:* White rump, white tail barred with gray, no wing stripe. *Breeding:* Rather dark streaks and bars on breast and belly.

Similar species. Lesser Yellowlegs is smaller, with a shorter, slighter, straight, black bill; breeding adult shows no barring on belly. Common Greenshank, occurring during spring in western Aleutian Islands, has greenish legs, black shoulder patch, shows white back in flight.

Voice. Usually 3- or 4-note whistle sounding like *whew-whew-whew*. Display song is a repeated whistle *whee-oodle*.

Habitat. *Breeding:* Muskegs, freshwater marshes. Nests on the ground in moss. *Migration:* Tidal flats, lakes, ponds.

Region	Sp	S	F	W
Southeastern ★	C	C	C	+
Southcoastal ★	C	C	C	-
Southwestern ★	C	C	C	-
Central ★	R	R	R	-
Western ★	R	R	R	-
Northern	-	+	-	-

Greater Yellowlegs, breeding

Greater Yellowlegs (left) and Lesser Yellowlegs, juveniles

Lesser Yellowlegs
Tringa flavipes

Field marks. 11". *All plumages:* Long yellow legs; thin, straight, black bill; white rump. *Breeding:* Barring sparse on flanks and lacking on belly.

Similar species. Greater Yellowlegs is larger, with longer, slightly upturned bill; breeding bird has barring on belly and more on flanks; non-breeding and juvenile has 2-toned bill. See Common Greenshank.

Voice. One or two notes like *tew tew.* Display song is *wheedle-bree.*

Habitat. *Breeding:* Muskegs, freshwater marshes. *Migration:* Tidal flats, lakes, ponds.

Region	Sp	S	F	W
Southeastern ★	C	R	C	-
Southcoastal ★	C	C	C	-
Southwestern	R	-	R	-
Central ★	C	C	C	-
Western ★	U	U	U	-
Northern ★	-	+	-	-

Lesser Yellowlegs

Lesser Yellowlegs, breeding

Wood Sandpiper
Tringa glareola

Region	Sp	S	F	W
Southeastern	-	-	-	-
Southcoastal	-	-	-	-
Southwestern ★	R	R	R	-
Central	-	-	-	-
Western	R	+	-	-
Northern	-	+	-	-

Field marks. 8". Warm brown upperparts spotted with white, wings whitish underneath, white rump, dull yellow legs.

Similar species. Solitary Sandpiper has greenish legs, wings dark underneath, dark rump. Lesser Yellowlegs has bright yellow legs. (These two species seldom occur in the same area as Wood Sandpiper.) Green Sandpiper (casual) has darker underwings, a larger white rump patch, and less barring on tail.

Voice. In flight, a 3-note whistle.

Habitat. Tundra, tidal flats. This Asiatic sandpiper is seen most often as a spring migrant and occasional breeder in western and central Aleutian Islands.

Wood Sandpiper

Solitary Sandpiper
Tringa solitaria

Field marks. 8". Conspicuous white eye ring, rather short olive bill, olive brown upperparts speckled with white, short greenish legs. In flight, blackish underwings contrast with white belly; dark rump and tail contrast with flashy white sides barred with black.

Behavior. Often flies high in the air when flushed; swooping, swallow-like flight; usually solitary or with 1 or 2 others.

Similar species. Lesser Yellowlegs has long, bright yellow legs and white rump. Wood Sandpiper (seldom occurs in same area) has whitish wings underneath and white rump. Spotted Sandpiper has white wing stripe, heavy spots underneath in breeding plumage, and short jerky wingbeats.

Voice. A high-pitched whistle, *wheet-wheet-wheet-wheet*.

Habitat. *Breeding:* Muskegs, freshwater marshes, lakes, ponds. Nests in deserted nests of other birds, such as thrushes. *Migration:* Muddy shorelines of ponds and streams in wooded areas. Rarely occurs on salt water.

Region	Sp	S	F	W
Southeastern ★	U	R	U	-
Southcoastal ★	U	R	U	-
Southwestern ★	+	R	-	-
Central ★	U	U	U	-
Western ★	+	R	-	-
Northern ★	+	+	-	-

Solitary Sandpiper

Wandering Tattler
Heteroscelus incanus

Region	Sp	S	F	W
Southeastern ★	U	R	U	-
Southcoastal ★	C	U	C	-
Southwestern ★	U	R	U	-
Central ★	U	U	U	-
Western ★	U	U	U	-
Northern ★	+	+	+	-

Field marks. 11". *All plumages:* Uniform slate gray on upperparts, wings, rump, and tail; whitish eyebrow; greenish yellow legs. *Breeding:* Heavily barred underparts.

Behavior. Usually found alone or with 1 or 2 others.

Similar species. Gray-tailed Tattler in breeding plumage has narrower, lighter barring underneath and no barring on belly and undertail; juveniles and nonbreeding adults look nearly identical to Wandering Tattler, but the sides are white, not gray. Voice is different.

Voice. A ringing series of whistled notes.

Habitat. *Breeding:* Gravel bars of mountain streams. Nests in gravel near streams. *Migration:* Rocky saltwater beaches.

Wandering Tattler, breeding

Wandering Tattler, nonbreeding

Gray-tailed Tattler
Heteroscelus brevipes

Field marks. 9 ½". *Breeding:* Similar to Wandering Tattler, but with narrower, lighter barring underneath and no barring on belly and undertail. *Nonbreeding and juvenile:* Similar to Wandering, but with white sides.

Similar species. Wandering Tattler has heavier barring over entire underparts; nonbreeding and juvenile birds have gray sides and can be distinguished by voice.

Voice. A double whistle, *too-weet;* also a call similar to Wandering Tattler.

Habitat. This Asiatic migrant is found mostly in western Aleutian Islands; also, Bering Sea Islands and on coast to Point Barrow. Sometimes seen with Wandering Tattler.

Region	Sp	S	F	W
Southeastern	-	-	-	-
Southcoastal	-	-	+	-
Southwestern	U	+	U	-
Central	-	-	-	-
Western	R	+	+	-
Northern	+	+	-	-

Gray-tailed Tattler, breeding

Common Sandpiper
Actitis hypoleucos

Field marks. 8". *Breeding:* Unspotted underparts, streaked breast and neck, grayish olive or dull yellow legs, dark bill. *In flight:* White wing stripe extends to base of wing; tail outlined in white.

Similar species. Nonbreeding and juvenile Spotted Sandpiper is almost identical to Common, but is generally slightly grayer above and has a shorter tail. White wing stripe of Spotted stops well before base of wing. (Spotted Sandpiper unlikely on Bering Sea islands.) Solitary Sandpiper has white speckling on back and no white wing stripe.

Habitat. This Asiatic migrant is found in western Aleutian and Bering Sea islands. Beaches, reefs, shores of lakes and ponds.

Region	Sp	S	F	W
Southeastern	-	-	-	-
Southcoastal	-	-	-	-
Southwestern ★	R	+	R	-
Central	-	-	-	-
Western	R	-	-	-
Northern	-	-	-	-

Common Sandpiper

Spotted Sandpiper
Actitis macularia

Region	Sp	S	F	W
Southeastern ★	C	C	C	+
Southcoastal ★	C	C	C	+
Southwestern ★	U	U	U	-
Central ★	C	C	C	-
Western ★	U	U	U	-
Northern ★	U	U	U	-

Field marks. 7 ½". *Breeding:* Large black spots on white underparts. *Nonbreeding and juvenile:* White wedge separating brown patch on side of breast from dark bend of wing; buff-colored bars on wings (most obvious in juveniles).

Behavior. When flushed, flies out over water with short, jerky wing-beats. Teeters almost constantly.

Similar species. Common Sandpiper is almost identical to nonbreeding and juvenile Spotted Sandpiper, but is generally slightly browner above, has longer tail, and wing stripe extends to base of wing; both species unlikely to occur in same area. Solitary Sandpiper has white speckling on back; lacks white shoulder wedge and wing stripe.

Voice. A series of high-pitched whistles dropping toward the end of the series.

Habitat. Shores of rivers, streams, and lakes; saltwater beaches. Nests near water in gravel or grass.

Spotted Sandpiper, nonbreeding

Spotted Sandpiper, breeding

Upland Sandpiper
Bartramia longicauda

Field marks. 11½". Long neck, small head, bill about length of head. *In flight:* long tail; blackish lower back; long, dark, pointed wings.

Behavior. Flies with wings held low like Spotted Sandpiper. Often holds wings up for a moment on alighting. Frequently perches on small trees or fence posts.

Similar species. Buff-breasted Sandpiper is much smaller, has unmarked buff color from throat to undertail, and lacks barred underparts.

Voice. On breeding grounds, a long, mournful, rolling whistle. Alarm call a mellow *quip-ip-ip-ip.*

Habitat. Open grassy fields and sparsely vegetated uplands. Never associated with water. Occurs primarily in interior Alaska, in areas such as Denali National Park and Preserve and open grassy ridges north of Fairbanks.

Region	Sp	S	F	W
Southeastern	+	+	+	-
Southcoastal	+	-	+	-
Southwestern	-	-	-	-
Central ★	U	U	U	-
Western ★	-	+	+	-
Northern	-	+	-	-

Upland Sandpiper

Whimbrel
Numenius phaeopus

Field marks. 17". Long downcurved bill, striped crown, brown or gray brown upperparts. In flight, appears uniform brown without pattern or buff tone. Note: A subspecies of Whimbrel from Siberia (*N. p. variegatus*) occurs regularly in southwestern and western Alaska; it has a conspicuous white lower back and dark-spotted white rump.

Similar species. Bristle-thighed Curlew has a rust tinge and bright buff-colored rump and tail. Far Eastern Curlew, casual in central and western Aleutian Islands, lacks conspicuous head stripes and is boldly marked with streaks and chevrons underneath.

Voice. A loud, repeated, whistled *pi-pi-pi-pip*.

Habitat. *Breeding:* Tundra. Nests in a depression or on a mound of vegetation in the tundra. *Migration:* Tidal flats and beaches.

Region	Sp	S	F	W
Southeastern	U	R	U	-
Southcoastal	C	U	C	-
Southwestern	C	C	C	-
Central ★	C	C	U	-
Western ★	C	C	U	-
Northern ★	U	U	-	-

Whimbrel

Bristle-thighed Curlew
Numenius tahitiensis

Field marks. 17". Long downcurved bill, conspicuous head stripes, rusty tinge, bright buff-colored rump and tail.

Similar species. Whimbrel lacks rusty tinge and bright buff rump and tail; has bars on rump and tail same color as back (Bristle-thighed lacks bars on rump). Far Eastern Curlew (casual) lacks conspicuous head stripes and bright buff rump and tail, has bold streaks and chevrons underneath.

Voice. A slurred whistle.

Habitat. *Breeding:* Only in western Alaska on the flat, dry tundra of exposed ridges. Nests in depressions on the tundra. *Migration:* Drier coastal tundra; tidal flats and beaches.

Region	Sp	S	F	W
Southeastern	+	-	-	-
Southcoastal	+	-	+	-
Southwestern	R	+	R	-
Central	+	-	-	-
Western ★	U	U	U	-
Northern	R	R	-	-

Bristle-thighed Curlew

Hudsonian Godwit
Limosa haemastica

Field marks. 15". *All plumages:* Large; long, slender, slightly upturned, pink-based bill. *In flight:* Black wing linings, white wing stripe, black band across white-based tail. *Breeding:* Dark cinnamon underparts, narrowly barred with black. *Nonbreeding:* Pale brownish gray above and on breast, whitish lower breast and belly.

Similar species. Bar-tailed Godwit lacks black tail band and has poorly defined wing stripe. Marbled Godwit also lacks vivid black tail band and white wing stripe. Black-tailed Godwit (casual in Aleutian and Bering Sea islands) has straight bill, cinnamon head and breast, white wing linings, bold black bars on belly.

Habitat. *Breeding:* Sedge-grass marshes, wet tundra, taiga bogs. *Migration:* Tidal flats and beaches.

Region	Sp	S	F	W
Southeastern	R	+	+	-
Southcoastal ★	U	U	U	-
Southwestern ★	+	R	R	-
Central	R	+	-	-
Western ★	U	U	U	-
Northern	R	R	R	-

Hudsonian Godwit

Hudsonian Godwit, breeding

Bar-tailed Godwit
Limosa lapponica

Field marks. 16". *All plumages:* Large; long, slightly upturned, pink-based bill; short legs for a godwit. *In flight:* Rather plain above, poorly defined wing stripe, brown rump and wing linings, whitish tail with narrow black bars. *Breeding male:* Rich rufous-colored underparts. *Breeding female:* Streaked, pinkish buff breast.

Similar species. Marbled Godwit is larger, with conspicuous cinnamon wing linings; breeding Marbled has heavily barred underparts (unbarred in Bar-tailed). Hudsonian Godwit has white wing stripe, black wing linings, and bold black tail band. Black-tailed Godwit (casual) has straight bill, bold white wing stripe, and white wing linings.

Habitat. *Breeding:* Wet lowland tundra. Nests on the ground in moss. *Migration:* Tidal flats.

Region	Sp	S	F	W
Southeastern	+	+	+	-
Southcoastal	R	+	R	+
Southwestern	C	U	C	-
Central	-	-	-	-
Western ★	C	C	C	-
Northern ★	U	U	U	-

Bar-tailed Godwit

Bar-tailed Godwit, breeding male

Bar-tailed Godwit, breeding female

Marbled Godwit
Limosa fedoa

Field marks. 16"-20". *All plumages:* Largest godwit; very long, straight to slightly upturned, pink-based bill; cinnamon brown overall. *In flight:* Conspicuous cinnamon wing linings. *Breeding:* Cinnamon-buff underparts, with dark bars on breast and flanks.

Similar species. Juvenile Bar-tailed Godwit in fall has paler breast and belly and lighter tail. Hudsonian Godwit has white wing stripe, black wing linings, and bold black tail band. Black-tailed Godwit has straight bill, bold white wing stripe, and white wing linings.

Voice. A loud *kerreck*.

Habitat. Tidal flats. No nests have been found in Alaska.

Region	Sp	S	F	W
Southeastern	R	+	+	-
Southcoastal	R	I	I	
Southwestern ★	R	R	R	-
Central	-	-	-	-
Western	-	-	-	-
Northern	-	-	-	-

Marbled Godwit

Marbled Godwit, breeding

Ruddy Turnstone
Arenaria interpres

Field marks. 9". *Breeding:* Striking pattern of black, white, and russet; black bib, rusty back, orange-red legs. *In flight:* Bold calico pattern of black, white, and rust on upperparts. *Nonbreeding and juvenile:* Brownish, but still show enough of the peculiar breast and wing pattern to be distinctive.

Similar species. Black Turnstone lacks rust color and has dark legs and mostly dark head and neck; nonbreeding and juvenile Black has dark breast markings cut straight across, not bilobed as in Ruddy.

Voice. Chattering call, slower and lower-pitched than Black Turnstone.

Habitat. *Breeding:* Drier tundra areas, dunes. Nests in a depression on the ground. *Migration:* Rocky shores; tidal flats and beaches.

Region	Sp	S	F	W
Southeastern	U	-	U	+
Southcoastal	C	R	U	-
Southwestern	C	U	C	-
Central	R	+	-	-
Western ★	C	C	C	-
Northern ★	U	U	U	-

Ruddy Turnstone, breeding

Ruddy Turnstone, nonbreeding

Ruddy Turnstone

Black Turnstone
Arenaria melanocephala

Field marks. 9". *Breeding:* Black head with white spot at base of bill; black upperparts and breast, white belly, dark legs. *Nonbreeding and juvenile:* Similar but overall grayer and lack the white spot at base of bill. *In flight:* All plumages show a striking black-and-white pattern on wings and back.

Similar species. Nonbreeding Ruddy Turnstone usually shows peculiar bilobed breast pattern and orange-red legs.

Voice. High and shrill chattering call.

Habitat. *Breeding:* Wet tundra. Nests on the ground in grassy areas near ponds. *Migration and winter:* Rocky shores; tidal flats and beaches.

Region	Sp	S	F	W
Southeastern	C	R	C	U
Southcoastal	C	U	C	R
Southwestern ★	C	U	C	R
Central	-	+	+	-
Western ★	C	C	C	-
Northern	+	-	-	-

Black Turnstone, breeding

Black Turnstone, nonbreeding

Surfbird
Aphriza virgata

Field marks. 10". *All plumages:* Chunky; short, yellow legs; short bill. *In flight:* Appears dark, with white wing stripe, white rump, and tail base that contrasts with black tip. *Breeding:* Heavily spotted and streaked on breast and flanks; reddish brown on back. *Nonbreeding:* Plain gray head, upperparts, and breast; spotted sides.

Similar species. Wandering Tattler has longer bill and no white wing stripe and rump. Black Turnstone is darker, lacks spotted sides, and shows more white on lower back and wing in flight. Nonbreeding Rock Sandpiper is smaller, longer-billed, and shows a vertical black bar on rump.

Habitat. *Breeding:* Alpine tundra along mountain ridges. Nests on the ground in rocky areas interspersed with small clumps of vegetation. *Migration and winter:* Rocky shores and rockier portions of tidal flats.

Region	Sp	S	F	W
Southeastern	U	R	U	R
Southcoastal ★	C	U	C	U
Southwestern ★	R	R	R	R
Central ★	U	U	U	-
Western ★	R	R	R	-
Northern	-	-	+	-

Surfbird, juvenile

Surfbird, breeding

Red Knot
Calidris canutus

Region	Sp	S	F	W
Southeastern	R	-	+	-
Southcoastal	C	+	R	-
Southwestern	+	+	R	-
Central	+	-	-	-
Western ★	U	U	U	-
Northern ★	R	R	R	-

Field marks. 10½". *All plumages:* Short, straight, black bill. *Breeding:* Brick red face and underparts; dark brown upperparts, with white and reddish feather edges. *Nonbreeding and juvenile:* Upperparts light gray, underparts white.

Similar species. Juvenile Black-bellied Plover has spotted, golden yellow upperparts, streaked breast and belly. Curlew Sandpiper (casual) has long, downcurved bill. Dowitcher has a much longer bill, and in nonbreeding and juvenile plumage has gray breast and sides.

Habitat. *Breeding:* Gravelly ridges in alpine tundra. Nests on the ground in shallow depressions in gravel or rubble. *Migration:* Tidal flats. Locally abundant on tidal flats of Copper and Bering river deltas in spring, where flocks of more than 40,000 have been seen.

Red Knot, juvenile

Red Knot, breeding

Sanderling
Calidris alba

Field marks. 8". *All plumages:* Short, heavy black bill; black legs. *In flight:* Conspicuous white wing stripe. *Breeding:* Reddish upperparts, head, and neck; white belly. *Nonbreeding:* Very pale, with snowy white underparts; black mark at bend of wing (may not be visible). *Juvenile:* Black-and-white checkered upperparts, pure white below.

Similar species. Other small sandpipers lack the conspicuous white wing stripe visible in flight and in winter are not as pale.

Voice. A sharp *wick-wick.*

Habitat. *Breeding:* Primarily in Canadian arctic islands and Greenland; very rarely in Alaska, at Point Barrow. *Migration and winter:* Sandy beaches, tidal flats, and rocky beaches.

Region	Sp	S	F	W
Southeastern	U	R	U	R
Southcoastal	U	U	U	R
Southwestern	U	-	U	R
Central	R	+	R	-
Western	U	R	U	-
Northern ★	U	R	U	-

Sanderling, juvenile

Sanderling, breeding

Semipalmated Sandpiper
Calidris pusilla

Field marks. 6½". *All plumages:* Short, thick bill; black legs. *Breeding:* Mottled grayish-brown and black upperparts with some rufous color.

Similar species. Least Sandpiper has yellowish legs. Western Sandpiper usually has longer, thinner bill with a slight droop at tip; breeding Western has V-shaped marks on flanks; in fall, Western often has reddish color remaining on upperparts near neck. Juvenile Red-necked Stint has slenderer bill. White-rumped Sandpiper has all-white rump (lacks vertical black line of Semipalmated), and wing tips extend beyond end of tail. Baird's Sandpiper has wing tips that extend beyond end of tail. Nonbreeding and juvenile Little Stints (casual) nearly identical to nonbreeding and juvenile Semipalmated.

Voice. Trills on breeding grounds simple and unmusical. Flight call a sharp *cheh,* lower and shorter than calls of Least and Western.

Habitat. *Breeding:* Wet tundra, sand dunes. Nests on the ground in tundra or short grass of sand dunes. *Migration:* Tidal flats and beaches, lakeshores.

Region	Sp	S	F	W
Southeastern	R	-	R	-
Southcoastal	U	R	U	-
Southwestern	R	-	R	-
Central ★	C	+	U	-
Western ★	U	U	U	-
Northern ★	C	C	U	-

Semipalmated Sandpiper, breeding

Semipalmated Sandpiper, juvenile

Western Sandpiper
Calidris mauri

Field marks. 6½". *All plumages:* Longish bill with slight droop at tip; black legs. *Breeding:* V-shaped marks on flanks; rusty color on crown, near ear, and upperparts; in fall, usually retains rusty color on shoulders until mid-August or September. *Juvenile:* Bright, rusty-edged feathers on shoulder.

Similar species. Breeding Semi-palmated Sandpiper lacks V-shaped marks on flanks and rusty shoulder color in fall; bill is shorter and thicker. Least Sandpiper has yellowish legs. White-rumped and Baird's sandpipers have wing tips that, at rest, extend beyond tip of tail.

Voice. Breeding song is more varied than that of Semipalmated Sandpiper, rising and falling in pitch. Flight call: grating, rather high *keeep.*

Habitat. *Breeding:* Drier areas of tundra. Nests on ground in short tundra vegetation. *Migration:* Tidal flats and beaches.

Region	Sp	S	F	W
Southeastern	C	R	C	-
Southcoastal	C	U	C	-
Southwestern	C	R	C	-
Central ★	R	+	R	-
Western ★	C	C	C	-
Northern ★	U	U	U	-

Western Sandpiper, juvenile

Western Sandpiper, breeding

Red-necked Stint
Calidris ruficollis

Field marks. 6". *Breeding:* Rufous-colored face, throat, and upper breast; rufous feather edges on back, whitish chin, short black bill, short dark legs. Only small sandpiper (except Little Stint) with unwebbed toes.

Similar species. Breeding Little Stint (casual) has orange feather edges on back, rusty face, and mostly white throat. Breeding Western Sandpiper usually lacks rufous color on throat and breast. Breeding Sanderling has duller orange-rufous on throat and breast that is marked with short stripes and spots (lower throat lacks dots or streaks in Red-necked Stint). Nonbreeding Little Stint and Western and Semi-palmated sandpipers look nearly identical to nonbreeding Red-necked Stint.

Habitat. *Breeding:* Wet tundra. Nests in depressions in the tundra. *Migration:* Tidal flats. Asiatic species.

Region	Sp	S	F	W
Southeastern	-	-	+	-
Southcoastal	I	I	I	
Southwestern	R	+	R	-
Central	-	-	-	-
Western ★	R	R	+	-
Northern ★	R	R	R	-

Red-necked Stint, breeding

Long-toed Stint
Calidris subminuta

Field marks. 5¼". *Breeding:* Crown, ear, and finely streaked breast band are washed with pale cinnamon; longer toes than other small sandpipers; white throat; pale legs.

Similar species. Breeding Least Sandpiper lacks the pale cinnamon and is much browner. Nonbreeding and juvenile Least are difficult to tell from similarly plumaged Long-toed Stint.

Voice. Low, short, trilled *chrrup.*

Habitat. This Asiatic shorebird is seen mostly as a migrant in the western Aleutian Islands, where it frequents the vegetated margins of ponds and the debris line along the seashore.

Region	Sp	S	F	W
Southeastern	+	-	-	-
Southcoastal	-	-	-	-
Southwestern	R	+	R	-
Central	-	-	-	-
Western	R	-	-	-
Northern	-	-	-	-

Long-toed Stint, breeding

Least Sandpiper
Calidris minutilla

Field marks. 5½". *All plumages:* Short, finely tapered bill; yellowish or greenish legs. *Breeding:* Sooty brown upperparts; foreneck and upper breast with brown streaks. *Juvenile:* Rufous-fringed upperparts.

Similar species. Western and Semipalmated sandpipers have longer bills and black legs, and appear lighter on upperparts, neck, and breast. Breeding Long-toed Stint is washed with pale cinnamon on crown around ear and breast; nonbreeding and juvenile very similar to Least.

Voice. A thin, rising *pree-eet*.

Habitat. *Breeding:* Sedge-grass marshes near tidal flats, freshwater marshes, muskegs. Nests on the ground in both wet and dry grassy areas. *Migration:* Tidal flats, lakes, ponds, marshes.

Region	Sp	S	F	W
Southeastern ★	C	U	C	-
Southcoastal ★	C	C	C	-
Southwestern ★	C	C	C	-
Central ★	C	U	U	-
Western ★	U	U	U	-
Northern ★	U	U	R	-

Least Sandpiper, nonbreeding

Least Sandpiper, breeding

White-rumped Sandpiper
Calidris fuscicollis

Field marks. *7½". All plumages:* Wing tips, at rest, extend well beyond tip of tail. *In flight:* White rump. *Breeding:* Rusty tinge on crown and around ear; dark brown streaks on breast and flanks.

Similar species. Baird's Sandpiper lacks all-white rump and streaks on flanks; has a buff-colored tinge on face, pronounced scaly appearance on back. All other similar-sized sandpipers have wing tips that do not extend beyond tip of tail.

Voice. A very high, mouselike squeak.

Habitat. *Breeding:* Wet grassy tundra. Nests on the ground in tundra moss. *Migration:* Tidal flats and beaches.

Region	Sp	S	F	W
Southeastern	+	-	-	-
Southcoastal	+	-	+	-
Southwestern	-	-	-	-
Central	R	-	-	-
Western	-	-	-	-
Northern ★	R	R	-	-

White-rumped Sandpiper, juvenile

White-rumped Sandpiper, breeding

Baird's Sandpiper
Calidris bairdii

Field marks. 7". *All plumages:* Wing tips, at rest, extend well beyond tip of tail; pronounced scaly appearance on back. *In flight:* Buff-white rump divided by broad black line. *Breeding:* Buff-colored tinge on face. *Juvenile:* Buff-colored foreparts.

Similar species. White-rumped Sandpiper has all-white rump and a rusty tinge on crown and around ear. All other similar-sized sandpipers have wing tips that do not extend beyond tip of tail.

Voice. Call is a louder, deeper version of Least Sandpiper's. Breeding song: a loud, long trill, *durreee, durreee,* given from high in the air.

Habitat. *Breeding:* Tundra, preferably drier portions. Nests on dry tundra. *Migration:* Lakes, ponds, tidal flats, and beaches, often in drier areas.

Region	Sp	S	F	W
Southeastern	U	-	U	-
Southcoastal	U	+	U	-
Southwestern	R	-	U	-
Central ★	U	U	U	-
Western ★	U	U	U	-
Northern ★	C	C	C	-

Baird's Sandpiper, juvenile

Baird's Sandpiper, breeding

Pectoral Sandpiper
Calidris melanotos

Field marks. 9". *All plumages:* Heavily streaked brown breast, with streaks sharply cut off from white belly; yellowish legs.

Similar species. Breeding Sharp-tailed Sandpiper has bold V marks on orange breast that extend to flanks. Juvenile Sharp-tailed Sandpiper has buff-colored breast only lightly streaked and not sharply cut off from white belly, and a ruddy-colored cap. Least Sandpiper is much smaller. Baird's and White-rumped have black legs and are lighter overall.

Voice. The male's "hooting" court-ship call given in low flights across the tundra is unique among North American shorebirds. To call, they fill their esophagus with air until breast and throat are inflated to at least twice normal size.

Habitat. *Breeding:* Grassy areas in wet tundra. Nests on the ground within tundra vegetation. *Migration:* Sedge-grass areas of tidal flats, grassy marshes, grassy edges of lakes and ponds.

Region	Sp	S	F	W
Southeastern	C	+	C	-
Southcoastal	C	+	C	-
Southwestern	R	R	C	-
Central	C	U	U	-
Western ★	C	C	C	-
Northern ★	C	C	C	-

Pectoral Sandpiper, breeding

Pectoral Sandpiper, juvenile

Sharp-tailed Sandpiper
Calidris acuminata

Field marks. 8½". *Breeding:* Orange breast with bold V marks that extend to flanks. *Juvenile:* Buff-colored breast only lightly streaked, not sharply cut off from white belly; ruddy-colored cap; white eyebrow, broader behind eye.

Similar species. Pectoral Sandpiper has dark breast streaks that are sharply cut off from white belly; lacks the ruddy cap and bold V marks and has a longer bill; white eyebrow, if present, is fainter and not broader behind eye.

Habitat. *Migration:* This Siberian bird frequents grassy areas of tidal flats, marshes, lakes, and ponds.

Region	Sp	S	F	W
Southeastern	+	-	R	-
Southcoastal	-	-	R	-
Southwestern	+	-	U	-
Central	-	-	+	-
Western	+	+	U	-
Northern	+	-	+	-

Sharp-tailed Sandpiper, juvenile

Rock Sandpiper
Calidris ptilocnemis

Field marks. 9". *All plumages:* Slightly downcurved bill; short legs. *Breeding:* Black patch on breast; rust-colored upperparts; pale head with dark ear patch. *Winter:* Brownish gray upperparts and breast; dark, slender bill with yellowish base, gray spots on sides; greenish yellow legs.

Similar species. Breeding Dunlin has black patch on belly, not breast; black legs. Winter-plumaged Dunlin has all-black bill and legs; lacks spots on sides. Purple Sandpiper (accidental) probably indistinguishable from Rock Sandpiper in winter.

Habitat. *Breeding:* Tundra. Nests on the ground in mossy or rocky tundra. *Migration and winter:* Tidal flats and beaches, usually in more rocky areas.

Region	Sp	S	F	W
Southeastern	C	-	C	C
Southcoastal	C	-	C	C
Southwestern ★	C	C	C	C
Central	-	-	-	-
Western ★	C	C	C	-
Northern	-	-	-	-

Rock Sandpiper, nonbreeding

Rock Sandpiper, breeding

Dunlin
Calidris alpina

Field marks. 8". *All plumages:* All-black bill, drooped near tip; black legs. *Breeding:* Black patch on belly, rich reddish upperparts. *Juvenile:* Reddish upperparts, dark brown spots on belly. *Winter:* Unpatterned grayish brown upperparts and breast, white below.

Similar species. Breeding Rock Sandpiper has black patch on lower breast and greenish yellow legs. Winter Rock Sandpiper has pale base on dark bill, greenish yellow legs, and gray spots on flanks. Winter-plumaged Curlew Sandpiper (casual) has all-white rump (Dunlin has broad black median line on white rump).

Habitat. *Breeding:* Wet grassy tundra and coastal sedge-grass marshes. Nests on the ground in grassy areas. *Migration and winter:* Tidal flats, and muddy and sandy beaches. Sometimes associated with Rock Sandpipers in rocky areas.

Region	Sp	S	F	W
Southeastern	C	-	C	U
Southcoastal ★	C	R	C	U
Southwestern ★	C	C	C	U
Central	+	+	+	-
Western ★	C	C	C	-
Northern ★	C	C	C	-

Dunlin, breeding

Dunlin, juvenile

Dunlin, nonbreeding

Stilt Sandpiper
Calidris himantopus

Field marks. 8". *All plumages:* Long, drooped bill; dull yellow to grayish green legs. *Breeding:* Chestnut cheek patch; heavily barred underparts. *Juvenile and winter plumage:* Whitish eyebrow. *In flight:* White rump.

Behavior. Feeds by constant probing, like dowitchers, usually in water.

Similar species. Lesser Yellowlegs has straight bill, bright yellow legs, and less distinct whitish eyebrow. Juvenile Curlew Sandpiper (casual) has bill tapered to fine tip (Stilt Sandpiper has blunt tip), black legs, and prominent white wing stripe (short and narrow in juvenile Stilt Sandpiper).

Habitat. *Breeding:* Relatively open, dry tundra, north of the tree line. Nests have been found in the Arctic National Wildlife Refuge. *Migration:* Tidal flats, lakeshores, ponds, sloughs.

Region	Sp	S	F	W
Southeastern	+	-	R	-
Southcoastal	+	-	R	-
Southwestern	+	-	-	-
Central	R	-	+	-
Western	+	+	-	-
Northern ★	R	R	R	-

Stilt Sandpiper, juvenile

Stilt Sandpiper, breeding

Buff-breasted Sandpiper
Tryngites subruficollis

Field marks. 8 ½". *All plumages:* Buff-colored underparts, white wing linings, yellow legs.

Behavior. Impressive display on the breeding grounds, with 1 or both wings raised to show the white wing linings.

Similar species. Upland Sandpiper is larger, with a smaller head and longer neck and tail; streaked and barred underparts and underwing. Juvenile Ruff is larger; has longer neck and legs and reddish-fringed upperparts (not pale sandy buff).

Habitat. *Breeding:* Dry tundra ridges. Nests on the ground in dry areas. *Migration:* Drier areas of tidal flats, sandy beaches, grassy fields, and meadows.

Region	Sp	S	F	W
Southeastern	+	-	+	-
Southcoastal			+	-
Southwestern	-	-	+	-
Central	R	-	+	-
Western	R	-	+	-
Northern ★	R	R	R	-

Buff-breasted Sandpiper

Ruff
Philomachus pugnax

Field marks. 11½". *In flight:* Conspicuous large, white patches on rump separated by a dark median line; feet project beyond tail. *Breeding male:* Huge erectile ruffs of white, orange, brown, or black. *Breeding female:* Lacks ruff; white underparts with variable amount of black on breast and foreneck, giving scaly appearance. *Nonbreeding:* Whitish area at base of short tapered bill; upperparts warm brown with scaly appearance. *Juvenile:* Reddish-fringed upperparts, buff-colored breast, white belly.

Similar species. Pectoral Sandpiper has heavily streaked breast that is cut off sharply from white belly. Both Yellowlegs have streaked breasts. Juvenile Sharp-tailed Sandpiper has ruddy-colored cap.

Habitat. This Asiatic shorebird has been found mostly in western and central Aleutian Islands, on Bering Sea islands, and on the Chukchi Sea coast. Only 1 nest has been found, in northern Alaska.

Region	Sp	S	F	W
Southeastern	+	-	+	-
Southcoastal	-	-	+	-
Southwestern	R	-	R	-
Central	-	-	-	-
Western	R	+	R	-
Northern ★	-	+	+	-

Ruff, breeding male

Ruff, nonbreeding

Ruff, juvenile

Short-billed Dowitcher
Limnodromus griseus

Field marks. 11½". *All plumages:* Long, straight bill. *In flight:* White on rump and lower back penetrates forward in a point (white rumps on most shorebirds cut straight across). *Breeding:* Reddish underparts, sides of breast spotted, lightly barred flanks. *Juvenile:* Upper feather edges broad and rusty; lower feathers washed with rust.

Similar species. Breeding Long-billed Dowitcher has heavier barring on its sides to upper breast; heavily spotted throat. Juvenile Long-billed Dowitcher has upper feather edges that are narrow and buff-colored; lower feathers washed with buff. The voices of Long-billed and Short-billed dowitchers are different. Common Snipe has shorter legs, stripes on head and back; lacks white on lower back and tail.

Voice. Low, mellow *tu-tu-tu.*

Habitat. *Breeding:* Muskegs. Nesting locations are not well known. One nest was found in a muskeg and consisted of a small hollow in the moss. *Migration:* Tidal flats and ponds, especially the muddy portions.

Region	Sp	S	F	W
Southeastern ★	C	R	C	-
Southcoastal ★	C	C	C	
Southwestern ★	C	C	C	-
Central	-	+	-	-
Western	-	+	-	-
Northern	-	-	-	-

Short-billed Dowitcher, breeding

Short-billed Dowitcher, juvenile

Long-billed Dowitcher
Limnodromus scolopaceus

Field marks. 11½". *All plumages:* Long, straight bill. *In flight:* White on rump and lower back penetrates forward in a point. *Breeding:* Reddish underparts, heavily spotted throat, obvious barring on sides to upper breast. *Juvenile:* Upper feather edges narrow and buff-colored; lower feathers washed with buff.

Similar species. Breeding Short-billed Dowitcher has mostly spots and light barring on sides, and light spotting on throat. Juvenile Short-billed Dowitcher has upper feather edges that are broad and rusty and lower feathers washed with rust. The voices of Short-billed and Long-billed dowitchers are different. Common Snipe has shorter legs, stripes on head and back, and dark rump.

Voice. A high, single or sometimes repeated *peep*.

Habitat. *Breeding:* Wet tundra. Nests on the ground in wet marshy areas. *Migration:* Tidal flats and ponds, especially muddy areas.

Region	Sp	S	F	W
Southeastern	U	-	U	+
Southcoastal	C	+	C	-
Southwestern	U	-	U	-
Central ★	C	U	U	-
Western ★	C	C	C	-
Northern ★	C	C	C	-

Long-billed Dowitcher, juvenile

Long-billed Dowitcher, breeding

Common Snipe
Gallinago gallinago

Region	Sp	S	F	W
Southeastern ★	C	C	C	U
Southcoastal ★	C	C	C	R
Southwestern ★	C	C	C	+
Central ★	C	C	C	-
Western ★	C	C	C	-
Northern ★	C	C	C	-

Field marks. 11". *All plumages:* Extremely long, straight bill; vivid buff-colored stripes on head and back. *In flight:* Short, dark tail (orange at close range); dark wings and lower back.

Behavior. Secretive bird, seldom seen except when flushed.

Similar species. Dowitchers have white rump and lower back; no buff-colored stripes on head and back.

Voice. When flushed, a raspy *zhak.* On breeding grounds, a prolonged series of short, shrill *wheets.* Produces a loud winnowing sound during courtship that sounds like *who who who who who who who* that increases and then decreases in intensity. This *who who* sound is made in flight by air rushing past stiffened tail feathers; pulsations are produced by wingbeats.

Habitat. *Breeding:* Muskegs, freshwater marshes. Nests on the ground, usually in grass. *Migration and winter:* Sedge-grass meadows at the head of tidal flats and freshwater marshes.

Common Snipe

Red-necked Phalarope
Phalaropus lobatus

Field marks. 7". *All plumages:* Thin, dark bill. *Breeding female:* Gray above, rufous patch on neck, white throat. *Breeding male:* Browner, less colorful than female; white line above eye. *Juvenile:* Dark mark through eye, dark crown and back, back heavily marked with pale lines.

Behavior. Lands on water, swims with ease, spins.

Similar species. Breeding Red Phalarope has a thicker, yellow bill with black tip; white patch on face and no white throat. Juvenile Red Phalarope has evenly striped upperparts (not wide, as in juvenile Red-necked). Wilson's Phalarope (casual) has white breast and belly and longer, thinner bill; shows no white wing stripe in flight (other phalaropes have white wing stripe).

Habitat. *Breeding:* Wet tundra, freshwater marshes, ponds, lakes. Nests on the ground in wet grassy areas near water. *Migration:* Inshore and offshore marine waters, tidal ponds and sloughs, lakes and ponds.

Region	Sp	S	F	W
Southeastern	C	U	C	+
Southcoastal ★	C	C	C	+
Southwestern ★	C	C	C	-
Central ★	C	C	C	-
Western ★	C	C	C	-
Northern ★	C	C	C	-

Red-necked Phalarope, breeding female

Red-necked Phalarope, juvenile

Red-necked Phalarope, breeding male

Red Phalarope
Phalaropus fulicaria

Field marks. 8". *Breeding female:* Brown above, rich reddish below, white face patch, yellow bill, dark throat. *Breeding male:* Variable, from just duller than female but with brownish, streaked crown to virtually white beneath; yellow bill. *Juvenile:* Gray, evenly striped back; dark mark through eye.

Behavior. Lands on water, swims with ease, spins.

Similar species. Breeding Red-necked Phalarope has white throat and dark, thinner bill; lacks white face patch. Juvenile Red-necked Phalarope has dark back, heavily marked with pale lines. Wilson's Phalarope (casual) has longer, thinner bill, white breast, and belly, and shows no white wing stripe in flight.

Habitat. *Breeding:* Wet tundra near ponds and lakes. Nests on the ground in tundra. *Migration:* Inshore and offshore marine waters, preferably offshore.

Region	Sp	S	F	W
Southeastern	R	-	R	-
Southcoastal	C	R	C	-
Southwestern	C	U	C	-
Central	+	+	-	-
Western ★	C	C	C	-
Northern ★	C	C	C	-

Red Phalarope, juvenile

Red Phalarope, breeding female

JAEGERS, GULLS, TERNS
Family *Laridae*

Jaegers are gull-like seabirds with a strongly hooked bill and sharp claws. Their wings are narrow, pointed, and dark, with white patches near the tip. Adults have characteristic projecting central tail feathers, but these may be missing or broken. Their color can range from very light (light phase) to very dark (dark phase). Jaegers fly in a fast, falconlike manner, forcing gulls and terns to drop or disgorge just-caught fish. The agility of the jaegers during these maneuvers is breathtaking. Jaegers are predators that also feed on songbirds, shorebirds, lemmings, and the eggs and young of other birds. They also scavenge on garbage thrown from ships and on waste from fish-processing boats.

Gulls are the familiar "seagulls" that frequent Alaska's waters. Adult gulls are mostly white below and gray above, often with black on the wing tips or head. The relative darkness of the mantle—the back and wings together—is helpful in identifying some gull species. Young gulls are usually darker than adults of the same species and, depending on species, can take as long as 4 years to reach maturity. Young gulls can be difficult to identify. They molt each fall and take on a distinctive appearance, a winter plumage (cited in the following descriptions as "first-winter," "second-winter," etc.). Gulls will eat almost anything. They can act as scavengers on beaches and garbage dumps or as predators on the eggs and young of other birds.

Terns look somewhat like gulls, but are more slender, with very pointed wings and sharp-pointed bills. They usually have long, forked tails, in contrast with the square-cut or rounded tails of the gulls. Terns do not have the color phases of the jaegers or the different plumages of the gulls. Most terns are white or whitish, with dark caps. Terns are more selective than jaegers and gulls in their diet, feeding mostly on fish. They typically hunt for fish by hovering over the water, then plunging headfirst after their prey.

Mew Gull

Pomarine Jaeger
Stercorarius pomarinus

Region	Sp	S	F	W
Southeastern	R	R	U	-
Southcoastal	C	R	C	
Southwestern	C	U	C	-
Central	-	+	-	-
Western ★	C	R	C	-
Northern ★	C	U	C	-

Field marks. 22". *Light-phase adult:* In flight, shows a dark breast band, white belly, and blunt central tail feathers that project 1 to 4 inches. *Light-phase juvenile:* Brown, heavily barred below; lacks projecting central tail feathers. *Dark-phase adult:* Blunt central tail feathers. *Dark-phase juvenile:* Identification extremely difficult; large size, wings broad at base, and steady flight with strong, shallow wingbeats helpful in identification.

Similar species. Adult Parasitic Jaeger has pointed central tail feathers; light-phase has less distinct breast band. Juvenile Parasitic has a more buoyant flight, with wings narrower at base and more angled. Adult Long-tailed Jaeger has no breast band; has long, projecting tail feathers. Juvenile Long-tailed is difficult to identify, but has a light, airy flight; shows less white in the spread wing and is smaller and paler than Pomarine juvenile.

Habitat. *Breeding:* Low, wet tundra in areas interspersed with lakes and ponds. Nests on the ground in slight depressions. *Migration:* Inshore and offshore marine waters.

Pomarine Jaeger, light-phase adult

Pomarine Jaeger, juvenile

Parasitic Jaeger
Stercorarius parasiticus

Field marks. 17". *Light-phase adult:* In flight, shows a rather diffuse breast band; pointed central tail feathers, shorter than those of adult Long-tailed Jaeger. *Dark-phase adult:* Pointed central tail feathers. *Juvenile:* More buoyant flight than Pomarine Jaeger, and wings appear narrower at base and more angled.

Similar species. Adult Pomarine Jaeger has short, blunt-tipped tail feathers. Juvenile Pomarine is larger, has more steady flight, and wings appear broader at base and less angled. Adult Long-tailed Jaeger lacks a breast band and has very long, pointed central tail feathers. Juvenile Long-tailed shows less white in the spread wing and is smaller and paler.

Habitat. *Breeding:* Wet tundra, tidal flats, beaches, coastal marshes. Nests on the ground in depressions. *Migration:* Tundra, tidal flats, beaches, coastal marshes, inshore and offshore marine waters.

Region	Sp	S	F	W
Southeastern ★	U	U	U	-
Southcoastal ★	U	C	C	-
Southwestern ★	C	C	C	-
Central ★	-	R	-	-
Western ★	C	C	C	-
Northern ★	C	C	C	-

Parasitic Jaeger, light-phase adult

Parasitic Jaeger, juvenile

Long-tailed Jaeger
Stercorarius longicaudus

Field marks. 21". *Adult:* Long, streaming central tail feathers; plain white breast; bluish gray legs. Dark-phase birds are extremely rare. *Juvenile:* Shows less white in the spread wing and is slightly smaller and paler than Parasitic Jaeger in similar plumage; has light, airy flight.

Similar species. Other light-phased adult jaegers have a breast band. Parasitic Jaeger may resemble a molting Long-tailed Jaeger with only partly developed tail feathers, but has a brown rather than gray-brown back, a breast band, and black legs. See Pomarine and Parasitic jaegers.

Habitat. *Breeding:* Wet coastal tundra and drier upland tundra of the Interior. Nests on the ground. *Migration:* Inshore and offshore marine waters.

Region	Sp	S	F	W
Southeastern	R	R	R	-
Southcoastal ★	R	R	R	I
Southwestern ★	U	U	U	-
Central ★	C	C	C	-
Western ★	C	C	C	-
Northern ★	C	C	C	-

Long-tailed Jaeger, juvenile

Long-tailed Jaeger, adult

Black-headed Gull
Larus ridibundus

Field marks. 14½". *Adult:* Similar to adult Bonaparte's Gull, but larger with a longer, thicker bill and slightly paler mantle. *In flight:* Shows dark gray lower surface of wing tips. *First-winter:* Yellowish bill with black tip.

Similar species. Adult Bonaparte's Gull is smaller, with shorter, fine-pointed bill; in flight, shows white lower surface of wing tips; first-winter bird has blackish bill with reddish base.

Habitat. This Asiatic gull is seen most often in western and central Aleutian Islands and Pribilof Islands.

Region	Sp	S	F	W
Southeastern	-	-	+	-
Southcoastal	+	+	+	-
Southwestern	R	R	+	-
Central	+	-	-	-
Western	R	+	-	-
Northern	-	+	-	-

Black-headed Gull, breeding

Black-headed Gull, first-winter

Bonaparte's Gull
Larus philadelphia

Region	Sp	S	F	W
Southeastern ★	C	U	C	+
Southcoastal ★	C	C	C	+
Southwestern ★	U	U	U	-
Central ★	U	U	U	-
Western ★	U	U	U	-
Northern	-	+	·	-

Field marks. 13". Small, fine-pointed black bill. *In flight:* Flies like a tern, with rapid wingbeats; hovers. Largely white wing tips flash conspicuously at considerable distances. *Breeding:* Black head, white crescent bordering eyes, red legs. *Winter adult:* White head with conspicuous black ear spot; wings with black on trailing edge only. *First-winter:* Striking pattern of black, gray, and white on upper wings; dark band at end of tail; black ear spot; blackish bill with reddish base.

Similar species. Black-headed Gull is larger, with a longer bill; in flight, shows dark gray lower surface of wing tips; first-winter bird has yellowish bill with black tip. Adult Franklin's Gull (casual) is larger, has darker mantle, and has white band across wing tips.

Habitat. *Breeding:* Coniferous woods near lakes and ponds. Nests in low conifers. *Migration and winter:* Tidal flats, beaches, inshore marine waters, lakes, salmon streams.

Bonaparte's Gull, breeding

Bonaparte's Gull, first-winter

Mew Gull
Larus canus

Region	Sp	S	F	W
Southeastern ★	C	C	C	C
Southcoastal ★	C	C	C	C
Southwestern ★	C	C	C	C
Central ★	C	C	C	-
Western ★	C	C	C	-
Northern ★	R	R	R	-

Field marks. 17". *Adult:* Yellowish bill without markings, dark gray mantle, prominent white spots on black wing tips (may appear as white band), greenish yellow legs, brown eyes. *First-winter:* Grayish brown; dark band on tail tip; pinkish gray legs and base of bill; dark eyes. *Second-winter:* Begins to resemble adult, but with mottled head; dark tip on gray bill.

Similar species. First-winter Ring-billed Gull has larger bill and narrower tail band. Second-winter and adult Ring-billed have pale eyes and a distinct black ring around bill. Other similar-looking gulls are much larger, with heavier bills. (Note: A Siberian subspecies—*L. c. kamtschatschensis*—that occurs in the western Aleutian Islands is suspected to be a separate species. It is decidedly larger than the Mew Gull, is darker on the mantle, and has a longer bill in which more than half of the top of the upper mandible is straight.)

Habitat. *Breeding:* Tundra, lakes, rivers, streams, islands. Nests on tundra, in trees, on stumps, in cavities in sand by water. *Migration and winter:* Inshore and offshore marine waters, tidal flats, beaches, lakes, rivers, rocky shores, reefs.

Mew Gull, breeding

Mew Gull, winter, adult

Mew Gull, juvenile

Mew Gull, second-summer

Ring-billed Gull
Larus delawarensis

Field marks. 19½". *Adult:* Yellow bill with distinct black ring, yellow legs, pale gray mantle. *First-winter:* Pale gray mantle, narrow tail band. *Second-winter:* Pale gray mantle, pale eyes, black ring around bill.

Similar species. Mew Gull has much smaller bill, dark eyes, darker mantle. Other gulls in similar immature plumages have darker mantle and broader tail band.

Habitat. Inshore marine waters, tidal flats, beaches.

Region	Sp	S	F	W
Southeastern	R	R	R	R
Southcoastal	R	R	R	R
Southwestern	-	+	+	-
Central	+	-	-	-
Western	-	-	-	-
Northern	-	-	-	-

Ring-billed Gull, second-winter

Ring-billed Gull, first-winter

Ring-billed Gull, adult

California Gull
Larus californicus

Field marks. 21½". *Adult:* Yellow bill with both a red and a black spot near tip, dark eyes, medium gray mantle, yellow-green legs. *First- and second-winter:* Resemble young Herring Gull, but are smaller, with a more slender bill that is flesh-colored for the basal two-thirds.

Similar species. Ring-billed Gull has paler mantle; adults and second-winter birds have a distinct ring around bill and have pale eyes (third-winter California Gull may show bill ring, but has dark eyes). See Herring Gull.

Habitat. Found mostly in southern part of southeastern Alaska along inshore marine waters and coastal beaches.

Region	Sp	S	F	W
Southeastern	R	U	U	+
Southcoastal	+	+	+	-
Southwestern	-	-	-	-
Central	-	-	-	-
Western	-	-	-	-
Northern	-	-	-	-

California Gull, adult

California Gull, first-winter

California Gull, second-winter

Herring Gull
Larus argentatus

Field marks. 24". *Adult:* Yellow bill with red spot; flesh-colored legs; cold, yellow eyes; jet black wing tips above and below, with two white spots; pale gray mantle. *Winter adult:* Dark streaks on head. *Juvenile and first-winter:* Dusky gray brown; all dark bill at first with pale base later; wide black tail band. *Second- and third-winter:* Gray back, dark wing tips, black tail band, light rump, pink or yellow bill with dark tip.

Similar species. See Ring-billed, California, Thayer's, and immature Lesser Black-backed gulls.

Habitat. *Breeding:* Lakes, rivers, islands, tidal flats, beaches. Nests on the ground in hollows; on sand, gravel, rocks, grassy fields, and cliff ledges; in trees. *Migration and winter:* Lakes, rivers, tidal flats, beaches, garbage dumps, inshore marine waters.

Region	Sp	S	F	W
Southeastern ★	C	C	C	C
Southcoastal ★	C	U	C	U
Southwestern	R	R	R	R
Central ★	U	U	U	-
Western ★	U	U	U	-
Northern ★	-	R	U	-

Herring Gull, juvenile

Herring Gull, second-winter

Herring Gull, adult

Thayer's Gull
Larus thayeri

Field marks. 24". Formerly considered a subspecies of the Herring Gull, this bird is difficult to separate from that species, but the following are some helpful marks. *All plumages:* Smallish bill, gently curving on top, with no thickening toward the tip. *Typical adult:* Wing tips black above and gray below; brown eyes.

Similar species. Typical adult Herring Gull has black or blackish wing tips from below, and cold yellow eyes. Typical adult Glaucous-winged Gull has gray wing tips from above, and a much larger, thicker bill. Some individuals of these 2 species develop characteristics that make them look nearly identical to the Thayer's Gull. (Note: Birds of a plumage with characteristics of the Iceland Gull, *Larus glaucoides,* have been observed in southeastern Alaska. It's not known whether these are pale Thayer's Gulls or stray Iceland Gulls from the eastern Arctic. The Thayer's Gull is under consideration for including with the Iceland Gull as a single species.)

Habitat. *Migration and winter:* Similar to the Herring Gull.

Region	Sp	S	F	W
Southeastern	C	+	C	U
Southcoastal	R	R	R	R
Southwestern	+	-	+	+
Central	-	-	-	-
Western	-	-	+	-
Northern	-	-	R	-

Thayer's Gull, adult

Thayer's Gull, first-winter

Slaty-backed Gull
Larus schistisagus

Field marks. 27". *Adult:* Dark slate-gray mantle, black wing tips, cream-colored eyes with pale pink eye ring. *In flight:* Broad white trailing edge on wings.

Similar species. Adult Herring Gull has pale gray mantle; cold, yellow eyes. A dark-backed form of the Herring Gull from Siberia *(L. a. vegae),* found in the northern Bering Sea, may be confused with the Slaty-backed Gull, but this form is clearly paler than the Slaty-backed and, in flight, shows a narrow white trailing edge on wings.

Habitat. This Eurasian gull is seen mostly along the Bering Sea coast of Alaska; more numerous in winter, when flocks of more than 30 may be seen along leads and edges of the pack ice.

Region	Sp	S	F	W
Southeastern	-	-	+	+
Southcoastal	+	+	+	+
Southwestern	R	R	R	U
Central	-	-	-	-
Western ★	R	R	R	U
Northern	R	R	R	-

Slaty-backed Gull, adult

Glaucous-winged Gull
Larus glaucescens

Region	Sp	S	F	W
Southeastern ★	C	C	C	C
Southcoastal ★	C	C	C	C
Southwestern ★	C	C	C	C
Central	-	R	R	-
Western ★	C	C	C	-
Northern	-	-	+	-

Field marks. 26". *Adult:* Pale gray mantle; upper and lower wing tips somewhat darker gray, with white spots; eyes usually brown, but may vary to yellow (not clear yellow); pink legs. *First-winter:* All-black bill, buff-colored mottling, pink legs. Second- and third-year immatures become increasingly like adults, maturing in fourth or fifth year. Intermediate-plumaged birds vary widely and can be difficult to identify. Also, species of larger gulls hybridize, which further complicates identification.

Similar species. Adult Glaucous Gull has whiter wing tips. First-winter Glaucous has obvious black tip to flesh-pink bill. Adult Herring Gull has thinner bill; cold, yellow eyes; black wing tips.

Habitat. *Breeding:* Tidal flats, beaches, inshore marine waters, islands, cliffs. Nests in colonies on flat, low islands, cliff ledges, and rocky beaches. *Migration and winter:* Various habitats, including coastal communities, garbage dumps, around canneries, salmon streams, inshore and offshore marine waters, tidal flats, beaches.

Glaucous-winged Gull, adult

Glaucous-winged Gull, second-winter

Glaucous Gull
Larus hyperboreus

Field marks. 27". *Adult:* Pure white wing tips. *Immature:* At a distance, looks uniform pale buff (first-year) or white (second-year), with flesh color on the basal two-thirds of the dark-tipped bill.

Similar species. Adult Glaucous-winged Gull has gray wing tips. Immature Glaucous-winged has all-black, mostly black, or irregularly tipped bills (not sharply cutoff black tips).

Habitat. *Breeding:* Cliffs near the coast, islands, tundra. Nests in colonies on cliff ledges, on the ground in slightly elevated portions of the tundra, or on islands in tundra lakes. *Migration and winter:* Tidal flats, beaches, inshore marine waters.

Region	Sp	S	F	W
Southeastern	R	R	R	R
Southcoastal	R	R	R	R
Southwestern ★	U	U	U	U
Central	R	R	R	-
Western ★	C	C	C	+
Northern ★	C	C	C	-

Glaucous Gull, first-winter

Glaucous Gull, adult

Black-legged Kittiwake
Rissa tridactyla

Region	Sp	S	F	W
Southeastern ★	U	U	U	U
Southcoastal ★	C	C	C	U
Southwestern ★	C	C	C	U
Central	-	-	+	-
Western ★	C	C	C	-
Northern	R	C	C	-

Field marks. 17". *Breeding:* Black wing tips that look as if they had been dipped in ink, unmarked yellow bill, black legs. *First-year:* White below, dark band across back of neck, dark ear spot, dark tail tip, black bill and legs, and an M-shaped mark across mantle.

Similar species. Adult Red-legged Kittiwake has red legs and feet, darker mantle, conspicuously dark underwings. First-year Red-legged Kittiwake lacks both the M-shaped mark across mantle and black tail tip. Adult Mew Gull has irregularly shaped black wing tip with white spots. Immature Sabine's Gull lacks narrow M-shaped mark across mantle. First year Ross's Gull lacks dark band on back of neck and has red legs.

Habitat. *Breeding:* Sea cliffs, inshore marine waters. Nests on cliff ledges. *Migration and winter:* Inshore and offshore marine waters, tidal flats, beaches, rocky shores, reefs.

Black-legged Kittiwake, first-winter

Black-legged Kittiwake, adult

Red-legged Kittiwake
Rissa brevirostris

Field marks. 15". *Adult:* Dark mantle with black wing tips, conspicuously dark underwings (good distant field mark), red legs and feet. *First-year:* Indistinct dark bar on back of neck, ragged white triangle in trailing edge of dark upperwing, all-white tail.

Similar species. Adult Black-legged Kittiwake has white underwings, black legs and feet. First-year Black-legged Kittiwake has M-shaped mark across mantle and dark tail tip. Immature Sabine's Gull has distinct 3-colored mantle and dark tail tip.

Habitat. *Breeding:* Pribilof Islands; Buldir and Bogoslof islands in the Aleutians. Nests on cliff ledges and cliff points. *Migration and winter:* Inshore and offshore marine waters.

Region	Sp	S	F	W
Southeastern	-	-	-	-
Southcoastal	-	+	+	R
Southwestern ★	U	C	U	U
Central	-	+	-	-
Western	-	R	+	-
Northern	-	-	-	-

Red-legged Kittiwake, adult

Ross's Gull
Rhodostethia rosea

Region	Sp	S	F	W
Southeastern	-	-	-	-
Southcoastal	+	-	-	-
Southwestern	+	-	+	+
Central	-	-	+	-
Western	R	+	R	-
Northern	+	+	C	-

Field marks. 13½". Short black bill, red legs, wedge-shaped tail, pale gray mantle. *Breeding:* Black neck ring, rosy tinge to underparts. *First- and second-winter:* Dark M pattern on the mantle, similar to Black-legged Kittiwake, but without dark bar on the neck (second-winter Ross's develops black neck ring).

Similar species. First-year Black-legged Kittiwake has dark band across back of neck; black legs. Juvenile Sabine's Gull has a forked tail.

Habitat. This Asiatic gull frequents the edges and leads of pack ice in the Arctic Ocean. Best place to see this bird is the Point Barrow vicinity in fall.

Ross's Gull, first-winter

Ross's Gull, breeding

Sabine's Gull
Xema sabini

Field marks. 13½". *All plumages:* Prominent tricolored pattern on upper wings with black, white, and gray; shallow fork in tail. *Breeding:* Dark hood; black bill with yellow tip. *Immature:* Lacks dark hood; browner on upper parts; dark tail tip.

Similar species. Bonaparte's and Black-headed gulls have a white triangular patch on forewing that extends to tip (in Sabine's, this area is black). Juvenile Black-legged Kittiwake has dark band across back of neck and a narrow M-shaped mark across mantle.

Habitat. *Breeding:* Wet tundra, lakes, ponds, tidal flats. Nests on the tundra near lakes and ponds. *Migration:* Inshore and offshore marine waters, tidal flats, beaches.

Region	Sp	S	F	W
Southeastern	R	+	R	-
Southcoastal	U	R	U	-
Southwestern ★	U	U	U	-
Central	-	+	-	-
Western ★	C	C	C	-
Northern ★	C	C	C	-

Sabine's Gull, immature

Sabine's Gull, breeding

Ivory Gull
Pagophila eburnea

Field marks. 16". *Adult:* Snowy white; black legs; dark, yellow-tipped bill. *Immature:* Small black spots on wings and tip of tail; dark smudge on face.

Similar species. Pale immature Thayer's Gull may look similar at a distance, but is much larger.

Habitat. Inshore and offshore marine waters; pack and drift ice of Chukchi, Bering, and Beaufort seas; coastal areas.

Region	Sp	S	F	W
Southeastern	-	+	+	-
Southcoastal	+	-	+	-
Southwestern	R	-	R	U
Central	-	-	-	-
Western	U	+	U	U
Northern	U	R	U	-

Ivory Gull, first-winter

Ivory Gull, first-summer

Caspian Tern
Sterna caspia

Field marks. 19"-23". Larger than a Mew Gull. Large red bill, short-crested black cap, slightly forked tail, black on undersides of wing tips. Nonbreeding birds have white streaking on cap.

Similar species. Other terns in Alaska are much smaller and lack a head crest.

Habitat. Ocean coasts, tidal estuaries, rivers, lakes. Since the early 1980s, has been annual in southeastern and southcoastal Alaska west to Cook Inlet. Probably breeds on the western Copper River Delta and Alsek River Delta.

Region	Sp	S	F	W
Southeastern	R	R	R	-
Southcoastal ★	R	R	R	-
Southwestern	-	-	-	-
Central	-	+	-	-
Western ★	+	+	-	-
Northern	-	-	-	-

Caspian Tern, breeding

Common Tern
Sterna hirundo

Field marks. 14½". The Common Tern seen in Alaska is a Siberian subspecies *(S. h. longipennis)* with all-black bill and black or brown legs and feet in breeding plumage. *Immature and nonbreeding:* Very similar to Arctic Tern, but neck and bill are longer, giving it a more pointed look in front, with more of the bird projecting in front of the wings. Common Tern has more obvious black posterior borders on each wing than does the Arctic Tern.

Similar species. Arctic Tern in flight has head barely projecting beyond wing tips, appearing to be neckless. Breeding Arctic Tern has red bill, legs, and feet.

Habitat. Seen most frequently during spring and summer in western and central Aleutian Islands and Pribilof Islands.

Region	Sp	S	F	W
Southeastern	-	-	-	-
Southcoastal	-	-	-	-
Southwestern	R	R	+	-
Central	-	-	-	-
Western	+	+	-	-
Northern	-	-	-	-

**Common Tern, breeding
(S. h. longipennis)**

Arctic Tern
Sterna paradisaea

Field marks. 15". *Breeding:* Black cap; bright red bill and feet. *In flight:* Head barely projects beyond wing tips, so bird appears neckless; long pointed wings; forked tail. *Juvenile:* White forehead, blackish crown and nape, dark bill, short tail.

Similar species. Juvenile Aleutian Tern is brownish above. Nonbreeding Common Tern in flight has longer neck and bill, giving it a more pointed look in front, with more of the bird projecting in front of the wings; has more obvious black posterior borders on each wing than does the Arctic Tern.

Voice. Nasal, bickering *keearr.*

Habitat. *Breeding:* Tidal flats, beaches, glacial moraines, rivers, lakes, marshes. Nests in colonies or scattered pairs on sand, gravel, or moss, or in rocks. *Migration:* Inshore and offshore marine waters, tidal flats, beaches, rivers, lakes.

Region	Sp	S	F	W
Southeastern ★	C	C	C	-
Southcoastal ★	C	C	C	-
Southwestern ★	C	U	C	-
Central ★	U	U	U	-
Western ★	C	C	C	-
Northern ★	U	U	U	-

Arctic Tern, juvenile

Arctic Tern, breeding

Aleutian Tern
Sterna aleutica

Field marks. 15". *Breeding:* White forehead; black cap, bill, legs, and feet; gray back and belly contrast sharply with white tail. *Juvenile:* Buff and brown above.

Similar species. Breeding Arctic Tern has black forehead; red bill, legs, and feet; back and tail about the same color. Juvenile Arctic Tern lighter above.

Voice. A loud ploverlike whistle and loud chirpings, unlike the nasal *keearr* of the Arctic Tern.

Habitat. *Breeding:* Coastal areas, marshes, islands, rivers, lagoons, inshore marine waters. Nests on ground in matted dry grass. *Migration:* Offshore marine waters.

Region	Sp	S	F	W
Southeastern	+	+	-	-
Southcoastal ★	U	U	U	-
Southwestern ★	U	U	U	-
Central	-	-	-	-
Western ★	U	U	U	-
Northern ★	-	+	-	-

Aleutian Tern, juvenile

Aleutian Tern, breeding

ALCIDS
Family *Alcidae*

Members of the alcid family are seabirds that come to shore only to breed. They nest in colonies, where females lay 1 or 2 eggs each. They have small, narrow wings that are used both for swimming underwater and for flight. On land, alcids stand almost erect and penguinlike. All are short-necked and heavy-bodied, with webbed feet placed far back on the body to facilitate swimming. Most are black and white; some have a brightly colored bill. Alcids feed mostly on small fish, crustaceans, and other marine invertebrates.

Dovekie
Alle alle

Field marks. 8". Stubby bill and thick neck. *Breeding:* Sharply black and white; entirely black head and breast. *Winter:* White of the throat extends up in a half-collar almost around the neck.

Similar species. Winter Least Auklet has obvious white stripe on either side of back and lacks the white half-collar.

Habitat. Small numbers occur during summer in the Bering Strait, where it is considered a rare probable breeder on islands.

Region	Sp	S	F	W
Southeastern	-	-	-	-
Southcoastal	-	-	-	-
Southwestern	+	+	+	+
Central	-	-	-	-
Western ★	R	R	R	-
Northern	-	+	-	-

Dovekie, breeding

Dovekie, winter

Common Murre
Uria aalge

Field marks. 16½". *All plumages:* Long, pointed, slender bill. *Breeding:* Entire head and neck dark; white underparts come to a blunt point on foreneck; flanks streaked with brown. *Winter:* White cheeks with distinct dark line extending behind eye.

Similar species. Thick-billed Murre has shorter, more curved bill; in breeding plumage, white underparts come to a sharp point on foreneck, has a pale line along upper mandible, and lacks brown streaks on flanks; in winter plumage, has less white on face and no dark line behind eye.

Habitat. *Breeding:* Coastal sea cliffs and islands, inshore marine waters. Nests in colonies on the ground on cliff ledges and on the flat tops of cliffs. *Winter:* Inshore and offshore marine waters.

Region	Sp	S	F	W
Southeastern ★	C	C	C	C
Southcoastal ★	C	C	C	C
Southwestern ★	C	C	C	C
Central	-	-	-	+
Western ★	C	C	C	C
Northern	-	+	-	-

Common Murre, breeding

Common Murre, winter

Thick-billed Murre
Uria lomvia

Field marks. 18". *All plumages:* Thick bill, curved on top; pale line along upper mandible. *Breeding:* Entire head and neck dark; white of belly comes to a sharp point on dark foreneck. *Winter:* White on cheeks, with no dark line behind eye.

Similar species. Common Murre has longer, straighter bill, with no pale line on upper mandible; in breeding plumage, white of under-parts comes to a blunt point on foreneck, and has brown streaks on flanks; in winter plumage, has dark line on white face behind eye.

Habitat. *Breeding:* Coastal sea cliffs and islands, inshore marine waters. Nests in colonies on the ground on cliff ledges and on the flat tops of cliffs. *Winter:* Inshore and offshore marine waters.

Region	Sp	S	F	W
Southeastern ★	R	R	R	R
Southcoastal ★	R	R	R	R
Southwestern ★	C	C	C	C
Central	-	-	-	-
Western ★	C	C	C	C
Northern	R	R	R	-

Thick-billed Murre, winter

Thick-billed Murre, breeding

Black Guillemot
Cepphus grylle

Field marks. 13". *All plumages:* Whitish underwings, unmarked white wing patch (except juvenile), slender bill, bright red mouth lining and feet. *Breeding:* Black with unmarked white wing patch. *Winter:* Very whitish at a distance; gray and white back. *Juvenile:* Dark bar across white wing patch (very similar to Pigeon Guillemot); duskier gray above, especially about the head.

Similar species. Pigeon Guillemot has darkish underwings; 1 or 2 black wedges extend into white wing patch. Winter murrelets are much smaller, with a shorter bill and dark crown.

Habitat. *Breeding:* Chukchi and Beaufort sea coasts. Nests in burrows and beach flotsam. *Winter:* Inshore and offshore marine waters; leads and edge of the ice pack.

Region	Sp	S	F	W
Southeastern	-	-	-	-
Southcoastal	-	-	-	-
Southwestern	R	-	-	R
Central	-	-	+	+
Western ★	U	U	U	U
Northern ★	U	U	U	U

Black Guillemot, breeding

Pigeon Guillemot
Cepphus columba

Field marks. 13". *All plumages:* Dark underwings; white wing patch with 1 or 2 black wedges; bright red mouth and feet; slender bill. *Breeding:* Black; white wing patch with 1 or 2 black wedges. *Winter:* Mottled gray and white plumage. *Juvenile:* Duskier gray above, with smaller white wing patches.

Similar species. Black Guillemot has whitish underwings; unmarked white wing patch (except juvenile). Winter murrelets are much smaller, with a shorter bill and dark crown.

Habitat. *Breeding:* Inshore marine waters, cliffs, islands. Nests in cliff crevices and between boulders above high tide line. *Winter:* Inshore and offshore marine waters.

Region	Sp	S	F	W
Southeastern ★	C	C	C	C
Southcoastal ★	C	C	C	C
Southwestern ★	C	C	C	C
Central	-	-	-	-
Western ★	C	C	C	-
Northern	-	-	-	-

Pigeon Guillemot, nonbreeding

Pigeon Guillemot, breeding

Marbled Murrelet
Brachyramphus marmoratus

Field marks. 9½". *Breeding:* Dark brown mottled with gray or red. *Winter:* Black cap extends below eyes. *Juvenile:* Similar to winter adult.

Similar species. Kittlitz's Murrelet has a shorter bill and, when flushed, shows white in the tail, whereas the Marbled Murrelet's tail is all dark. Breeding Kittlitz's Murrelet has a lighter brown plumage mottled with white; in winter plumage, dark cap does not extend below eyes, and it shows a nearly complete dark ring around its upper breast. Ancient Murrelet lacks white stripe on either side of back.

Voice. Soft, short whistle that carries far over open water.

Habitat. *Breeding:* Inshore marine waters. Nests on the ground along the steep tundra-edged coasts of southwestern Alaska or in the thick moss on branches of old-growth coniferous trees in southeastern and southcoastal Alaska. *Winter:* Inshore and offshore marine waters.

Region	Sp	S	F	W
Southeastern ★	C	C	C	C
Southcoastal ★	C	C	C	C
Southwestern ★	U	U	U	U
Central	-	-	+	-
Western ★	+	+	+	-
Northern	-	-	-	-

Marbled Murrelet, breeding

Marbled Murrelet, winter

Kittlitz's Murrelet
Brachyramphus brevirostris

Field marks. 9". *Breeding:* Light brown plumage mottled with white. *Winter:* White on face extends above the eye; dark ring nearly around upper breast. *Juvenile:* Similar plumage pattern as winter adult, but grayer overall.

Similar species. Marbled Murrelet, when flushed, shows all-dark tail; in breeding plumage, is darker brown mottled with gray or red; in winter, dark cap extends below eyes and lacks dark breast ring. Ancient Murrelet lacks white stripe on either side of back.

Voice. Deep squawk.

Habitat. *Breeding:* Inshore marine waters and adjacent mountains and sea cliffs. Little is known about the nesting habits, but 1 egg is usually laid on bare rock above timberline, on an unvegetated glacial moraine, or on the grassy ledge of an island sea cliff. *Winter:* Inshore and offshore marine waters.

Region	Sp	S	F	W
Southeastern ★	U	U	U	U
Southcoastal ★	C	C	C	U
Southwestern ★	U	U	U	R
Central	-	-	-	-
Western ★	U	U	U	-
Northern	R	R	R	-

Kittlitz's Murrelet, breeding

Kittlitz's Murrelet, winter

Ancient Murrelet
Synthliboramphus antiquus

Field marks. 10". *All plumages:* Black cap contrasts with gray back; cream-colored bill; has broader wings and lacks the rocking flight of other murrelets. *Breeding:* White stripe over eye; black throat patch. *Winter:* Sides of neck white; loses white stripe over eye.

Similar species. Marbled and Kittlitz's murrelets in winter and juvenile plumage have a white stripe on either side of their back; rock back and forth in flight; have an all-black bill.

Habitat. *Breeding:* Inshore marine waters and islands, including Aleutian, Shumagin, and Semidi islands and Forrester Island. Nests in colonies and lays egg in crevices or burrows. *Winter:* Inshore and offshore marine waters.

Region	Sp	S	F	W
Southeastern ★	U	U	U	U
Southcoastal ★	U	U	U	U
Southwestern ★	C	C	C	C
Central	-	-	-	-
Western	+	R	R	-
Northern	-	-	-	-

Ancient Murrelet, breeding

Cassin's Auklet
Ptychoramphus aleuticus

Field marks. 7½". *On water:* Appears all dark; at close range, tiny white crescent over eye, dark bill with pale area on base of lower mandible. *In flight:* Dark upperparts, including head and throat; white belly.

Similar species. In breeding plumage, all other auklets have brightly colored bills and white stripe or stripes on face.

Habitat. *Breeding:* Inshore coastal waters and islands. Breeds in scattered colonies from Buldir Island in the western Aleutian Islands to Forrester Island in southeastern Alaska. Largest colonies are found in the Sandman Reefs and Shumagin Islands, south of the Alaska Peninsula, and at Forrester Island. Nests are similar to those of the Ancient Murrelet, but the burrows tend to be deeper. *Winter:* Inshore and offshore marine waters.

Region	Sp	S	F	W
Southeastern ★	U	U	U	U
Southcoastal	R	R	R	-
Southwestern ★	C	C	C	C
Central	-	-	-	-
Western	-	-	-	-
Northern	-	-	-	-

Cassin's Auklet, breeding

Parakeet Auklet
Aethia psittacula

Field marks. 10". *Breeding:* Broad, stubby, reddish bill; single line of white plumes behind eye; mottled breast; dark head, throat, and upperparts. *Winter:* White throat, dark bill.

Similar species. Breeding Cassin's Auklet has dark bill and no white lines on face; in winter, has a darker throat.

Habitat. *Breeding:* Inshore marine waters and islands, especially in Aleutian, Shumagin, and Pribilof islands. Nests under loose boulders and in crevices in sea cliffs. *Winter:* Inshore and offshore marine waters.

Region	Sp	S	F	W
Southeastern	R	+	-	+
Southcoastal ★	U	U	U	+
Southwestern ★	C	C	C	U
Central	-	-	-	-
Western ★	C	C	C	-
Northern	-	-	+	-

Parakeet Auklet, breeding

Least Auklet
Aethia pusilla

Field marks. 6". *All plumages:* Very small, with stubby bill. *Breeding:* Red bill; white plumes on front of face and single line of plumes behind eye; white throat; mottled underparts. *Winter:* Obvious white stripe on either side of dark back; white underparts; black bill.

Similar species. Breeding Cassin's Auklet is larger, has dark throat and larger bill, lacks white plumes on front of face. Winter Cassin's Auklet lacks stripes on back. Whiskered Auklet has all-gray body and forehead crest.

Habitat. *Breeding:* Inshore marine waters, islands. Nests in cliff crevices, among boulders above high tide line, and on talus slopes. *Winter:* Inshore and offshore marine waters.

Region	Sp	S	F	W
Southeastern	-	-	-	-
Southcoastal	+	+	+	+
Southwestern ★	C	C	C	C
Central	-	-	-	-
Western ★	C	C	C	-
Northern	-	+	+	-

Least Auklet, breeding

Whiskered Auklet
Aethia pygmaea

Field marks. 7". *Breeding:* Thin, quail-like crest on forehead; 3 white plumes on each side of face; all-gray body with darker head. *Juvenile:* May have traces of the 3 white head stripes.

Similar species. Breeding Crested Auklet has only single white plume on side of face and a much thicker crest on forehead; head is same dark shade as body. Juvenile Crested Auklet is difficult to distinguish from Juvenile Whiskered Auklet unless traces of 3 white head stripes are visible. Cassin's and Least auklets have white or mottled underparts.

Habitat. *Breeding:* Inshore marine waters, islands. Nests in cliff crevices, on talus slopes, and between boulders above high tide. *Winter:* Inshore and offshore marine waters.

Region	Sp	S	F	W
Southeastern	-	-	-	-
Southcoastal	-	-	-	-
Southwestern ★	U	U	U	U
Central	-	-	-	-
Western	-	+	-	-
Northern	-	-	-	-

Whiskered Auklet, breeding

Crested Auklet
Aethia cristatella

Field marks. 9½". *Breeding:* Uniformly dark all over, stubby orange bill, thick crest on forehead, single white line of plumes behind eye.

Similar species. Breeding Whiskered Auklet has thinner crest and 3 white lines of plumes on side of face; head darker than body. Cassin's, Parakeet, and Least auklets have white or mottled white underparts.

Habitat. *Breeding:* Inshore marine waters, island cliffs, beaches. Nests in crevices of talus slopes and cliffs and among beach boulders. *Winter:* Inshore and offshore marine waters.

Region	Sp	S	F	W
Southeastern	-	-	-	-
Southcoastal	-	+	+	U
Southwestern ★	C	C	C	C
Central	-	-	+	-
Western ★	C	C	C	-
Northern	-	R	R	-

Crested Auklet, breeding

Rhinoceros Auklet
Cerorhinca monocerata

Region	Sp	S	F	W
Southeastern ★	U	U	U	+
Southcoastal ★	R	R	R	-
Southwestern ★	R	R	R	R
Central	-	-	-	-
Western	-	-	-	-
Northern	-	-	-	-

Field marks. 15". *Breeding:* Long, bright, yellowish orange-to-pink bill; short, pale, upright horn at base of bill; two white lines of plumes on head. *In flight:* Shows a white belly. Winter-plumaged adults show the long, colorful bill, but in juveniles the bill is darker.

Similar species. Other auklets are smaller and have shorter, stubbier bills. Puffins have much deeper bills.

Habitat. *Breeding:* Inshore marine waters, islands. Nests in deep burrows on sea islands. *Migration:* Inshore and offshore marine waters. Breeds mainly in southeastern Alaska, primarily on St. Lazaria and Forrester islands. Sizable colonies also exist in the Barren and Chiswell islands and on Middleton Island in the Gulf of Alaska.

Rhinoceros Auklet, breeding

Tufted Puffin
Fratercula cirrhata

Field marks. 15". *Breeding:* White face with long, curved, yellowish tufts that hang behind the eye; massive, brightly colored bill; black body and orange legs. *Winter:* Dusky sides, orange-tipped bill, grayish feathers behind eyes.

Similar species. Horned Puffin has white sides. Rhinoceros Auklet has considerably narrower bill.

Habitat. *Breeding:* Inshore marine waters, islands. Nests principally in burrows in the soil, but rock crevices are also used. *Winter:* Inshore and offshore marine waters.

Region	Sp	S	F	W
Southeastern ★	U	U	U	R
Southcoastal ★	C	C	C	R
Southwestern ★	C	C	C	U
Central	-	-	-	-
Western ★	C	C	C	-
Northern	-	+	-	-

Tufted Puffin, breeding

Horned Puffin
Fratercula corniculata

Field marks. 14½". *All plumages:* White sides and belly. *Breeding:* Large, triangular orange-red and yellow bill; white face; clear white underparts; broad black collar. *Winter:* Face and bill darker, bill red only at tip; juvenile has an all-dark bill.

Similar species. Breeding Tufted Puffin is all dark and lacks white sides; in winter, has dusky sides.

Habitat. *Breeding:* Inshore marine waters, islands. Nests on sea islands in rock crevices or in burrows among boulders, on sea cliffs, and on grassy slopes. *Winter:* Inshore and offshore marine waters.

Region	Sp	S	F	W
Southeastern ★	R	R	R	R
Southcoastal ★	U	U	U	R
Southwestern ★	C	C	C	U
Central	-	-	-	-
Western ★	C	C	C	-
Northern ★	-	R	+	-

Horned Puffin, breeding

PIGEONS, DOVES
Family *Columbidae*

Pigeons and doves are short-legged birds with pointed wings and a small, rounded head that they bob when walking. They drink by immersing their bill in water and quickly drinking without raising their head, unlike most other birds, which must tip their head back to drink. Pigeons and doves spend a lot of their time on the ground searching for seeds and insects.

Rock Dove
Columba livia

Field marks. 13". Blue-gray or ash-gray body most common; white rump, dark head, 2 dark wing bars, dark tail tip. Colors of certain individuals may vary from mostly white to browns and blacks. *In flight:* Typically glides with wings up in a V.

Similar species. Much less common Band-tailed Pigeon and Mourning Dove lack the 2 dark wing bars.

Habitat. Cities, towns. Nests on building ledges.

Region	Sp	S	F	W
Southeastern ★	C	C	C	C
Southcoastal ★	C	C	C	C
Southwestern	-	-	-	-
Central ★	C	C	C	C
Western	-	-	-	-
Northern	-	-	-	-

Rock Dove

Band-tailed Pigeon
Columba fasciata

Field marks. 14½". Yellow bill with black tip; white crescent on hind neck; yellow feet. *In flight:* Tail shows wide, pale gray band at tip.

Similar species. Rock Dove has 2 dark wing bars; dark tail tip; white rump; red feet and bill. Mourning Dove is smaller and slimmer and has a pointed tail bordered with white.

Voice. A deep owl-like hooting.

Habitat. Open woodlands, forest edges. Nests in conifers or deciduous trees.

Region	Sp	S	F	W
Southeastern ★	R	R	R	-
Southcoastal	-	+	+	-
Southwestern	-	-	-	-
Central	-	-	-	-
Western	-	-	+	-
Northern	-	+	-	-

Band-tailed Pigeon

Mourning Dove
Zenaida macroura

Field marks. 12". Slim; uniformly gray-brown; long pointed tail bordered with white; black blotches on wings. *Immature:* Browner, with a scaly appearance above.

Similar species. Rock Dove has 2 dark wing bars. Band-tailed Pigeon is larger; has white crescent on neck; yellow bill with black tip.

Voice. A mournful *coo-a-coo, coo, coo.*

Habitat. Open woodlands; commonly perches in trees.

Region	Sp	S	F	W
Southeastern	R	R	R	-
Southcoastal	R	R	R	+
Southwestern	-	-	+	-
Central	R	R	R	-
Western	-	-	+	-
Northern	-	-	-	-

Mourning Dove

TYPICAL OWLS
Family *Strigidae*

Typical owls are large-headed and short-necked birds of prey. Many are nocturnal, more often heard than seen. Their large forward-facing eyes are immovable, so the entire head must move to look in another direction. Owls excel at hunting; they approach prey silently because the modified downy edges of their primary feathers eliminate sounds that, in other birds, are caused by straight-edged primaries. Owls feed on small mammals, other birds, and insects.

Western Screech-Owl
Otus kennicottii

Field marks. 8½". Small brownish owl with conspicuous ear tufts. Strictly nocturnal and seldom seen; best located at night by voice.

Voice. A series of short notes accelerating toward the end of the series, like a "bouncing ball." Both sexes also duet by trilling.

Habitat. Coniferous forests. Nests in holes in trees.

Region	Sp	S	F	W
Southeastern ★	R	R	R	R
Southcoastal	+	+	+	+
Southwestern	-	-	-	-
Central	-	-	-	-
Western	-	-	-	-
Northern	-	-	-	-

Western Screech-Owl

Great Horned Owl
Bubo virginianus

Field marks. 18"-25". Very large; prominent ear tufts; white throat; barring underneath.

Similar species. Other large owls lack ear tufts. Smaller Long-eared Owl (casual) is slimmer, has more closely set ear tufts, lacks a white throat, and has vertical chest markings rather than horizontal.

Voice. A series of deeply resonant *hoo* notes, often 5 in males and 8 in females; also a scream.

Habitat. Coniferous and deciduous forests. Nests in abandoned hawk nests or cliff crevices.

Region	Sp	S	F	W
Southeastern ★	U	U	U	U
Southcoastal ★	C	C	C	C
Southwestern ★	U	U	U	U
Central ★	C	C	C	C
Western ★	U	U	U	U
Northern	-	-	+	-

Great Horned Owl

Snowy Owl
Nyctea scandiaca

Region	Sp	S	F	W
Southeastern	+	-	+	R
Southcoastal	R	+	R	U
Southwestern ★	R	R	R	U
Central	R	-	+	R
Western ★	U	U	U	U
Northern ★	U	U	U	+

Field marks. 22"-25". *All plumages:* White, rounded head without ear tufts. *Adult male:* Almost immaculate white. *Adult female:* Scattered brown spots and bars. *Immature:* Heavily marked with brown; white face.

Similar species. An arctic subspecies of Great Horned Owl *(B. v. algistus)* is very pale, but has gray facial disk and horns; occurs from Kotzebue to Bristol Bay along forest fringes.

Voice. On breeding grounds, utters loud croaking and whistling sounds.

Habitat. Open country. *Breeding:* Tundra. *Winter:* Marshes and beaches. Nests on the ground on dry tundra hummocks or promontories or on rocky ledges or cliffs.

Snowy Owl, adult

Snowy Owl, immature

Northern Hawk Owl
Surnia ulula

Field marks. 16". Heavily barred underparts, long tail, black–bordered facial disks, no ear tufts.

Behavior. When perched, often flicks tail. Hunts from exposed perch, often in broad daylight.

Similar species. Boreal Owl is smaller; lacks barred underparts.

Voice. Hawklike cry *ki-ki-ki-ki*.

Habitat. Open coniferous and deciduous forests. Nests in tree cavities, on the tops of tree stubs, and occasionally on cliffs or among limbs of a conifer.

Region	Sp	S	F	W
Southeastern ★	R	+	R	R
Southcoastal ★	U	U	U	C
Southwestern ★	R	R	R	U
Central ★	C	C	C	C
Western ★	U	U	U	U
Northern	+	-	+	-

Northern Hawk Owl

Northern Pygmy-Owl
Glaucidium gnoma

Field marks. 7". Very small owl; sparrow-sized. Gray brown or rusty brown upperparts, with white spots and 2 black "eye" patches on upper back. Whitish underparts streaked with black. Long, narrow tail with narrow white bars.

Voice. Single, short whistle repeated at intervals of about 2 seconds.

Habitat. Open coniferous forests and forest edges. Usually seen hunting during the day.

Region	Sp	S	F	W
Southeastern ★	U	U	U	U
Southcoastal	-	+	+	-
Southwestern	-	-	-	-
Central	-	-	-	-
Western	-	-	-	-
Northern	-	-	-	-

Northern Pygmy-Owl

Barred Owl
Strix varia

Field marks. 17"-24". Barring across neck and upper breast, lengthwise streaks on belly, dark eyes, no ear tufts.

Similar species. Great Gray Owl is larger, and has yellow eyes and obvious white patch on throat. Great Horned Owl has ear tufts and yellow eyes.

Voice. Emphatic hoots that gradually rise in intensity in the pattern *hoo hoo hoo hoo hoo hoo ho hooo.*

Habitat. Has been seen or heard several times in coniferous forests around Juneau, Petersburg, Wrangell, and Ketchikan. Nesting has been noted near Ketchikan.

Region	Sp	S	F	W
Southeastern ★	R	R	R	R
Southcoastal	-	-	-	-
Southwestern	-	-	-	-
Central	-	-	-	-
Western	-	-	-	-
Northern	-	-	-	-

Barred Owl, adult

Barred Owl, immature

Great Gray Owl
Strix nebulosa

Field marks. 24"-33". Very large facial disk with concentric gray circles; dusky gray with streaked underparts; obvious white patch on throat; yellow eyes; no ear tufts.

Similar species. Barred Owl has dark eyes and lacks white throat patch.

Voice. A deep *hooo* note at irregular intervals and a hoarse catlike scream.

Habitat. Coniferous and deciduous forests and forest edges. Nests on tops of broken-off trees and in raven nests.

Region	Sp	S	F	W
Southeastern ★	+	+	+	+
Southcoastal ★	R	R	R	R
Southwestern	-	-	-	-
Central ★	U	U	U	U
Western	-	-	-	-
Northern	-	-	-	-

Great Gray Owl

Short-eared Owl
Asio flammeus

Field marks. 15". Buff-brownish color with vertical streaks on breast and belly; light facial disks. *In flight:* Pale, buff patches on upper side of wing; black marks on underwing at the bend (wrist); dark trailing edge of upper wing; dark wing tip from below.

Behavior. Commonly seen hunting over open areas during the day. Flies with very deep wing strokes (moth-like flapping).

Similar species. Northern Harrier flies with shallow strokes, then glides with wings held in a shallow V; has a white rump patch, which the Short-eared Owl lacks.

Voice. A sharp bark, *kyow!*

Habitat. Open country. Lowland tundra, tidal flats, muskegs, freshwater marshes. Nests on ground in grass-lined depressions.

Region	Sp	S	F	W
Southeastern	C	R	C	R
Southcoastal ★	C	C	C	R
Southwestern ★	C	C	C	R
Central ★	C	C	C	-
Western ★	C	C	C	-
Northern ★	C	C	C	-

Short-eared Owl

Short-eared Owl, in flight

Boreal Owl
Aegolius funereus

Field marks. 10". *Adult:* Black framing of facial disks; yellow bill; white spots on forehead. *Juvenile:* Chocolate brown below; white eyebrows and cheek spots.

Similar species. Northern Sawwhet Owl has dark bill and streaked forehead; lacks black framing of facial disks. Western Screech-Owl has ear tufts (may be laid down).

Voice. A series of rapid *hoos,* often rising in pitch at end. Resembles sound made by winnowing Common Snipe.

Habitat. Coniferous and mixed coniferous-deciduous forests. Nests in tree holes.

Region	Sp	S	F	W
Southeastern	+	+	+	R
Southcoastal ★	U	U	U	U
Southwestern ★	U	U	U	U
Central ★	C	C	C	C
Western ★	R	R	R	R
Northern	-	-	-	-

Boreal Owl, adult

Boreal Owl, juvenile

Northern Saw-whet Owl
Aegolius acadicus

Field marks. 7½". *Adult:* Looks like a small Boreal Owl without the black framing of facial disks; dark bill; streaked forehead. *Juvenile:* White area on dark forehead; chocolate brown above; buff-colored belly.

Similar species. Boreal Owl has black framing of facial disks; yellowish bill; spotted forehead.

Voice. Similar in quality to Boreal Owl, but is of separate notes, not run together in a tremolo. A monotonous series of notes, *too-too-too-too-too*, etc., on 1 pitch. Also an upslurred whistle.

Habitat. Coniferous and deciduous forests. Nests in holes in trees.

Region	Sp	S	F	W
Southeastern ★	R	R	R	R
Southcoastal ★	R	R	R	R
Southwestern	-	-	+	-
Central	+	-	-	-
Western	-	-	+	-
Northern	-	-	-	-

Northern Saw-whet Owl, juvenile

Northern Saw-whet Owl, adult

GOATSUCKERS
Family *Caprimulgidae*

Members of the goatsucker family are typically nocturnal birds. But the species of goatsucker most likely to be seen in Alaska—the Common Nighthawk—often feeds on flying insects during the day. The name *goatsucker* comes from the European folklore belief that the birds, with their gaping mouth and fondness for pastures, sucked milk from livestock at night.

Common Nighthawk
Chordeiles minor

Field marks. 9". *Adult in flight:* Long, narrow, pointed wings; conspicuous white spot halfway between bend of the wing and wing tip. *Male:* White throat and white band across tail. *Perched on ground:* Mottled brown (above) and barred brown (below); tiny bill; if on branch, perches lengthwise.

Similar species. Lesser Nighthawk (accidental) has shorter tail and pale wing patch closer to wing tip. Whip-poor-will and Jungle Nightjar (both accidental) have rounded wing tips.

Voice. Loud, buzzy *peent*.

Habitat. Open woodlands. Mostly seen near the mouths of mainland rivers in southeastern Alaska from mid-August through mid-September.

Region	Sp	S	F	W
Southeastern ★	+	+	R	-
Southcoastal	-	+	+	-
Southwestern	-	-	-	-
Central	+	+	+	-
Western	-	+	-	-
Northern	-	+	-	-

Common Nighthawk

SWIFTS
Family *Apodidae*

Swifts resemble swallows, but their wings are narrow, slightly bowed, and held very stiffly. Swifts appear to beat their wings alternately, but this is an illusion. They typically fly in rapid, "twinkling" spurts, interspersed with glides. Swifts feed exclusively on insects while flying.

Black Swift
Cypseloides niger

Field marks. 7". Appears entirely black; deeply notched tail; long, narrow wings.

Similar species. Male Purple Martin (casual) has short, broad wings and slower flight, and it perches often.

Habitat. Mountains, open woodlands. Nests on cliffs in niches or cavities.

Region	Sp	S	F	W
Southeastern ★	R	R	R	-
Southcoastal	-	+	-	-
Southwestern	-	-	-	-
Central	-	-	-	-
Western	-	-	-	-
Northern	-	-	-	-

Black Swift, in flight

Black Swift

Vaux's Swift
Chaetura vauxi

Field marks. 4". Smaller than any of
Alaska's swallows; no apparent tail;
pale brown underparts; paler on
throat and upper breast.

Similar species. Chimney Swift
(accidental) is slightly larger and
usually more uniformly brown.

Habitat. Mountains, open woodland. Nests on inner walls of hollow
trees.

Region	Sp	S	F	W
Southeastern ★	U	U	U	-
Southcoastal	-	-	+	-
Southwestern	-	-	-	-
Central	-	-	-	-
Western	-	-	-	-
Northern	-	-	-	-

Vaux's Swift, flying

Vaux's Swift

HUMMINGBIRDS
Family *Trochilidae*

Hummingbirds are the smallest birds found in Alaska. They are known for their ability to hover and to fly backward while rapidly beating their wings. Their long, slender bill and extensile tongue are especially adapted for sipping nectar from flowers. Their annual arrival in Alaska occurs just when the early blueberry blossoms open. The Rufous Hummingbird probably aids in pollination of these plants, as well as others such as western columbine and Indian paintbrush. Hummingbirds also feed on small insects.

Anna's Hummingbird
Calypte anna

Field marks. 4". *Adult male:* Rose red crown and throat; green back; grayish green underparts. *Female:* Lacks extensive red; tiny red spots on throat; green back; grayish white underparts.

Similar species. Rufous Hummingbird lacks rose red crown; has rufous color on back, belly, or tail.

Habitat. Forest edges and openings wherever flowers occur. Most often seen at sugar-water feeders. Spring and summer observations indicate possible breeding in Alaska.

Region	Sp	S	F	W
Southeastern	R	R	R	+
Southcoastal	+	+	+	+
Southwestern	-	+	+	-
Central	-	-	-	-
Western	-	-	-	-
Northern	-	-	-	-

Anna's Hummingbird, male

Anna's Hummingbird, female

Rufous Hummingbird
Selasphorus rufus

Field marks. 3½". *Adult male:* Flaming, orange-red throat patch; orange-rufous upperparts and sides. *Adult female:* Small red to golden-green spots on throat; green back; dull rufous sides; considerable rufous at base of tail. *Juvenile:* Similar to adult female.

Similar species. Anna's Hummingbird lacks rufous coloration; male Anna's has rose red crown.

Habitat. Forest edges and openings from sea level to the mountains, wherever flowers are available. Nests in various trees and bushes.

Region	Sp	S	F	W
Southeastern ★	C	C	C	+
Southcoastal ★	C	C	C	-
Southwestern	-	-	-	-
Central	-	R	-	-
Western	+	-	-	-
Northern	-	-	-	-

Rufous Hummingbird, male

Rufous Hummingbird, female

KINGFISHERS
Family *Alcedinidae*

Only one species, the Belted Kingfisher, occurs in Alaska. These birds catch fish by diving into the water headfirst. Kingfishers may hunt for fish by watching from a branch over the water or by hovering. When fish are scarce, they may feed on insects, small rodents, and even berries.

Belted Kingfisher
Ceryle alcyon

Field marks. 13". *Both sexes:* Large head and bill; crest on head (may be lowered); blue-gray above, white below; white collar; gray breast band. *Female:* Additional band, rufous-colored, across belly. *In flight:* Jerky wingbeats; often hovers over water.
Voice. Harsh, rattling call.
Habitat. Rivers, streams, lakes, ponds, sloughs, inshore marine waters. Nests in burrows that it excavates in sandy, clay, or gravelly banks.

Region	Sp	S	F	W
Southeastern ★	C	C	C	C
Southcoastal ★	U	U	U	U
Southwestern ★	U	U	U	U
Central ★	C	C	C	-
Western ★	U	U	U	-
Northern	-	-	+	-

Belted Kingfisher, female

WOODPECKERS
Family *Picidae*

Woodpeckers are highly specialized for climbing the trunks and branches of trees and for digging out wood-boring insects. The bill is hard, straight, and chisel-like; the tongue is slender and fitted with a horny spear at the tip for impaling insect larvae. Woodpeckers have short legs, with sharp claws for climbing, and most have 4-toed feet (2 toes in front and 2 behind). Stiff, pointed tail feathers serve as a brace against tree trunks. In flight, woodpeckers have a characteristic undulating pattern. Their presence is usually evident from their loud territorial drumming during breeding season or their quieter hammering while foraging for insects.

Red-breasted Sapsucker
Sphyrapicus ruber

Field marks. 9". Red hood covers head, neck, and breast. White wing patches appear as a stripe down wing when the bird is perched. *In flight:* White rump.

Behavior. Digs rows of holes in trunks of alder, cottonwood, and willow trees; eats soft cambium layer and sap that oozes from holes. Also, snatches insects from the air in flycatcher fashion.

Similar species. Yellow-bellied Sapsucker (casual) has 2 white horizontal stripes across face and straw yellow belly.

Voice. Squealing *chee-ar.*

Habitat. Coniferous and mixed deciduous-coniferous forests. Nests in holes in trees.

Region	Sp	S	F	W
Southeastern ★	C	C	C	R
Southcoastal	+	+	+	+
Southwestern	-	-	-	-
Central	+	-	-	-
Western	-	-	-	-
Northern	-	-	-	-

Red-breasted Sapsucker

Downy Woodpecker
Picoides pubescens

Field marks. 6½". Black bars on white outer tail feathers. Stubby bill, obviously shorter than head. Vivid black and white markings above; unmarked white back and underparts. Male has a bright red patch on back of head.

Similar species. Hairy Woodpecker is larger, bill is nearly as long as head, has unmarked white outer tail feathers. Three-toed Woodpecker has barring on sides and back. Black-backed Woodpecker has black back and barred sides.

Voice. A *pick,* softer than that of Hairy Woodpecker.

Habitat. Coniferous and deciduous forests, shrub thickets. Nests in holes in trees.

Region	Sp	S	F	W
Southeastern ★	U	U	U	U
Southcoastal ★	U	U	U	U
Southwestern ★	R	R	R	R
Central ★	U	U	U	U
Western ★	R	R	R	R
Northern	-	-	-	-

Downy Woodpecker

Hairy Woodpecker
Picoides villosus

Field marks. 9". Unmarked white outer tail feathers. Large bill nearly as long as head. Vivid black-and-white markings above; unmarked white back and underparts. Male has bright red patch on back of head.

Similar species. Downy Woodpecker is smaller, with stubby bill obviously shorter than head; has barring on outer tail feathers. Three-toed Woodpecker has barring on sides and back. Black-backed Woodpecker has black back and barred sides.

Voice. A far-carrying *pick*.

Habitat. Coniferous and deciduous forests. Nests in holes in trees.

Region	Sp	S	F	W
Southeastern ★	U	U	U	U
Southcoastal ★	U	U	U	U
Southwestern	-	-	-	-
Central ★	U	U	U	U
Western	-	-	-	-
Northern	-	-	-	-

Hairy Woodpecker

Three-toed Woodpecker
Picoides tridactylus

Region	Sp	S	F	W
Southeastern ★	U	U	U	U
Southcoastal ★	R	R	R	R
Southwestern ★	U	U	U	U
Central ★	U	U	U	U
Western ★	U	U	U	U
Northern	-	-	-	-

Field marks. 8½". Dull black-and-white-barred back; barred sides. Male has yellow patch on crown. As name says, has 3 toes; other woodpeckers—except Black-backed—have 4.

Similar species. Hairy and Downy woodpeckers have an unmarked white back and no barring on sides. Black-backed Woodpecker has a black back.

Voice. A sharp *pik* or *kik*.

Habitat. Coniferous and mixed deciduous-coniferous forests. Nests in tree cavities, usually of conifers.

Three-toed Woodpecker

Black-backed Woodpecker
Picoides arcticus

Field marks. 9½". Solid, glossy black back; barred sides; 3 toes. Male has yellow patch on crown.

Similar species. All other black-and-white woodpeckers have white on their back.

Voice. A sharp *kyik* or *tschik*.

Habitat. Coniferous and mixed deciduous-coniferous forests; often found in burned-over areas. Nests in tree cavities, usually of conifers.

Region	Sp	S	F	W
Southeastern	R	+	R	-
Southcoastal ★	+	+	+	+
Southwestern	+	-	-	-
Central ★	R	R	R	R
Western	-	-	-	-
Northern	-	-	-	-

Black-backed Woodpecker

Northern Flicker
Colaptes auratus

Field marks. 12½". Black and brown barring above; white rump patch (obvious in flight); black spotting below; broad black patch on chest. Two forms are found in Alaska: Red-shafted male has a red mustache and pinkish orange underwings and tail; bird is most numerous in southeastern Alaska. Yellow-shafted male has a black mustache and yellow underwings and tail; bird occurs throughout forested regions of the state, most commonly in central Alaska.

Voice. Loud, far-carrying series of rapid *wucks* or a deliberate *wicka-wicka-wicka*.

Habitat. Coniferous and deciduous forests. Only woodpecker that commonly feeds on the ground. Nests in holes in trees or stumps.

Region	Sp	S	F	W
Southeastern ★	U	U	U	+
Southcoastal ★	U	U	U	+
Southwestern	-	-	+	-
Central ★	C	C	C	+
Western	-	-	+	-
Northern	-	-	+	-

Northern Flicker

TYRANT FLYCATCHERS
Family *Tyrannidae*

Flycatchers typically perch in an upright position on bare branches and make frequent short flights after flying insects, usually returning to the same perch. They have broad, flat bills especially adapted for catching insects. Flycatchers of the genus *Empidonax* look very much alike and thus are extremely difficult to identify. During breeding season their songs and calls can be used for identification. But during migration these birds are usually silent, and at this time only very experienced birders can tell one species from another solely by the subtle differences in appearance and behavior.

Olive-sided Flycatcher
Contopus cooperi

Field marks. 7½". Stout; large bill; dark chest patches separated by narrow white stripe; white tufts of feathers on lower back (usually hidden by wings).

Similar species. Western Wood-Pewee is smaller and has white wing bars.

Voice. Song is loud and distinctive; emphatic whistled *whip-three-beers,* with the middle note the highest in pitch. Call is incessant *pilt, pilt.*

Habitat. Coniferous forests. Nests in conifers.

Region	Sp	S	F	W
Southeastern ★	R	R	R	-
Southcoastal ★	R	R	R	-
Southwestern ★	R	R	R	-
Central ★	U	U	U	-
Western ★	R	R	R	-
Northern	-	+	-	-

Olive-sided Flycatcher

Western Wood-Pewee
Contopus sordidulus

Field marks. 6¼". Slightly larger and even duller than flycatchers of the genus *Empidonax,* also members of this family. No white eye ring. Adult has whitish wing bars; first-winter bird has buff wing bars.

Similar species. Olive-sided Flycatcher is larger, lacks white wing bars. Most *Empidonax* flycatchers have white eye rings.

Voice. A nasal *pee-wee.*

Habitat. Open coniferous and deciduous forests, forest edges. Nests on horizontal limbs and occasionally in upright crotches of deciduous or coniferous trees.

Region	Sp	S	F	W
Southeastern ★	U	U	U	-
Southcoastal ★	U	U	U	-
Southwestern	-	-	-	-
Central ★	U	U	U	-
Western	+	+	-	-
Northern	+	+	-	-

Western Wood-Pewee

Alder Flycatcher
Empidonax alnorum

Field marks. 6". Very pale yellow belly and whitish throat; faint eye ring; brownish olive above. Best identified by song.

Similar species. Hammond's and Least flycatchers have more obvious white eye rings.

Voice. Song: A *fee-bee-o,* with accent on second syllable. Call: Short, sharp *whit* or *wee-o.*

Habitat. Alder and willow thickets, usually in moist areas. Nests in upright crotches of shrubs.

Region	Sp	S	F	W
Southeastern ★	U	U	U	-
Southcoastal ★	U	U	U	-
Southwestern ★	U	U	U	-
Central ★	C	C	C	-
Western ★	U	U	U	-
Northern	+	+	-	-

Alder Flycatcher

Least Flycatcher
Empidonax minimus

Field marks. 5 ¼". Strongly marked eye ring; olive gray above; white throat and gray breast; faint yellow on belly. Best identified by song.

Behavior. Flicks tail upward.

Similar species. Alder Flycatcher and Willow Flycatcher (casual) have fainter eye rings and brownish backs. See Hammond's and Pacific-slope flycatchers.

Voice. Song: An explosive *che-bek,* with emphasis on second syllable. Call: A clear *whit* or *wit.*

Habitat. Deciduous woodlands. Singing males have been recorded at numerous localities in recent years, indicating possible breeding in Alaska.

Region	Sp	S	F	W
Southeastern	R	R	-	-
Southcoastal	-	+	+	-
Southwestern	-	-	-	-
Central	+	+	-	-
Western	-	-	-	-
Northern	-	-	-	-

Least Flycatcher

Hammond's Flycatcher
Empidonax hammondii

Field marks. 5". Clear white eye ring; grayish olive back: grayish white throat; very pale yellow belly. Best identified by song.

Behavior. Flicks wings and tail simultaneously.

Similar species. See Alder, Least, Willow (casual), and Pacific-slope flycatchers.

Voice. Song: Typical 3-part song begins and ends with a double note and has a short or slightly rolling middle part described as *seedick, prrt, pewit.* Call: Note is lower pitched and quite different from that of the Alder Flycatcher, but similar to the song of the Least Flycatcher, and sounds like *che-bink.*

Habitat. Riparian deciduous forests. Also dry upland mixed or deciduous forests with closed canopy. Nests on tree limbs, 15 to 50 feet above the ground. Hammond's Flycatcher is an early migrant, arriving in central Alaska about the first of May; Alder Flycatcher is a late migrant, arriving near the end of May.

Region	Sp	S	F	W
Southeastern ★	U	U	U	-
Southcoastal	+	-	-	-
Southwestern	-	-	-	-
Central ★	C	C	C	-
Western	-	-	-	-
Northern	-	+	-	-

Hammond's Flycatcher

Pacific-slope Flycatcher
Empidonax difficilis

Field marks. 5 ½". Extensive yellowish underparts, including throat; almond-shaped eye ring; olive green upperparts. Best identified by song.

Behavior. Flicks wings and tail simultaneously.

Similar species. Other members of the genus *Empidonax* lack the almond-shaped eye ring, yellowish throat, and greenish upperparts. The songs of others contain lower, more burry notes.

Voice. Song: 3 thin notes, *pseet-ptsick-seet*. Call: Sharp, lisping *ps-seet*.

Habitat. Open coniferous forests. Nests on rock ledges near streams, in the roots of upturned trees, and on stumps or buildings.

Region	Sp	S	F	W
Southeastern ★	C	C	C	-
Southcoastal	-	+	-	-
Southwestern	-	-	-	-
Central	-	-	-	-
Western	-	-	-	-
Northern	-	-	-	-

Pacific-slope Flycatcher

Say's Phoebe
Sayornis saya

Field marks. 7½". Gray-brown on back and breast; light cinnamon on belly; black tail.

Voice. Song: Fast *pit-tsee-ar.* Call: Mellow, whistled *pee-ur.*

Habitat. Open areas and cliffs in mountains and uplands. Nests on shelves or in crevices of cliffs and on buildings.

Region	Sp	S	F	W
Southeastern ★	R	R	R	+
Southcoastal ★	R	R	R	-
Southwestern	-	+	+	-
Central ★	U	U	U	-
Western ★	U	U	U	-
Northern ★	U	U	U	-

Say's Phoebe

Eastern Kingbird
Tyrannus tyrannus

Field marks. 8½". Dark gray above and white below; white band at tip of black tail.

Similar species. Western Kingbird (casual) is olive gray above with yellow belly; black tail has white edges and lacks white tail tip.

Voice. Call is a loud, harsh *dzeeb,* at times uttered in rapid progression.

Habitat. Open areas with trees, shrubs, or posts for perching.

Region	Sp	S	F	W
Southeastern	-	R	R	-
Southcoastal	-	+	+	-
Southwestern	-	+	-	-
Central	-	+	+	-
Western	-	+	-	-
Northern	-	+	+	-

Eastern Kingbird

LARKS
Family *Alaudidae*

Larks are sparrow-sized ground birds that rarely perch in trees or bushes. They are usually found in rather open country. They run along the ground rather than hop. Larks feed on insects and seeds. They are famous in the field, and in poetry, for their complex and melodious songs.

Sky Lark
Alauda arvensis

Region	Sp	S	F	W
Southeastern	-	-	-	-
Southcoastal	-	-	-	-
Southwestern ★	R	+	+	-
Central	-	-	-	-
Western	+	-	-	-
Northern	-	-	-	-

Field marks. 7". Brown, heavily streaked above and on the breast; slight crest on head; bill thinner than sparrows'. In flight, shows blackish tail with white outer tail feathers.

Similar species. American Pipit is longer tailed and bobs when it walks; lacks head crest. See female Lapland and Smith's longspurs.

Voice. Song: Continuous trills and warblings, given in flight. Call: Liquid *chirrup.*

Habitat. This Asiatic lark occurs most often in the western Aleutian Islands.

Sky Lark

Horned Lark
Eremophila alpestris

Field marks. 7½". *Adult:* Black stripe curving downward from bill to below eye; black shield below light throat; black tail with white outer tail feathers; black horns (actually tufts of feathers) may or may not be visible. *Juvenile:* Brown upperparts covered with numerous white spots; lacks adult head pattern.

Voice. Song: A series of tinkling notes given from high in the air. Call: High-pitched *tsee-titi*.

Habitat. *Breeding:* Alpine tundra. Nests on the ground in the tundra. *Migration:* Drier grassy areas of tidal flats, alpine meadows.

Region	Sp	S	F	W
Southeastern ★	U	R	U	-
Southcoastal	R	R	R	-
Southwestern ★	R	R	R	-
Central ★	C	C	C	-
Western ★	U	U	U	-
Northern ★	U	U	U	-

Horned Lark

SWALLOWS
Family *Hirundinidae*

Swallows are excellent fliers that capture insects on the wing. They have long, pointed wings; a flattish head; a small, flat bill; and a wide mouth. Most have notched or forked tails. Most species are gregarious, and many nest in colonies. When not breeding, they may occur in large flocks, often with mixed species. They commonly perch on wires.

Tree Swallow
Tachycineta bicolor

Field marks. 5½". Steely blue upperparts; white underparts. Dark cap extends down over eyes; notched tail. *Immature:* Similar pattern to adult, but with brownish upperparts.

Similar species. Violet-green Swallow has white on face that extends around eye, white patch on either side of rump that shows from above in flight. Female Purple Martin (casual) is larger and has grayish collar and underparts (not clear white). Common House-Martin (accidental) has large white rump patch. Other swallows lack sharp distinction between cap and throat.

Habitat. Wooded areas near water, especially if dead trees are abundant. Lakes, larger streams, marshes, and wet muskegs. Nests in tree cavities and sometimes in buildings and bird boxes. Closely tied to human settlements in tundra areas.

Region	Sp	S	F	W
Southeastern ★	C	C	C	-
Southcoastal ★	C	C	C	-
Southwestern ★	C	C	C	-
Central ★	C	C	C	-
Western ★	C	C	C	-
Northern	+	+	+	-

Tree Swallow

Violet-green Swallow
Tachycineta thalassina

Region	Sp	S	F	W
Southeastern ★	U	U	U	-
Southcoastal ★	C	C	C	-
Southwestern ★	U	U	U	-
Central ★	C	C	C	-
Western	+	-	-	-
Northern	-	+	-	-

Field marks. 5½". White on face extends behind and over eye. Green and violet upperparts; white underparts. *In flight:* White patch on either side of rump shows from above; notched tail shows. *Female:* Duller, especially around head. *Juvenile:* Gray upperparts, breast often sooty brown, face has dusky mottling.

Similar species. Tree Swallow lacks white patch on either side of rump; lacks white around eye. Female Purple Martin (casual) is larger and has grayish collar and underparts (not clear white as in adult Violet-green).

Habitat. Open woodlands; near human settlement. Nests in holes, cavities, and crevices in trees, cliffs, and buildings.

Violet-green Swallow

Northern Rough-winged Swallow
Stelgidopteryx serripennis

Region	Sp	S	F	W
Southeastern ★	R	R	+	-
Southcoastal	+	+	-	-
Southwestern	-	+	-	-
Central	-	-	-	-
Western	-	-	-	-
Northern	-	+	-	-

Field marks. 5½". All brown above; brownish gray throat; notched tail. *In flight:* Appears batlike, with deep wingbeats.

Behavior. Usually occurs in single pairs; not colonial like the Bank Swallow.

Similar species. Bank Swallow is smaller; has a white throat; flies more directly, with quicker wingbeats. Young Tree Swallow usually has white throat and darker back; commonly seen with adults.

Habitat. Near water and open land. Nests in burrows in sand, gravel, or clay and in other cavities.

Northern Rough-winged Swallow

Bank Swallow
Riparia riparia

Field marks. 5". Alaska's smallest and dullest swallow. Brown upperparts; white throat; clearly defined dark breast band; white belly and undertail.

Similar species. Northern Rough-winged Swallow flies less directly and with deeper wingbeats; has brownish gray throat; does not nest in colonies. Other swallows lack dark breast band.

Habitat. Usually near water, especially rivers. Nests in holes in clay and sand banks near rivers, creeks, and lakes and along highways.

Region	Sp	S	F	W
Southeastern ★	U	U	U	-
Southcoastal ★	U	U	U	-
Southwestern ★	U	U	U	-
Central ★	C	C	C	-
Western ★	U	U	U	-
Northern	+	+	+	-

Bank Swallow

Cliff Swallow
Petrochelidon pyrrhonota

Field marks. 5½". Dark chestnut throat; whitish forehead; conspicuous buff-colored rump patch; dark, almost square-tipped tail.

Habitat. Water and open land; near human settlement. Nests on buildings, under bridges, and on cliffs, especially along rivers. Makes gourd-shaped nests of mud.

Region	Sp	S	F	W
Southeastern ★	R	R	R	-
Southcoastal ★	U	U	U	-
Southwestern ★	U	U	U	-
Central ★	C	C	C	-
Western ★	U	U	U	-
Northern ★	U	U	U	-

Cliff Swallow

Barn Swallow
Hirundo rustica

Field marks. 6". Deeply forked tail; light orange underparts; chestnut throat; steely, iridescent blue back. Asian forms occurring in southwestern and western Alaska have whitish underparts.

Behavior. Flies in a leisurely manner, with relatively slow wingbeats for a swallow.

Habitat. Marshes, open land, and water; near human settlement. Places cup-shaped nest of mud and grass in buildings and under bridges.

Region	Sp	S	F	W
Southeastern ★	C	C	C	-
Southcoastal ★	C	C	C	-
Southwestern	+	+	-	-
Central	+	+	+	-
Western	+	+	+	-
Northern	-	+	-	-

Barn Swallow

JAYS, MAGPIES, CROWS
Family *Corvidae*

Members of this family are medium-sized to large birds with sharply tapered but sturdy bills of moderate length. They feed on meat (including carrion), the eggs and young of other birds, insects, fruits, and seeds. These birds are gregarious, aggressive, and very vocal, so people almost always know of their presence.

Gray Jay
Perisoreus canadensis

Region	Sp	S	F	W
Southeastern	+	-	R	R
Southcoastal ★	R	R	R	R
Southwestern ★	U	U	U	U
Central ★	C	C	C	C
Western ★	U	U	U	U
Northern ★	+	+	+	+

Field marks. 11". *Adult:* Dark back and crown; white forehead and cheeks; pale gray below. *Juvenile:* From fledging until September, very dark gray overall.

Similar species. Adult Northern Shrike has black mask on otherwise all-gray head. Clark's Nutcracker (casual) has much longer bill and tail; wings and tail are black with white patches.

Voice. A variety of shrill, high-pitched notes and whistles, including a soft *whee-oh* and a harsh, scolding *cla, cla, cla, cla.*

Habitat. Openings in coniferous and deciduous forests; campgrounds. Nests in conifers.

Gray Jay, adult

Gray Jay, juvenile

Steller's Jay
Cyanocitta stelleri

Region	Sp	S	F	W
Southeastern ★	C	C	C	C
Southcoastal ★	C	C	C	C
Southwestern	-	-	-	-
Central	-	-	+	-
Western	-	-	-	-
Northern	-	-	-	-

Field marks. 13". Dark blue to black; conspicuous crest.

Behavior. Flight is series of wing-flappings interspersed with long, straight glides.

Voice. Harsh *shack-shack-shack-shack-shack* or *chook-chook-chook.* Other sounds include a simple *too-leet;* an imitation of a Red-tailed Hawk, *tee-ar;* mechanical-sounding rattle (female); high muted whistle (male); and a "whisper song," consisting of a medley of whistled and gurgled notes interspersed with snapping or popping sounds run together (male's courtship song).

Habitat. Coniferous and mixed coniferous–deciduous forests. Nests 10 feet or more above the ground in conifers.

Steller's Jay

Black-billed Magpie
Pica pica

Field marks. 20". *Adult:* Very long tail. *In flight:* 2 white stripes on back and white patches in wings give striking contrast to blackish upperparts; at close range, a blue gloss on wings gives an even more striking appearance. *Juvenile:* Similar black-and-white pattern, but much shorter tail.

Voice. A rapid, nasal *mag? mag? mag?* or *yak yak yak.*

Habitat. Shrub thickets, open woodlands, and forest edges along saltwater beaches. Nests are huge, domed-shaped structures of branches, placed in bushes or trees.

Region	Sp	S	F	W
Southeastern ★	U	+	U	C
Southcoastal ★	C	C	C	C
Southwestern ★	C	C	C	C
Central ★	C	C	C	C
Western	-	-	-	R
Northern	-	+	-	-

Black-billed Magpie

American Crow
Corvus brachyrhynchos

Field marks. 17"-21". All black, with slight purplish gloss.

Similar species. Northwestern Crow is usually smaller and more slender; has faster wingbeat and different voice. See Common Raven.

Voice. A distinctive *caw* that is not as hoarse as the *kaah* call of the Northwestern Crow.

Habitat. Meadows, fields, and woodlands. An extension of the interior British Columbia population occurs at Hyder and in the adjacent Salmon River Valley at the end of Portland Canal in southeastern Alaska.

Region	Sp	S	F	W
Southeastern ★	R	R	R	-
Southcoastal	-	-	-	-
Southwestern	-	-	-	-
Central	-	-	-	-
Western	-	-	-	-
Northern	-	-	-	-

American Crow

Northwestern Crow
Corvus caurinus

Region	Sp	S	F	W
Southeastern ★	C	C	C	C
Southcoastal ★	C	C	C	C
Southwestern ★	R	R	-	-
Central	-	-	-	-
Western	-	-	-	-
Northern	-	-	-	-

Field marks. 17". All black; dull violet gloss above; tail tip cut more or less straight across.

Behavior. Feeds heavily on the blue bay mussel, which it opens by carrying aloft and dropping on rocks below.

Similar species. Common Raven is much larger, with heavier bill and wedge-shaped or rounded tail; takes 2 or 3 hops to become airborne (crow jumps directly into air); voice is different. If in or near Hyder, Alaska, see American Crow.

Voice. Common call a rather hoarse *kaah;* several other sounds, including an unusual catlike, mewing *mraaa.*

Habitat. Marine shores; rarely ventures inland. Coniferous forests; beaches, tidal flats, rocky shores, reefs. Nests in conifers or sometimes under boulders or windfalls close to shore.

Northwestern Crow

Common Raven
Corvus corax

Field marks. 22"-27". All black; heavy bill; wedge-shaped or rounded tail.

Behavior. Often soars high in the sky.

Similar species. Northwestern and American crows are smaller, with a proportionally smaller bill; tail tip more or less cut straight across; jump directly into air (raven takes 2 or 3 hops); voice is different.

Voice. Common call is hoarse, croaking *kraaak.* Others include hollow, knocking sound and melodious *kloo-klok,* usually in flight.

Habitat. Marine shores to mountain ridges and glaciers; garbage dumps. Nests in trees or on cliffs.

Region	Sp	S	F	W
Southeastern ★	C	C	C	C
Southcoastal ★	C	C	C	C
Southwestern ★	C	C	C	C
Central ★	C	C	C	C
Western ★	C	C	C	C
Northern ★	C	C	C	U

Common Raven

CHICKADEES
Family *Paridae*

Chickadees are small, dull-colored, acrobatic birds with black bibs and dark caps. They are quite tame and readily come to feeders, where their favorite food is sunflower seeds. Otherwise they eat insects, seeds, and berries. They typically inhabit the forested regions of Alaska. In winter they travel about in small groups.

Black-capped Chickadee
Poecile atricapillus

Field marks. 5". Solid black cap and bib; gray back; pale buff sides; white edges on feathers in middle portion of wing (not always visible).

Similar species. Mountain Chickadee (casual) has a white stripe above eye.

Voice. Most commonly a clear *tsick-a-dee-dee-dee*. Male in spring sings clear, 2-noted whistle, *fee-bee*.

Habitat. Prefers deciduous woods; secondarily, coniferous forests, particularly the edges. In southeastern Alaska, most often found in cottonwoods and alders along mainland river systems. Nests in holes in the dead wood of trees or tree stubs.

Region	Sp	S	F	W
Southeastern ★	U	U	U	U
Southcoastal ★	U	U	U	U
Southwestern ★	U	U	U	U
Central ★	C	C	C	C
Western ★	U	U	U	U
Northern	-	-	+	-

Black-capped Chickadee

Gray-headed Chickadee
Poecile cinctus

Region	Sp	S	F	W
Southeastern	-	-	-	-
Southcoastal	-	-	-	-
Southwestern	-	+	-	-
Central ★	R	R	R	R
Western ★	R	R	R	R
Northern	-	-	-	-

Field marks. 5½". Larger, longer tailed, washed-out version of more frequently encountered Boreal Chickadee. Gray-brown cap; brownish back; very little brown on sides; white of cheek extends onto sides of neck.

Similar species. Boreal Chickadee is smaller and darker, with gray (not white) on sides of neck and bright reddish-brown flanks. Black-capped Chickadee has black cap and gray (not brownish) back.

Voice. Series of fretful notes *dee-deer.*

Habitat. *Breeding:* Deciduous woodlands at or near timberline and poplar/willow groves along rivers. *Winter:* Willow and alder thickets along river valley. Nests in the holes of dead trees. Rarely seen.

Gray-headed Chickadee

Boreal Chickadee
Poecile hudsonicus

Region	Sp	S	F	W
Southeastern	+	+	+	+
Southcoastal ★	R	R	R	R
Southwestern ★	U	U	U	U
Central ★	C	C	C	C
Western ★	U	U	U	U
Northern	-	-	-	-

Field marks. 5". Brown cap; gray around ear; brown back; dull reddish-brown flanks.

Similar species. Chestnut-backed Chickadee has white (not gray) on sides of neck; brighter reddish-brown back. Siberian Tit has very little brown on sides; white of cheek extends onto sides of neck; gray-brown cap.

Voice. A slow, wheezy *tsick-a-dee-dee-dee.*

Habitat. Coniferous forests, deciduous-coniferous woodlands. Nests in holes in trees.

Boreal Chickadee

Chestnut-backed Chickadee
Poecile rufescens

Field marks. 5". Reddish brown back and sides; dark brown cap.
Similar species. Boreal Chickadee has gray (not white) around ear, and duller back.
Voice. Common call is *tsida-tsida-see*.
Habitat. Coniferous forests, deciduous trees, and thickets. Nests in holes in trees.

Region	Sp	S	F	W
Southeastern ★	C	C	C	C
Southcoastal ★	C	C	C	C
Southwestern	-	-	-	-
Central	-	-	-	-
Western	-	-	-	-
Northern	-	-	-	-

Chestnut-backed Chickadee

NUTHATCHES
Family *Sittidae*

Nuthatches are small, tree-climbing birds with short tails and long, straight bills. With unusually long toes and claws, they can run nimbly up and down tree trunks and on the underside of limbs, searching for insects, insect eggs, or the seeds of pine and spruce. They often make short flights to catch insects on the wing. The nuthatch name derives from their habit of inserting nuts in the crevices of bark and hammering the nuts with their bill until the shell is broken.

Red-breasted Nuthatch
Sitta canadensis

Field marks. 4½". Prominent white stripe above eye, black stripe through eye, blue-gray back, reddish underparts. *Male:* Black crown. *Female:* Gray crown.

Voice. More often heard than seen. Call can be heard for considerable distances: a high nasal *yank-yank-yank.*

Habitat. Coniferous and deciduous trees. Nests in tree cavities.

Region	Sp	S	F	W
Southeastern ★	U	U	U	R
Southcoastal ★	R	R	U	R
Southwestern	+	-	+	
Central ★	+	+	+	+
Western		-	+	
Northern	-	-	-	-

Red-breasted Nuthatch

CREEPERS
Family *Certhiidae*

Creepers are small, tree-climbing birds with long, stiff tail feathers and a long, slender bill. They search the cracks in tree bark for insects by starting at the bottom of a tree and working upward in a spiral fashion. Then they fly to the base of the next tree and repeat the pattern. Sometimes they forage along the underside of branches.

Brown Creeper
Certhia americana

Field marks. 5½". Long, slender, downcurved bill. Upperparts brown with grayish white streaks; underparts whitish with some buff on flanks and undertail; blends with tree bark.

Voice. Song: High-pitched song consists of about 6 notes falling and then rising: *see-see-see-whee-see-see.* Call: Faint, high-pitched *ts-ts.*

Habitat. Coniferous forests, mixed deciduous-coniferous woodlands. Nests in trees behind strips of loosened bark.

Region	Sp	S	F	W
Southeastern ★	U	U	U	U
Southcoastal ★	U	U	U	U
Southwestern ★	U	U	U	U
Central ★	R	R	R	R
Western	-	-	-	-
Northern	-	-	-	-

Brown Creeper

WRENS
Family *Troglodytidae*

Wrens are small, restless, brownish birds that hold their tail straight up when not in flight. They spend much of their time on or near the ground, looking for insects and spiders to feed on.

Winter Wren
Troglodytes troglodytes

Field marks. 4". Small, all-brown bird with short, uptilted tail; dusky bars on belly and flanks.
Behavior. When approached, usually bobs up and down nervously.
Voice. Song: Rapid succession of high, tinkling warbles and trills. Call: A loud *chimp-chimp*.
Habitat. The ground or low branches of heavily forested areas. Beaches in the Aleutian and Pribilof islands, where it feeds among beach rocks and nests in cliffs and talus slopes. Usually nests among the roots of an upturned tree, or in old stumps, brush piles, and abandoned buildings.

Region	Sp	S	F	W
Southeastern ★	C	C	C	U
Southcoastal ★	U	U	U	U
Southwestern ★	C	C	C	C
Central	-	-	-	-
Western	-	-	-	-
Northern	-	-	+	-

Winter Wren

DIPPERS
Family *Cinclidae*

Dippers are stocky, wrenlike birds with short tails. They are perching birds that have adapted to feeding underwater. They can walk, completely submerged, along the bottom of a rushing stream by grasping stones or rough places with their long toes while probing under stones for aquatic insects, small fish, and fish eggs. Dippers can also propel themselves underwater with swimming motions of their wings.

American Dipper
Cinclus mexicanus

Field marks. 7 ½". Slate gray with short tail.

Voice. Song: Melodious; resembles a long rendition of some of the best notes of thrushes and wrens; both sexes sing most of the year. Call: Loud, sharp *zeet* given singly or repeatedly.

Habitat. Fast-moving streams and occasionally ponds, lakeshores, saltwater beaches, especially in winter when streams are frozen. Nests on rock walls or perpendicular banks bordering streams, often behind waterfalls.

Region	Sp	S	F	W
Southeastern ★	C	C	C	C
Southcoastal ★	C	C	C	C
Southwestern ★	C	C	C	C
Central ★	U	U	U	U
Western ★	U	U	U	U
Northern ★	R	R	R	R

American Dipper

OLD WORLD WARBLERS
Family *Sylviidae*

Old World Warblers are small, rather drab-looking birds with thicker, straighter bills than similar looking Wood Warblers. They lack conspicuous markings and are difficult to identify. They are active birds, flitting from branch to branch after insects. Alaska is the sole breeding place in North America for the Arctic Warbler, which migrates across Bering Strait and through eastern Asia.

Arctic Warbler
Phylloscopus borealis

Region	Sp	S	F	W
Southeastern	-	-	-	-
Southcoastal	-	+	-	-
Southwestern ★	U	U	U	-
Central ★	C	C	C	-
Western ★	C	C	C	-
Northern ★	C	C	C	-

Field marks. 4¼". *Adult:* Dark line through eye; whitish stripe over eye; brownish or greenish above, with whitish underparts; short, white wing bar (may be faint). *Juvenile:* Yellow underparts, eyebrow, and wing bar.

Similar species. Orange-crowned Warbler is darker below, with some yellowing underneath at base of tail; lacks short, white wing bar.

Voice. Song is a trill introduced by a note sounding like *zick,* or *zick-zick-zick;* trill sounds raspier than other warblers', with each note containing a *z* sound.

Habitat. Willow thickets. Nests on ground in grass or moss in streamside willow thickets.

Arctic Warbler

KINGLETS
Family *Regulidae*

Kinglets are no longer than a hummingbird but rounder. They are very active birds that often hover, by rapidly beating their wings, to feed on insects.

Golden-crowned Kinglet
Regulus satrapa

Field marks. 3½". *Both sexes:* White stripe above the eye; olive green above; grayish olive on sides and flanks. *Male:* Orange crown bordered with yellow and black. *Female:* Yellow crown with black border.

Behavior. Flicks its wings almost constantly.

Similar species. Ruby-crowned Kinglet lacks white stripe above eye; has conspicuous white eye ring.

Voice. Common call is thin *see-see-see*.

Habitat. Coniferous forests. Nests in branches of conifers.

Region	Sp	S	F	W
Southeastern ★	C	C	C	U
Southcoastal ★	U	U	U	U
Southwestern ★	U	U	U	U
Central	-	R	R	+
Western	+	-	+	-
Northern	-	-	-	-

Golden-crowned Kinglet

Ruby-crowned Kinglet
Regulus calendula

Field marks. 4". Conspicuous white eye ring; 2 white wing bars; olive above, gray below. Male has red crown, usually concealed.

Behavior. Flicks its wings nervously.

Similar species. Golden-crowned Kinglet lacks white eye ring; has white stripe above eye; orange or yellow crown bordered in black.

Voice. Song: Usually in 3 parts—*tee tee tee, chur chur chur, teedadee teedadee teedadee*. Call: Harsh, usually 2-syllabled, chatter.

Habitat. Coniferous forests, mixed coniferous-deciduous woodlands, shrub thickets. Widespread in Alaska, occurring wherever spruce forests exist. Nests in conifers, usually 20 to 60 feet above the ground.

Region	Sp	S	F	W
Southeastern ★	C	C	C	+
Southcoastal ★	C	C	C	+
Southwestern ★	R	R	R	-
Central ★	U	U	U	-
Western ★	U	U	U	-
Northern	+	-	+	-

Ruby-crowned Kinglet

THRUSHES
Family *Turdidae*

Thrushes are songbirds characterized by large eyes and slender bills. Color varies widely among adults of these species, but birds in juvenile plumage all have spotted breasts. They feed on insects, worms, spiders, seeds, and berries. Some species are considered important distributors of plants because they eat berries without destroying the seeds and later pass them intact.

Siberian Rubythroat
Luscinia calliope

Field marks. 6". *Both sexes:* White stripe above and below eye; cinnamon brown upperparts. *Male:* Bright red throat. *Female:* White throat.

Behavior. Often cocks tail upward.

Similar species. Female Bluethroat also has a whitish throat, but it is bordered by black; has rusty patches at base of tail.

Habitat. This small Asiatic thrush is an annual migrant through the western Aleutian Islands. Also seen on Pribilof Islands and at Gambell on St. Lawrence Island. Summer observations at Attu Island may indicate breeding.

Region	Sp	S	F	W
Southeastern	-	-	-	-
Southcoastal	-	-	-	-
Southwestern	R	+	+	-
Central	-	-	-	-
Western	+	-	-	-
Northern	-	-	-	-

Siberian Rubythroat, male

Bluethroat
Luscinia svecica

Field marks. 5½". *Both sexes:* Plain brown above, with rusty patches at base of tail, conspicuous in flight; white stripe above eye. *Male:* Bright blue throat patch with chestnut spot in center. *Female:* White throat bordered by black.

Similar species. Female Siberian Rubythroat lacks rusty patches at base of tail and has no black border surrounding white throat.

Voice. Song: Musical, introduced by notes sounding like *dip, dip, dip.* Call: Alarm call is *buyt-tock.*

Habitat. Shrub thickets in the uplands and foothills of western and northern Alaska. Nests on the ground.

Region	Sp	S	F	W
Southeastern	-	-	-	-
Southcoastal	-	-	-	-
Southwestern	+	-	+	-
Central	-	-	-	-
Western ★	U	U	U	-
Northern ★	U	U	U	-

Bluethroat, female

Bluethroat, male

Northern Wheatear
Oenanthe oenanthe

Field marks. 6". *All plumages:* White rump patch; black-and-white tail pattern like an inverted T, obvious in flight. *Male:* Black stripe through eye; black wings; gray back. *Female:* Brownish above; dark brown wings; no mask. *Juvenile:* Like female, but with brownish yellow underparts.

Behavior. Has habit of frequently bobbing, spreading its tail feathers, and moving its tail up and down.

Voice. Song: Short, abrupt twitter, sounding like an ungreased door hinge. Call: Alarm call is *tuck, tuck*.

Habitat. Above timberline, rock fields in the tundra and rocky mountain ridges. Nests in crevices under rocks or in rubble.

Region	Sp	S	F	W
Southeastern	-	-	+	-
Southcoastal ★	R	R	R	-
Southwestern	R	+	R	-
Central ★	U	U	U	-
Western ★	C	U	C	-
Northern ★	U	U	U	-

Northern Wheatear, female

Northern Wheatear, male

Mountain Bluebird
Sialia currucoides

Field marks. 7". *Male:* Bright sky-blue all over. *Female:* Overall grayish brown appearance, but with bright blue wings and tail.

Voice. Song: A quiet warbling. Calls: Include soft *phew, ior,* and *terr.*

Habitat. Open woodlands. Perches conspicuously on dead limbs, treetops, fences, and utility wires. Nests in tree holes, rock crevices, and buildings.

Region	Sp	S	F	W
Southeastern ★	R	+	R	+
Southcoastal	+	-	+	-
Southwestern	-	-	-	-
Central ★	R	R	+	-
Western	-	-	+	-
Northern	+	-	-	-

Mountain Bluebird, female

Mountain Bluebird, male

Townsend's Solitaire
Myadestes townsendi

Field marks. 8½". *Adult:* Slim, gray bird with short bill, long tail, and white eye ring. *In flight:* Conspicuous buff-colored wing patch and white outer tail feathers. *Juvenile:* Pale spots on head and body.

Similar species. Northern Mockingbird (casual) lacks white eye ring; has white wing patches; lighter overall.

Voice. Song: Loud and melodious, with fluted rising and falling phrases. Often sings in fall. Call: Bell-like *heep.*

Habitat. Open forests, usually near timberline, especially during breeding season. Nests on the ground under overhanging banks, rocks, tree roots.

Region	Sp	S	F	W
Southeastern ★	R	R	R	+
Southcoastal ★	R	R	R	+
Southwestern	-	-	-	-
Central ★	R	R	R	+
Western	+	-	-	-
Northern	-	-	-	-

Townsend's Solitaire

Gray-cheeked Thrush
Catharus minimus

Field marks. 7½". Grayish cheeks; indistinct eye ring; gray-brown above.

Similar species. Swainson's Thrush has conspicuous buff-colored eye ring. Hermit Thrush has reddish tail, often slowly raised and lowered. Veery (casual) lacks heavy spotting on undersides that is found on other thrushes of the genus *Catharus*.

Voice. Song: Thin, nasal *wee-oh, chee, chee, wee-oh* that usually rises abruptly at end. Call: *Wee-a* and, when alarmed, *chuck*.

Habitat. Mixed deciduous-coniferous woodlands, shrub thickets, coniferous forests. Forages for food in open areas near thickets and on the tundra. Nests in bushes or low trees.

Region	Sp	S	F	W
Southeastern ★	U	U	U	-
Southcoastal ★	U	U	U	-
Southwestern ★	C	C	C	-
Central ★	C	C	C	-
Western ★	C	C	C	-
Northern ★	C	C	C	-

Gray-cheeked Thrush

Swainson's Thrush
Catharus ustulatus

Field marks. 7". Conspicuous buff eye ring and area in front of eyes that creates a spectacled appearance; brown back and tail.

Similar species. Other thrushes lack spectacled appearance. Gray-cheeked Thrush has grayish cheeks and lacks conspicuous eye ring. Hermit Thrush has reddish tail.

Voice. Song: Breezy, flutelike phrases starting with clear, long note on 1 pitch, then spiraling up the scale, becoming fainter until the last notes fade out. Call: *Whit,* easily imitated.

Habitat. Mixed deciduous-coniferous woodlands, shrub thickets, coniferous forests. Nests low in trees or bushes close to the trunk.

Region	Sp	S	F	W
Southeastern ★	C	C	C	-
Southcoastal ★	U	U	U	-
Southwestern ★	U	U	U	-
Central ★	C	C	C	-
Western ★	R	R	R	-
Northern	-	+	-	-

Swainson's Thrush

Hermit Thrush
Catharus guttatus

Field marks. 7". Reddish tail; conspicuous whitish eye ring.

Behavior. Often slowly raises and lowers tail; flicks wings.

Similar species. Other thrushes lack reddish tail. Swainson's Thrush has conspicuous buff eye ring and spectacled appearance. Gray-cheeked Thrush has grayish cheeks. Veery (casual) lacks heavy spotting on undersides of other thrushes of the genus *Catharus.*

Voice. Song: Loud, slow, repetitive phrases spiraling down the scale. Call: Soft *cheep* or *chup-chup,* or catlike *mew.*

Habitat. Edges of coniferous forests, mixed deciduous-coniferous woodlands, shrub thickets. Nests usually on ground, sometimes in trees.

Region	Sp	S	F	W
Southeastern ★	C	C	C	+
Southcoastal ★	C	C	C	-
Southwestern ★	C	C	C	-
Central ★	U	U	U	-
Western ★	R	R	R	-
Northern	+	+	-	-

Eyebrowed Thrush
Turdus obscurus

Field marks. 7 ½". *Male:* Distinct white stripe above eye; orange breast and sides; center of lower breast and belly white; dark gray throat. *Female:* Similar to male but duller; white throat with dark streaks.

Similar species. American Robin is larger, lacks white stripe above eye, and has white on belly only.

Habitat. This Asiatic thrush occurs annually during spring on western Aleutian Islands and occasionally on other islands of the Bering Sea.

Region	Sp	S	F	W
Southeastern	-	-	-	-
Southcoastal	-	-	-	-
Southwestern	R	-	+	-
Central	-	-	-	-
Western	+	-	-	-
Northern	+	-	-	-

Eyebrowed Thrush

American Robin
Turdus migratorius

Field marks. 10". *Adult:* Brick red breast, dark gray back, yellow bill. *Male:* Blackish head and brighter underparts than female. *Juvenile:* Black spots on pale orange breast.

Similar species. Eyebrowed Thrush is smaller, with distinct white stripe above eye; center of lower breast white; unlikely to occur in same area.

Voice. Song: A procession of 2- or 3- syllable phrases that suggest *cheer-up* or *cheerily* with variations in pitch. Call: Common calls are an alarm *pip, pip* and a sibilant flight call, *swee-weep.*

Habitat. From above timberline to forest edges, muskegs, tundra, salt-water beaches, and tidal flats. Nests in crotches of trees; less commonly on horizontal limbs or ledges of buildings or bridges.

Region	Sp	S	F	W
Southeastern ★	C	C	C	R
Southcoastal ★	C	C	C	R
Southwestern ★	C	C	C	-
Central ★	C	C	C	+
Western ★	C	C	C	-
Northern ★	R	R	R	-

American Robin

Varied Thrush
Ixoreus naevius

Field marks. 9½". *Adult:* Orange-buff stripe above and behind eye; orange-brown wing bars and patches (conspicuous in flight). *Male:* Black breast band. *Female:* Gray breast band.

Voice. Song is a long, somewhat burry, whistled note, followed after a pause by another note on a lower or higher pitch. Whistle and hum at the same time provides a fair imitation.

Habitat. Forests from sea level to alpine; prefers shady, damp forests. Forages on the tundra, muskegs, tidal flats, and beaches. Usually nests in conifers, from 5 to 15 feet above the ground.

Region	Sp	S	F	W
Southeastern ★	C	C	C	R
Southcoastal ★	C	C	C	R
Southwestern ★	C	C	C	R
Central ★	C	C	C	-
Western ★	C	C	C	-
Northern	+	-	-	-

Varied Thrush

WAGTAILS, PIPITS
Family *Motacillidae*

Wagtails and pipits are sparrow-sized ground birds with slender bills. They walk instead of hop, and they wag their long tails back and forth, flipping them around (wagtails) or pumping them up and down (pipits). They have dark tails and white outer tail feathers. They feed mostly on insects.

Yellow Wagtail
Motacilla flava

Field marks. 6½". *Adult:* Olive gray back, white line above eye, yellow underparts. *Juvenile:* Whitish throat outlined with dark U-shaped band; buff underparts.

Voice. Call is a loud single note, *tzeep,* often heard as bird flies overhead.

Habitat. Willow thickets on the tundra. Nests on open tundra under grass, overhanging banks.

Region	Sp	S	F	W
Southeastern	-	-	-	-
Southcoastal	-	+	+	-
Southwestern ★	R	R	R	-
Central	+	+	+	-
Western ★	C	C	C	-
Northern ★	U	U	U	-

Yellow Wagtail

White Wagtail
Motacilla alba

Field marks. 7". *Breeding male:* Black crown and throat, black line through eye, gray back. In flight, shows mostly dark wings. *Female:* Similar to male, but has less black on throat. *Juvenile:* Brownish above, with two faint wing bars.

Similar species. Breeding male Black-backed Wagtail has black back, usually a white chin, and in flight shows mostly white wings. Breeding female Black-backed Wagtail can look nearly identical, but in flight shows mostly white wings (may be difficult to see). Juveniles of the 2 species look identical.

Voice. When disturbed, flies up in great undulating arcs, uttering a loud *tizzick*.

Habitat. This Eurasian species occurs in open areas with short vegetation, usually along the coast. Nests in crevices near or on the ground or in niches in old buildings.

Region	Sp	S	F	W
Southeastern	-	-	-	-
Southcoastal	-	-	+	-
Southwestern	+	+	-	-
Central	+	-	-	-
Western ★	R	R	R	-
Northern	R	-	R	-

White Wagtail, male

Black-backed Wagtail
Motacilla lugens

Field marks. 7". *Breeding male:* Black crown and throat, black line through eye, black back, usually white chin. In flight, shows mostly white wings.

Similar species. Breeding male White Wagtail has gray back and usually black chin; shows mostly dark wings in flight. Breeding female White Wagtail can look nearly identical, but in flight shows mostly dark wings (may be difficult to see). Juveniles of the 2 species look identical.

Voice. Similar to White Wagtail.

Habitat. This Asiatic species occurs along creeks and ponds near the coast, mostly in spring in western Aleutian Islands.

Region	Sp	S	F	W
Southeastern	-	+	-	-
Southcoastal	-	+	-	-
Southwestern ★	R	+	+	-
Central	-	-	-	-
Western ★	+	+	-	-
Northern	-	-	-	-

Black-backed Wagtail, male

Red-throated Pipit
Anthus cervinus

Field marks. 6". *Breeding:* Reddish or pinkish color on face, throat, and breast; heavily striped back; black streaks on sides and sometimes belly; pale legs. *In fall:* Loses all or most of the reddish or pinkish color, but retains other field marks.

Similar species. American Pipit in fall looks similar to fall Red-throated, but lacks heavy stripes on back and usually has dark legs. Olive-backed Pipit (casual) has olive back with fainter streaked upperparts; more prominent eye stripe. Pechora Pipit (casual) has 2 distinctive whitish streaks on back, and buff rather than white outer tail feathers.

Voice. Call is a sharp, high-pitched *speez* or *bee-iis.*

Habitat. Shrubby areas on the tundra. Nests on the ground in tussock-sheltered areas.

Region	Sp	S	F	W
Southeastern	-	-	+	-
Southcoastal	-	-	R	-
Southwestern	R	-	R	-
Central				-
Western ★	U	U	U	-
Northern	-	+	+	-

Red-throated Pipit

American Pipit
Anthus rubescens

Field marks. 6½". *Breeding:* Plain, pale grayish back; buff breast with few streaks; dark legs. *In fall:* Dark brown back with faint streaks; heavy streaking on breast and flanks; usually dark legs.

Similar species. In spring, other pipits are more heavily streaked above or below. (Note: a subspecies of American Pipit from Asia may occur in the western Aleutians. This bird has heavy streaks below and pinkish legs.) In fall, Red-throated Pipit has heavy stripes on back and has pale legs. Olive-backed Pipit (casual) has prominent white eye stripe and pale legs. Pechora Pipit (casual) has 2 distinctive whitish streaks on back, and buff rather than white outer tail feathers.

Voice. Song: Series of simple notes, given in flight. Call: A soft *tsi-tsip,* hence "pipit."

Habitat. Tundra, tidal flats, saltwater beaches, fields, alpine meadows, lakeshores, ponds, rivers, streams. Nests on ground on drier ridges and foothills and above timberline. One of the most common and widely distributed birds in Alaska.

Region	Sp	S	F	W
Southeastern ★	C	C	C	+
Southcoastal ★	C	C	C	+
Southwestern ★	C	C	C	+
Central ★		C	C	C	-
Western ★		C	C	C	-
Northern ★		C	C	C	-

American Pipit, fall

American Pipit, spring

WAXWINGS
Family *Bombycillidae*

Waxwings are crested birds with a black mask and with a yellow tip to the tail. The red, waxlike spots on the wings of the adult give the birds their name. They are gregarious and often travel about in large flocks, looking for berries. Waxwings also like to eat insects, which they catch either in flycatcher fashion, by flying out from a perch, or like swallows, by circling high in the air. In interior Alaska they feed on the seeds of paper birch.

Bohemian Waxwing
Bombycilla garrulus

Field marks. 8". *Adult:* Crest; black eye patch, yellow tail tip, chestnut under tail, small white wing patches, very gray belly. *Juvenile:* Similar to adult, but darker with streaked underparts.

Similar species. Cedar Waxwing has white undertail (not chestnut) and no white in wings; yellowish buff belly.

Voice. Call is a high, sibilant rattle, often given in flight.

Habitat. *Breeding:* Wet muskegs. Nests in conifers. *Winter:* Usually any habitat where there are trees or shrubs with berries.

Region	Sp	S	F	W
Southeastern ★	U	R	U	U
Southcoastal ★	U	U	U	R
Southwestern ★	R	R	R	-
Central ★	C	C	C	R
Western ★	R	R	R	-
Northern	-	-	-	-

Bohemian Waxwing

Cedar Waxwing
Bombycilla cedrorum

Field marks. 7". *Adult:* Crest; black eye patch, yellow tail tip, white undertail, yellowish buff belly, no white in wings. *Juvenile:* Similar to adult, but grayer, and has streaked underparts and little or no black around eye.

Similar species. Bohemian Waxwing has chestnut undertail, gray belly, small white patches in wing.

Voice. Similar to Bohemian Waxwing, but higher pitched and even more sibilant.

Habitat. Openings and edges of coniferous forests. Nests in trees, usually in isolated trees in open areas.

Region	Sp	S	F	W
Southeastern ★	R	R	R	+
Southcoastal	-	-	+	+
Southwestern	-	-	-	-
Central	-	-	+	-
Western	-	-	-	-
Northern	-	+	-	-

Cedar Waxwing

SHRIKES
Family *Laniidae*

Shrikes are predatory songbirds with hooked bills that have a sharp, tooth-like projection near the tip. They prey on smaller birds, rodents, and large insects such as bumblebees. Shrikes are nicknamed butcher birds because of their habit of impaling their prey on thorns or barbed wire for later use. Although solitary, they are easily seen because they usually perch on top of small trees or on exposed branches.

Northern Shrike
Lanius excubitor

Field marks. 10". *Adult:* Robin-sized gray bird. Black mask, black wings and tail, hooked bill. *Juvenile:* Faint mask. Brownish above; brownish barring on underparts.

Similar species. Northern Mockingbird (casual) lacks strongly hooked bill and black mask; has light eyes (dark in shrike). Brown Shrike (accidental) is reddish brown, has buff-colored sides, and lacks black wings.

Voice. Song is variable, often consisting of low warbles and harsh squeaks; may mimic other birds. Warning note *sheck-sheck;* when alarmed, a mewing *jaaeg.*

Habitat. Openings and edges of coniferous forests and mixed deciduous-coniferous woodlands, shrub thickets on the tundra, trees near freshwater and saltwater marshes. Usually nests in small deciduous trees. May be found singly or in pairs in spruce forests over much of Alaska.

Region	Sp	S	F	W
Southeastern	U	-	U	U
Southcoastal ★	U	U	U	U
Southwestern ★	U	U	U	U
Central ★	U	U	U	R
Western ★	U	U	U	U
Northern ★	U	U	U	+

Northern Shrike, adult

Northern Shrike, juvenile

STARLINGS
Family *Sturnidae*

Starlings are Old World equivalents of North American blackbirds. The European Starling was introduced into the United States in the late 19th century and is now well established in Alaska. They are gregarious and often fly about in huge flocks. Starlings feed on insects, seeds, berries, and refuse.

European Starling
Sturnus vulgaris

Field marks. 8". *Breeding adult:* Yellow bill; blackish, highly iridescent plumage, with flashes of green and violet. *Winter adult:* Dark bill; blackish plumage spotted with white. *Juvenile:* Dusky brown overall, with dark bill. *In flight:* Short tail, pointed wings.

Behavior. Flies in a rapid, direct manner without undulation.

Similar species. Blackbirds have longer tails, dark bills year-round, and more rounded wings; fly in undulating pattern; lack iridescence and white spots. Brown-headed Cowbird has much shorter bill and longer tail.

Voice. Low-pitched, chirpy chatter without musical quality, interspersed with whistles, clicks, and mimicked songs and calls. Call note is a loud grating *veer.*

Habitat. Open woodlands, fields, beaches, tidal flats, garbage dumps. Nests in natural cavities such as woodpecker and Bank Swallow holes, and in buildings.

Region	Sp	S	F	W
Southeastern ★	U	U	U	U
Southcoastal ★	R	R	R	R
Southwestern	-	-	+	-
Central ★	R	R	R	+
Western	+	+	+	-
Northern	-	+	-	-

European Starling, breeding

European Starling, winter adult

VIREOS
Family *Vireonidae*

Vireos look somewhat like dull warblers, but have a heavier bill with a hooked upper mandible. They move more slowly and deliberately when feeding than do the more active warblers. Vireos eat insects, spiders, and berries.

Warbling Vireo
Vireo gilvus

Field marks. 5". Dull olive-gray above; whitish below; whitish line over eye. Drabness alone aids identification. Knowing distinctive voice helps.

Similar species. Red-eyed Vireo has black-and-white eye stripes. Philadelphia Vireo (accidental) has yellowish throat and breast and black line through eye. Solitary Vireo (accidental) has white spectacles and wing bars. Tennessee Warbler has tiny, pointed bill and greener upperparts.

Voice. Song is a short, husky warble, with a characteristic up-and-down pattern.

Habitat. Deciduous trees, mostly along the mainland rivers of southeastern Alaska. Nests in forked branches of trees.

Region	Sp	S	F	W
Southeastern ★	U	U	U	-
Southcoastal	+	+	+	-
Southwestern	-	-	-	-
Central	-	-	+	-
Western	-	-	-	-
Northern	-	-	-	-

Warbling Vireo

Red-eyed Vireo
Vireo olivaceus

Field marks. 6". Olive-green above; white below. Gray cap outlined in black; whitish line above eye; black stripe through eye; red eyes.

Similar species. Warbling Vireo lacks distinct black-and-white eye stripes. Philadelphia Vireo (accidental) has yellowish throat and breast.

Voice. Song is a series of 2- or 3-syllable whistles, given monotonously for hours.

Habitat. Deciduous trees, mostly along the mainland rivers of southeastern Alaska. Nests in forked branches of trees.

Region	Sp	S	F	W
Southeastern ★	R	R	R	-
Southcoastal	-	+	+	-
Southwestern	-	-	-	-
Central	-	+	-	-
Western	-	-	-	-
Northern	-	-	-	-

Red-eyed Vireo

WOOD WARBLERS
Family *Parulidae*

Wood Warblers are small, active birds that feed mostly on insects. They have small, thin bills. In Alaska, most of them have varying degrees of yellow plumage. In spring and summer, the male has bright, flashy breeding plumage, while the female plumage is duller. But in fall, the plumage of both sexes becomes duller, and identification of sexes and even species becomes more difficult.

Yellow Warbler

Tennessee Warbler
Vermivora peregrina

Field marks. 5". *Breeding male:* Gray head. White line above eye, dark line through eye. Bright olive-green above; white below. *Breeding female:* Similar to male, but with less gray on head and with some yellow on upper breast. *Nonbreeding adult:* In fall, breast is suffused with yellowish color and head becomes greenish; retains dark line through eye.

Similar species. Orange-crowned Warbler has less distinct line through eye; undertail is greenish yellow (white in Tennessee Warbler). Vireos have larger, heavier bills with hooked tip. Arctic Warbler is slightly larger, with stouter bill; unlikely to occur in same area.

Voice. Song begins with buzzy paired notes in series and ends in a dry trill.

Habitat. Deciduous and mixed deciduous-coniferous woodlands. Nests on or near the ground, often in a muskeg.

Region	Sp	S	F	W
Southeastern ★	R	R	R	-
Southcoastal	+	+	+	-
Southwestern	-	-	+	-
Central	+	+	+	-
Western	-	-	-	-
Northern	-	-	-	-

Tennessee Warbler, nonbreeding

Tennessee Warbler, breeding male

Orange-crowned Warbler
Vermivora celata

Field marks. 5". Dingy, greenish yellow warbler with no distinct markings.

Similar species. Dull female or immature Yellow Warbler somewhat similar, but shows yellow markings in outer tail feathers and more distinct edges to wing feathers. Nonbreeding Tennessee Warbler shows dark line through eye and white underneath at base of tail (in Orange-crowned, this area is greenish yellow). Arctic Warbler has whitish eyebrow and short white wing bar.

Voice. Song: Simple trill going up or down the scale toward the end. Call: Sharp *stick*.

Habitat. Deciduous woodlands, shrub thickets, coniferous forest edges where low deciduous growth is present. Nests on the ground or in low shrubs.

Region	Sp	S	F	W
Southeastern ★	C	C	C	+
Southcoastal ★	C	C	C	+
Southwestern ★	C	C	C	-
Central ★	C	C	C	-
Western ★	U	U	U	-
Northern	+	+	+	-

Orange-crowned Warbler

Yellow Warbler
Dendroica petechia

Field marks. 5". *All plumages:* Yellow markings on tail feathers (best seen in flight); distinct yellowish edges to wing feathers; yellowish wing bars. *Male:* Bright yellow underparts with reddish streaks. *Female:* Yellow underparts with streaks faint or absent. *Immature:* Dull olive-green plumage.

Similar species. Orange-crowned Warbler lacks yellow markings in tail feathers and distinct yellowish edges to wing feathers. Female and immature Wilson's Warbler have no wing bars or yellow markings in tail.

Voice. Song: Lively and cheerful, with single and double whistles, *sweet-sweet-sweet-sweet-setta-see-see-whew!* Call: Loud, down-slurred *cheep.*

Habitat. Deciduous woodlands and shrub thickets. Nests in shrubs or trees, usually near the ground.

Region	Sp	S	F	W
Southeastern ★	C	C	C	-
Southcoastal ★	U	U	U	-
Southwestern ★	C	C	C	-
Central ★	C	C	C	-
Western ★	C	C	C	-
Northern ★	R	R	R	-

Yellow Warbler, male

Yellow Warbler, female

Magnolia Warbler
Dendroica magnolia

Field marks. 5". *All plumages:* Tail crossed by band of white. *Breeding male:* Gray crown; wide black band through eyes; black back; bright yellow below with black streaks; white wing bars. *Breeding female:* Similar to male, but duller. *Immature and fall adult:* Grayish head; yellow underparts with faint streaks; white wing bars; narrow gray band across breast.

Similar species. Adult Yellow-rumped Warbler is white and black below. Cape May Warbler (accidental) has yellow on face; lacks white in tail.

Voice. Song is a rising *wisha-wisha-wisha-witsy* or *pretty-pretty-Rachel*.

Habitat. Coniferous forests and mixed deciduous-coniferous woodlands. Nests are usually placed in small conifers, less than 14 feet above the ground.

Region	Sp	S	F	W
Southeastern ★	R	R	R	-
Southcoastal	-	+	+	-
Southwestern	-	-	-	-
Central	-	+	-	-
Western	-	-	+	-
Northern	-	-	+	-

Magnolia Warbler, immature

Magnolia Warbler, breeding male

Yellow-rumped Warbler
Dendroica coronata

Field marks. 5½". *All plumages:*
Yellow rump; yellow on sides of
breast. *Breeding male:* Gray upperparts streaked with black; white
belly; black streaks on breast and
flanks. Two recognized subspecies:
Myrtle Warbler has white throat;
Audubon's Warbler has yellow throat.
Female: Similar pattern, but duller.
Fall immature: Very drab brownish
gray, with scattered streaks.
Similar species. Magnolia Warbler
is yellow below. Cape May Warbler
(accidental) has yellow on face. Palm
Warbler in fall (casual) is ground-
dwelling and constantly wags its tail
while feeding.
Voice. Song is tinkling trill that
either rises or falls in pitch at end.
Habitat. Coniferous forests, mixed
deciduous-coniferous woodlands,
shrub thickets. Nests in conifers,
usually 4 to 10 feet above the
ground.

Region	Sp	S	F	W
Southeastern ★	C	C	C	+
Southcoastal ★	U	U	U	+
Southwestern ★	U	U	U	-
Central ★	C	C	C	-
Western ★	C	C	C	-
Northern	+	+	-	-

Yellow-rumped Warbler, fall

Yellow-rumped Warbler, male, "Myrtle"

**Yellow-rumped Warbler,
female, "Audubon's"**

Townsend's Warbler
Dendroica townsendi

Region	Sp	S	F	W
Southeastern ★	C	C	C	+
Southcoastal ★	U	U	U	+
Southwestern	-	-	+	-
Central ★	C	C	C	-
Western	-	-	-	-
Northern	-	-	+	-

Field marks. 5". *All plumages:* Dark crown, and dark cheeks bordered by yellow, give the face a distinctive masked appearance. *Adult male:* Black throat, cheeks, and cap; yellow below, with streaked sides. *Adult female:* Olive cap and back, dusky cheeks, yellow throat, dark streaks on upper breast and sides. *Immature:* Similar to female, but duller.

Similar species. Black-throated Green Warbler (accidental) has more black on underparts and much fainter cheeks and crown than adult Townsend's.

Voice. Song: *Weazy weazy weazy twea* or *dee dee dee-de de.* Call: Soft *chip.*

Habitat. Coniferous forests, mixed deciduous-coniferous woodlands. Nests in conifers.

Townsend's Warbler, adult male

Townsend's Warbler, adult female

Blackpoll Warbler
Dendroica striata

Field marks. 5½". *Breeding male:* Olive above, white below, with black streaks on back and flanks. Black cap, white cheeks, white wing bars. *Breeding female:* Similar pattern to male, but mostly drab olive green; streaked on back and sides; white wing bars. *In fall:* Similar to breeding female, but greener upperparts, greenish yellow underparts, pale legs (only streaked warbler in Alaska with pale legs).

Similar species. Townsend's Warbler has distinctive black mask. Yellow-rumped Warbler has yellow on rump and sides of breast.

Voice. Song: High pitched *zi-zi-zi* repeated 6 to 12 times. Call: Low *chip* and thin *zeep.*

Habitat. Coniferous forests, mixed deciduous-coniferous woodlands, shrub thickets. Nests in small conifers or on the ground near conifers.

Region	Sp	S	F	W
Southeastern ★	R	+	R	-
Southcoastal ★	R	R	R	-
Southwestern ★	C	C	C	-
Central ★	U	U	U	-
Western ★	C	C	C	-
Northern	+	+	+	

Blackpoll Warbler, female

Blackpoll Warbler, breeding male

American Redstart
Setophaga ruticilla

Region	Sp	S	F	W
Southeastern ★	U	U	U	-
Southcoastal	-	+	+	-
Southwestern	-	-	-	-
Central	+	+	-	-
Western	-	-	-	-
Northern	-	-	+	-

Field marks. 5". *Breeding male:* Bright orange patches on wings and tail; black head, back, and breast; white belly. *Female and immature:* Olive gray above, white below; yellow patches on sides, wings, and tail.

Behavior. Often flits about, droops its wings, and spreads its tail feathers.

Voice. Song: Thin, high-pitched series of notes, often slurred at the end (somewhat like Yellow Warbler but more on 1 pitch). Call: Thin, slurred *tseep.*

Habitat. Has occurred mostly in the deciduous forests along the mainland rivers of southeastern Alaska. Nests in deciduous trees, usually 5 to 20 feet up.

American Redstart, female

American Redstart, breeding male

Northern Waterthrush
Seiurus noveboracensis

Field marks. 6". Prominent buff-colored eyebrow stripe. Dark brown above; heavily streaked below. Tiny spots on throat.

Behavior. Frequently "teeters" while walking.

Similar species. Ovenbird (accidental) behaves and looks similar, but lacks eyebrow stripe.

Voice. Song: Very loud, far-carrying sequence of quickly uttered, identical, short, chattering phrases repeated many times and speeded-up toward the end. Call: Loud, sharp *chink*.

Habitat. Deciduous trees and heavy brush bordering streams, lakes, ponds, and swamps. Nests on the ground beneath logs, roots, or stumps or in mossy banks.

Region	Sp	S	F	W
Southeastern ★	U	U	U	-
Southcoastal ★	U	U	U	-
Southwestern ★	C	C	C	-
Central ★		C	C	C	-
Western ★		C	C	C	-
Northern	+	-	-	-

Northern Waterthrush

MacGillivray's Warbler
Oporornis tolmiei

Field marks. 5". *Adult:* Slate gray hood; conspicuous white eye ring; olive above, yellow below. *Female and immature:* Duller hood than male.

Similar species. Female Common Yellowthroat has yellow throat and lacks hooded appearance. Male Mourning Warbler (accidental) has lighter gray hood and lacks white eye ring; female and immature Mourning Warblers difficult to distinguish, but highly unlikely to occur in Alaska.

Voice. Song: Chanting *tree tree tree tree sweet sweet.* Call: Loud *tik;* sharper than calls of most other warblers.

Habitat. Shrub thickets. Nests near the ground in shrubs or weed clumps.

Region	Sp	S	F	W
Southeastern ★	U	U	U	-
Southcoastal	+	-	+	-
Southwestern	-	-	-	-
Central	-	-	+	-
Western	-	-	-	-
Northern	-	+	+	-

MacGillivray's Warbler, immature

MacGillivray's Warbler, adult male

Common Yellowthroat
Geothlypis trichas

Field marks. 5". *Male:* Black mask; bright yellow throat. *Female:* Yellow throat; olive above; whitish belly. *Immature:* Male has partly developed mask; female has throat tinged with yellow.

Voice. Song: Well-enunciated *witchity-witchity-witchity-witch.* Call: Low *djip.*

Habitat. Freshwater marshes and estuarine meadows along mainland rivers of southeastern Alaska and on islands near the mouths of these rivers. Nests on or near the ground in grasses and weeds.

Region	Sp	S	F	W
Southeastern ★	U	U	U	-
Southcoastal ★	-	+	+	-
Southwestern	-	-	-	-
Central	-	+	-	-
Western	-	+	-	-
Northern	-	-	-	-

Common Yellowthroat, female

Common Yellowthroat, male

Wilson's Warbler
Wilsonia pusilla

Region	Sp	S	F	W
Southeastern ★	C	C	C	-
Southcoastal ★	C	C	C	+
Southwestern ★	C	C	C	-
Central ★	C	C	C	-
Western ★	U	U	U	-
Northern ★	+	+	+	-

Field marks. 4½". *Both sexes:* Olive above; entirely bright yellow below. *Male:* Glossy black cap. *Female and immature:* May have olive cap; yellow on face extends above eyes.

Behavior. Holds tail cocked up like wren. Twitches tail in circular motion. Flicks wings.

Similar species. Yellow Warbler has plain head, yellow wing bars, and yellow tail patches.

Voice. Song: Evenly spaced series of notes, *chip chip chip chip chip.* Call: Soft *timp.*

Habitat. Shrub thickets, mixed deciduous-coniferous woodlands. Nests on or near the ground in shrub thickets.

Wilson's Warbler, male

TANAGERS
Family *Thraupidae*

Tanagers look like very large warblers with a thick bill. They are very secretive; despite the striking yellow-and-black color of the male Western Tanager, this bird is difficult to spot. Tanagers feed on insects and berries.

Western Tanager
Piranga ludoviciana

Region	Sp	S	F	W
Southeastern ★	U	U	U	-
Southcoastal	+	-	+	-
Southwestern	-	-	-	-
Central	-	+	+	-
Western	-	-	-	-
Northern	+	-	-	-

Field marks. 7". *Breeding male:* Bright yellow below and back of neck; red face; black wings and tail; 2 wing bars, with the upper yellow and the lower white. *Breeding female:* Dull greenish back; duller yellow below (may range to grayish white in some); 2 white or yellowish wing bars.

Voice. Song: Robinlike but harsh and burry. Call: *Per-dick.*

Habitat. Open coniferous forests. Edge of Western Hemlock/Sitka Spruce forests of mainland rivers of southeastern Alaska. Nests in forked conifer branches.

Western Tanager, breeding female

Western Tanager, breeding male

SPARROWS, BUNTINGS
Family *Emberizidae*

This diverse bird family is represented in Alaska by sparrows, juncos, longspurs, and buntings. They all have short, conical bills designed for crushing seeds, and they feed mostly on the ground. Sparrows are small, more or less streaked, brownish, and rather drab looking. Juncos are without streaks; they have pale bills and white outer tail feathers. Longspurs, especially the males, have rather striking facial patterns. Buntings are mostly white with varying amounts of black, brown, and buff. When not breeding, most members of this family travel in flocks, sometimes quite large.

American Tree Sparrow
Spizella arborea

Field marks. 6". *Adult:* Single dusky spot in middle of unstreaked breast; 2 white wing bars; red cap; dark upper bill, yellow lower bill. *Juvenile:* Streaks on breast, sides, and crown.

Similar species. Adult Chipping Sparrow lacks spot on breast; has white line above eye and black line through eye.

Voice. Song: Usually begins with several *seet* notes followed by a variable, rapid warble. Call: *Tseet.*

Habitat. Shrub thickets. Near timberline to sea level, on the tundra wherever willows occur. Nests on the ground or in low bushes.

Region	Sp	S	F	W
Southeastern ★	U	+	U	R
Southcoastal ★	U	R	U	R
Southwestern ★	U	U	U	R
Central ★	C	C	C	+
Western ★	C	C	C	-
Northern ★	U	U	U	-

American Tree Sparrow, adult

Chipping Sparrow
Spizella passerina

Field marks. 5½". *Adult:* Reddish cap; broad white stripe over eye, and black stripe through eye; clean gray underparts. *Fall immature:* Streaked crown; less distinct eye stripe; brown cheek patch.

Similar species. Adult American Tree Sparrow has spot in center of breast; lacks obvious white stripe over eye. Savannah Sparrow may resemble juvenile Chipping Sparrow, but Savannah has yellowish about the face.

Voice. Song is an even trill, drier and less musical than that of the junco.

Habitat. Openings and edges of woodlands. Nests in deciduous or coniferous trees. Found mostly along the mainland rivers of southeastern Alaska and the upper Tanana River Valley of eastern central Alaska.

Region	Sp	S	F	W
Southeastern ★	R	R	R	+
Southcoastal ★	+	+	+	+
Southwestern	-	-	-	-
Central ★	U	U	U	-
Western	+	-	+	-
Northern	-	+	+	

Chipping Sparrow, adult/juvenile

Savannah Sparrow
Passerculus sandwichensis

Field marks. 5½". Yellowish line over eye (usually); streaked above and below; short, slightly notched tail.

Similar species. Song Sparrow is usually larger and darker, with rounded tail tip and no yellow on face. Lincoln's Sparrow has no yellow on face, and side of head looks gray.

Voice. Song is a quiet buzzing *tsit-tsit-tsit-tseee-tseee.*

Habitat. Open places, especially grassy fields. Widespread in Alaska from seashore to mountain ridges. Nests on ground, usually in open grassy areas.

Region	Sp	S	F	W
Southeastern ★	C	C	C	+
Southcoastal ★	C	C	C	+
Southwestern ★	C	C	C	+
Central ★	C	C	C	+
Western ★	C	C	C	-
Northern ★	C	C	C	-

Savannah Sparrow

Fox Sparrow
Passerella iliaca

Region	Sp	S	F	W
Southeastern ★	C	C	C	R
Southcoastal ★	C	C	C	R
Southwestern ★	C	C	C	-
Central ★	C	C	C	+
Western ★	C	C	C	-
Northern ★	U	U	U	-

Field marks. 7". Brown or grayish brown back; very heavily spotted-to-streaked underparts, often in a pattern of shapes that look like inverted Vs. Northern and Interior subspecies has a bright reddish-brown tail that contrasts sharply in color with the back; it has a striped back and a partially striped head. Coastal subspecies are much darker and browner, without the strong contrast between the back and tail colors and with no stripes on the head or back. The darkest and smallest Fox Sparrow is found in lower southeastern Alaska, while subspecies to the north is grayer and larger.

Similar species. Song Sparrow has an all-dark bill (Fox has a light lower mandible). Song Sparrow has a more elongated body, flatter head, and longer, thinner bill. Song Sparrow has a striped head and back (plain in southern Fox Sparrow).

Voice. Song: Opens with 1 or more clear whistles and follows with several short trills or *churrs.* Call: Sharp *chink.*

Habitat. Shrub thickets. Nests on ground under shrubs or low in trees or shrubs.

Fox Sparrow

Song Sparrow
Melospiza melodia

Region	Sp	S	F	W
Southeastern ★	C	C	C	C
Southcoastal ★	C	C	C	C
Southwestern ★	C	C	C	C
Central	-	-	+	-
Western	-	-	-	-
Northern	-	-	-	-

Field marks. 6"-7½". Brownish back; heavy streaks on breast, with usually a prominent spot in center of breast streaks. Head and back streaked; dark bill. Size varies in subspecies: Aleutian Island Song Sparrows are the largest and have a long, thin bill; those from southern Alaska are obviously smaller than the Fox Sparrow.

Behavior. Pumps tail in flight.

Similar species. Fox Sparrow has a light lower mandible. Northern and Interior Fox Sparrows have a reddish brown tail. Coastal Fox Sparrows lack stripes on head or back. Various subspecies of Song and Fox sparrows may occur together during migration. See Savannah, Lincoln's, and Swamp (casual) sparrows.

Voice. Song: Staccato but musical, usually beginning with 2 or 3 loud notes that sound like *sweet, sweet, sweet,* followed by a trill, then several short notes. Call: Harsh single note, *chimp.*

Habitat. Marine beaches; only occasionally ventures inland. Beach rocks, shrub thickets. Nests on ground in grass clumps.

Song Sparrow

Lincoln's Sparrow
Melospiza lincolnii

Field marks. 5½". Side of head looks gray; buff-colored band on breast and sides. Small, trim, finely streaked bird.

Similar species. Song and Fox sparrows are larger and darker; lack gray face. Savannah Sparrow usually has yellow on face; lacks gray face. Immature Swamp Sparrow (casual) has blackish stripes on head, with gray central stripe and reddish wings.

Voice. Song: Low, gurgling stanza that ends after some rising phrases. Call: *Tik* and buzzy *tzeee*.

Habitat. Shrubs; saltwater and freshwater marshes. Nests on the ground in marshy places.

Region	Sp	S	F	W
Southeastern ★	C	C	C	+
Southcoastal ★	C	C	C	+
Southwestern ★	U	U	U	-
Central ★	C	C	C	-
Western ★	U	U	U	-
Northern	-	+	-	-

Lincoln's Sparrow

Golden-crowned Sparrow
Zonotrichia atricapilla

Field marks. 6½". *Adult:* Golden crown bordered by wide black stripe on either side. *Juvenile:* Very dull; finely streaked on top of head; faint yellow may be visible on forehead; dark bill.

Similar species. Juvenile White-crowned and White-throated (casual) sparrows have prominent head stripes. White-crowned Sparrow has pale bill.

Voice. Song is normally 3 high, whistled notes of minor tone quality, running down the scale, as in "Three Blind Mice."

Habitat. Willow and alder thickets, at timberline and along the seacoast. Nests on ground under shrubs. Favors brushy areas in migration.

Region	Sp	S	F	W
Southeastern ★	C	U	C	R
Southcoastal ★	C	C	C	R
Southwestern ★	C	C	C	-
Central ★	U	U	U	+
Western ★	C	C	C	-
Northern	R	R	R	-

Golden-crowned Sparrow, juvenile

Golden-crowned Sparrow, adult

White-crowned Sparrow
Zonotrichia leucophrys

Field marks. 6". *Adult:* Conspicuous black-and-white-striped head; plain gray below, streaked above; pale bill. *Juvenile:* Head striped with rusty-brown and gray; pale bill.

Similar species. Adult White-throated Sparrow (casual) has white throat, yellow near eyes, and dark bill. Juvenile Golden-crowned Sparrow lacks prominent head stripes; has faint yellow on forehead and a dark bill.

Voice. Song is a series of 6 whistled notes, sounding lazy and wheezy, rising on the second and third notes and falling on the last 3 notes.

Habitat. Forest edges and brush patches. Nests on the ground in grass clumps or low shrubs.

Region	Sp	S	F	W
Southeastern	U	-	U	R
Southcoastal ★	U	R	U	R
Southwestern ★	C	C	C	+
Central ★	C	C	C	+
Western ★	C	C	C	-
Northern ★	U	U	U	-

White-crowned Sparrow, juvenile

White-crowned Sparrow, adult

Harris's Sparrow
Zonotrichia querula

Field marks. 7½". *Adult:* Black crown, face, and throat; streaked sides; white underneath. *Immature:* Much less black; may have dark blotch on upper breast; buff-colored head; white underneath, with streaked sides.

Similar species. Other large sparrows have much more streaking below and lack the pure white underparts.

Habitat. Most often seen at feeders in southeastern Alaska.

Note. Now considered casual by Gibson (1999).

Region	Sp	S	F	W
Southeastern	R	-	R	R
Southcoastal	+	-	+	+
Southwestern	-	-	-	-
Central	-	-	+	-
Western	-	-	-	-
Northern	+	+	-	-

Harris's Sparrow, immature

Harris's Sparrow, adult

Dark-eyed Junco
Junco hyemalis

Field marks. 5 ½". *All plumages:*
Flashy white outer tail feathers, conspicuous in flight; pink bill. *Adult:*
No streaks, wing bars, or head
markings. Juncos breeding north of
Yakutat Bay are all slate gray with
white belly; those from Yakutat Bay
south have a black (male) or gray
(female) hood, reddish brown back,
and buff-pink sides. These 2 subspecies are called Slate-colored and
Oregon, respectively. *Juvenile:* Colored like adult, but heavily streaked.
Voice. Song is a loud, musical trill, all
on 1 pitch.
Habitat. *Breeding:* Coniferous forests
and forest edges, clearings, muskegs.
Nests on the ground. *Winter:* Easily
attracted to feeders. Both Slate-
colored and Oregon subspecies
occur together in southeastern
Alaska when not breeding.

Region	Sp	S	F	W
Southeastern ★	C	C	C	U
Southcoastal ★	C	C	C	U
Southwestern ★	U	U	U	R
Central ★	C	C	C	R
Western ★	U	U	U	-
Northern ★	+	R	R	-

**Dark-eyed Junco,
slate-colored subspecies**

**Dark-eyed Junco,
Oregon subspecies, male**

Lapland Longspur
Calcarius lapponicus

Field marks. 6½". *All plumages:* White in outer tail feathers, but less than other birds with white outer tail feathers found in similar habitat; white underparts. *Breeding male:* Black crown, face, and throat; chestnut hindneck; white stripe on face and neck. *Breeding female:* Similar pattern to male, but much fainter.

Similar species. Smith's Longspur has buff-colored underparts and different head pattern; lacks chestnut hindneck. American Pipit and Horned Lark have more conspicuous white outer tail feathers and thin bills. Savannah Sparrow has heavily streaked breast and no white in tail.

Voice. Song: Beautiful series of tinkling notes given in flight. Call: On breeding grounds, a liquid *teew;* migrants utter a dry rattle.

Habitat. *Breeding:* Tundra. Nests on small clumps of grass or dry knolls. *Migration:* Grassy fields, wetlands, alpine meadows, ridges; often with Horned Larks and Snow Buntings.

Region	Sp	S	F	W
Southeastern	C	-	C	+
Southcoastal ★	C	R	C	+
Southwestern ★	C	C	C	+
Central ★	C	C	C	-
Western ★	C	C	C	-
Northern ★	C	C	C	-

Lapland Longspur, breeding male

Lapland Longspur, breeding female

Smith's Longspur
Calcarius pictus

Region	Sp	S	F	W
Southeastern	+	-	+	-
Southcoastal	-	-	-	-
Southwestern	-	-	-	-
Central ★	R	R	R	-
Western	-	-	-	-
Northern ★	U	U	U	-

Field marks. 6". *Breeding male:* Conspicuous black-and-white head pattern; bright buff underparts; white outer tail feathers. *Breeding female:* Streaked buff underparts; white outer tail feathers; may show some white on shoulder.

Behavior. Breeding male sings from the ground, rather than from the air like Lapland Longspur.

Similar species. Breeding male Lapland Longspur has different head pattern; chestnut hindneck and white underparts. Breeding female Lapland Longspur shows reddish on back of neck and whitish underparts.

Voice. Song: Warblerlike, with sweet notes. Call: On breeding grounds, is distinct 2-note rattle.

Habitat. In the Brooks Range: Damp tussock meadows, usually on wide alpine valley floors, often on flat meadows surrounding lakes. In central Alaska: Dry ridgetop tundra. Nests on the ground.

Smith's Longspur, breeding female

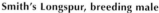

Smith's Longspur, breeding male

Rustic Bunting
Emberiza rustica

Field marks. 5¾". *All plumages:* Rusty band or streaks across breast; rusty streaks on sides; white outer tail feathers. *Breeding male:* Black top and sides of head; white stripe behind eye; white throat and underparts; slight crest on head. *Breeding female:* Similar to male, but with brown-and-white head pattern.

Similar species. Little Bunting (accidental) is smaller with smaller bill, has creamy white eye ring, heavy black steaks below.

Voice. Call is a sharp *tsip, tsip, tsip.*

Habitat. This Asiatic bunting occurs most often in the western Aleutian Islands. It is a ground-dwelling bird that occurs singly or in pairs, in or near dense cover.

Region	Sp	S	F	W
Southeastern	-	-	+	-
Southcoastal	+	-	-	+
Southwestern	R	-	R	-
Central	-	-	+	+
Western	+	-	-	-
Northern	-	-	-	-

Rustic Bunting, female

Rustic Bunting, breeding male

Snow Bunting
Plectrophenax nivalis

Region	Sp	S	F	W
Southeastern ★	U	R	U	U
Southcoastal ★	U	R	U	R
Southwestern ★	C	C	C	C
Central ★	C	U	U	R
Western ★	C	C	C	U
Northern ★	C	C	C	-

Field marks. 6½". *Breeding male:* Black back; white head and underparts; in flight, shows striking black-and-white plumage, white patches in wings and tail, white rump. *Breeding female and winter:* More brown, but still shows extensive white in wings and tail when in flight.

Similar species. Breeding male McKay's Bunting has mostly white on back; breeding female McKay's Bunting has less mottling on back and shows more white; both sexes show more white in tail and wings than Snow Bunting.

Voice. Song is a short musical warble, often with some phrases repeated, and is given on the ground or in flight.

Habitat. *Breeding:* Tundra. Coastline of northern, western, and southwestern Alaska. Nests in various locations, including buildings, empty gas drums, and birdhouses. In mountains, nests beneath rocks or in rock crevices. *Migration and winter:* Prefers open fields, shoreline, and roadsides.

Snow Bunting, breeding male

Snow Bunting, winter

McKay's Bunting
Plectrophenax hyperboreus

Region	Sp	S	F	W
Southeastern	-	-	-	-
Southcoastal	+	-	-	+
Southwestern ★	U	R	U	U
Central	-	-	-	-
Western ★	R	R	R	R
Northern	-	-	-	-

Field marks. 7". *Breeding male:* Mostly white except for some black on inner wing, black wing tips, and black tip of central tail feathers. *Breeding female:* Similar to male, but with some mottling on back. *Winter:* Some brown on head, breast, and rump.

Similar species. Breeding Snow Bunting shows much more black or mottling on back. In both summer and winter, Snow Bunting shows much more black in tail and wings.

Habitat. *Breeding:* Islands of the Bering Sea. Nests in small depressions on the ground or in rock crevices. *Migration and winter:* Mainland bordering the Bering Sea.

McKay's Bunting, male

BLACKBIRDS
Family *Icteridae*

The blackbirds found in Alaska are sparrow- to robin-sized. The males are mostly black. These birds forage mostly on the ground for seeds and insects.

Red-winged Blackbird
Agelaius phoeniceus

Region	Sp	S	F	W
Southeastern ★	U	U	U	R
Southcoastal ★	R	R	R	+
Southwestern	-	-	+	-
Central ★	U	U	U	+
Western	-	+	+	-
Northern	+	+	-	-

Field marks. 8". *Adult male:* All black; red shoulder patch with buff-colored rear border. *Female:* Heavily streaked underparts; dark brown upperparts; pale line above eye. *Immature male:* Resembles female in pattern, but larger and darker, with dull orange-red shoulder patch.

Similar species. Other blackbirds in Alaska are distinguished from female and immature Red-winged by a lack of streaking on underparts. Juvenile Brown-headed Cowbird is streaked below, but is smaller and lacks pale line above eye.

Voice. Song: Loud, liquid, ringing *ok-a-lee.* Call: *Chuck,* and a thin *teeyee.*

Habitat. Freshwater marshes and water edges with thick vegetation. Nests in shoreline vegetation or bushes.

Red-winged Blackbird, adult male

Red-winged Blackbird, female

Rusty Blackbird
Euphagus carolinus

Field marks. 9". *All plumages:* Conspicuous yellow eyes. *Breeding male:* All black with faint greenish gloss. *Adult female:* Plumage varies from similar to male to dull slate gray. *In fall:* Close, rust-colored bars, especially on undersides; rust-colored crown; buff-colored eye-brow.

Similar species. Male Brewer's Blackbird (casual) has whitish eyes and purplish reflection on head. Female Brewer's has dark eyes. Common Grackle (accidental) is larger, with a much larger bill and long, wedge-shaped tail.

Voice. Song: Short; ends with a note sounding like a squeaky hinge. Call: Harsh *chack.*

Habitat. Willow thickets near rivers in coastal areas; swampy areas inland. Nests in conifers, willows, or alders near water. After nesting season, may frequent garbage dumps.

Region	Sp	S	F	W
Southeastern ★	U	R	U	R
Southcoastal ★	U	R	U	R
Southwestern ★	U	U	U	-
Central ★	U	U	U	R
Western ★	U	U	U	+
Northern ★	R	R	R	-

Rusty Blackbird, fall

Rusty Blackbird, breeding male

Brown-headed Cowbird
Molothrus ater

Field marks. 7". *All plumages:* Short, conical, finchlike bill. *Adult male:* Brown head, shiny black body. *Adult female:* Overall brownish gray. *Juvenile:* Light brown; streaked underparts.

Similar species. Other blackbirds have a longer, more pointed bill. Female Red-winged Blackbird may resemble juvenile Brown-headed Cowbird, but is larger and has pale line above eye.

Voice. Male gives a variety of high, squeaking whistles and gurgling notes. Female gives a rattling call and soft *tsip.*

Habitat. Open woodlands, fields, and pastures. Often associated with horses and cows, feeding upon insects stirred up by the hoofed animals. Lays eggs in nests of other small birds.

Region	Sp	S	F	W
Southeastern ★	R	R	R	+
Southcoastal	-	+	+	+
Southwestern	-	-	+	-
Central	+	+	+	-
Western	-	+	+	-
Northern	-	+	+	-

Brown-headed Cowbird, adult female

Brown-headed Cowbird, adult male

FINCHES
Family *Fringillidae*

Members of the finch family have a short, heavy, conical beak, which is used for cracking seeds, their main food. They also eat insects and berries. In contrast with sparrows, which feed mainly on the ground, most finches spend much of the time foraging in trees for the seeds produced in cones. Many species travel about in large flocks, and their abundance from one year to the next may vary considerably, depending on the cone crop.

Brambling
Fringilla montifringilla

Field marks. 5¾". *All plumages:* Conspicuous white rump and lower back; rust-colored or orange breast and throat; white wing bars. *In fall:* Pale yellow bill with dark tip.

Voice. A soft, single *tshuck*. In flight, repeats note rapidly.

Habitat. This Asiatic finch is seen most often in western Aleutian Islands.

Region	Sp	S	F	W
Southeastern	+	-	+	+
Southcoastal	+	-	+	+
Southwestern ★	R	+	R	+
Central	-	-	-	-
Western	+	-	-	-
Northern	+	-	+	-

Brambling, female

Gray-crowned Rosy Finch
Leucosticte tephrocotis

Region	Sp	S	F	W
Southeastern ★	U	U	U	R
Southcoastal ★	U	U	U	R
Southwestern ★	C	C	C	C
Central ★	U	U	U	+
Western ★	U	U	U	-
Northern ★	R	R	R	-

Field marks. 6". *Male:* Gray crown; rosy wash on belly and often on flanks and shoulder. Body color may be dark brown or cinnamon brown, depending on subspecies. *Female:* Similar to male, but duller and with less gray on head. *Juvenile:* Entirely dull brown, without head markings and rosy wash.

Similar species. Other finches lack gray crown. Juveniles may be difficult to identify, but most other similar-looking finches are streaked.

Voice. Song: Canarylike warble. In flight: Harsh *cheep, cheep* notes.

Habitat. Alpine tundra, mountain ridges above timberline, near snowfields; beaches in the Aleutian Islands and Bering Sea islands. Nests in cliff crevices or rock slides. *Winter:* Lower elevations; often seen in flocks near towns.

Gray-crowned Rosy Finch, male

Pine Grosbeak
Pinicola enucleator

Field marks. 9". *All plumages:* Plump, stocky birds about the size of a robin; thick, stubby bill; 2 conspicuous white wing bars. *Male:* Rosy red; gray belly. *Female:* Gray; head and rump tinged with yellow. *Immature male:* Resembles female, but with reddish head and rump.

Similar species. Male White-winged Crossbill is smaller, with crossed bill.

Voice. Song: Series of musical warbles. Call: 3- to 4-note descending whistle.

Habitat. Coniferous forests. Nests in conifers, usually not more than 10 to 15 feet above ground. *Winter:* Travels in flocks and feeds on buds and fruits of trees. Fond of Mountain Ash berries.

Region	Sp	S	F	W
Southeastern ★	U	U	C	C
Southcoastal ★	U	U	U	U
Southwestern ★	U	U	U	U
Central ★	U	U	U	U
Western ★	U	U	U	U
Northern	R	R	R	-

Pine Grosbeak, female

Pine Grosbeak, male

Red Crossbill
Loxia curvirostra

Field marks. 6". *All plumages:* Large-headed and heavy-billed; crossed mandibles; stubby tail. *Male:* Brick red body; black wings and tail. *Female:* Dull olive gray; yellowish rump. *Juvenile:* Dull, brown; streaked above and below.

Behavior. Often feeds in treetops or flies high in air between trees, so presence best detected by call and a spotting scope.

Similar species. White-winged Crossbill has white wing bars in all plumages.

Voice. Repeated *kip-kip* or *jeep-jeep* and whistled notes sometimes interspersed with warbled passages.

Habitat. Coniferous forests. Nests in conifers, usually well out on branches. May nest almost any time of year. Abundance varies from year to year depending on cone crop.

Region	Sp	S	F	W
Southeastern ★	C	C	C	C
Southcoastal ★	R	R	R	R
Southwestern	-	R	+	-
Central	-	+	+	-
Western	-	-	+	-
Northern	-	-	-	-

Red Crossbill, female

Red Crossbill, male

White-winged Crossbill
Loxia leucoptera

Region	Sp	S	F	W
Southeastern ★	U	U	U	U
Southcoastal ★	U	U	U	U
Southwestern ★	U	U	U	U
Central ★	U	U	U	U
Western ★	U	U	U	U
Northern	-	-	+	-

Field marks. 6". *All plumages:* Conspicuous white wing bars; heavy-billed, with crossed mandibles; black wings and stubby tail. *Male:* Bright pink body; black wings and tail. *Female:* Grayish olive plumage; dark streaks above and below.

Behavior. Presence usually detected by calls when feeding near tops of coniferous trees.

Similar species. Red Crossbill lacks white wing bars. Pine Grosbeak is larger, with stubby bill.

Voice. Song: Variable, melodious, with warbling trilling, decidedly richer and sweeter than Red Crossbill's. Flight call: Soft *twee* or a loud, harsh *cheet, cheet.*

Habitat. Coniferous forests. Nests in conifers from 5 to 80 feet up. May nest almost any time of year. Abundance varies from year to year depending on cone crop.

White-winged Crossbill, male

White-winged Crossbill, female

Common Redpoll
Carduelis flammea

Field marks. 5". *Both sexes:* Bright red cap, blackish chin, dark streaks on sides and rump. *Male:* Pinkish wash on breast.

Similar species. Hoary Redpoll has shorter bill, unstreaked rump, and less streaking on sides; usually looks paler than Common Redpoll, but there is much overlap between these 2 species and some individuals cannot be identified in the field.

Voice. Song: Trill, followed by a rattling *chit-chit-chit-chit.* Call: Loud *chit-chit-chit-chit* and a *swee-e-et,* often given in flight.

Habitat. Tundra shrub thickets, mixed deciduous-coniferous woodlands, open fields and grasslands, near cities and towns especially in winter. Nests on the ground or in lower brances of bushes. Abundance varies from year to year depending on seed crop.

Region	Sp	S	F	W
Southeastern ★	C	U	C	C
Southcoastal ★	C	U	C	C
Southwestern ★	C	C	C	C
Central ★	C	C	C	C
Western ★	C	C	C	C
Northern ★	U	U	U	-

Common Redpoll

Hoary Redpoll
Carduelis hornemanni

Field marks. 5½". *Both sexes:* Bright red cap; blackish chin; some streaking on sides; very short bill (gives face pushed-in look); white rump and undertail with no streaks. *Male:* Indistinct tinge of pinkish wash on breast.

Similar species. Common Redpoll has longer bill, streaking on rump, and heavier streaking on sides; appears darker. Overlap in these characteristics makes some individuals indistinguishable from one another in the field.

Voice. Similar to Common Redpoll.

Habitat. Tundra shrub thickets, mixed deciduous-coniferous woodlands, open fields and grasslands, near cities and villages especially in winter. Nests on ground or in the lower branches of bushes. Abundance varies from year to year, depending on seed crop.

Region	Sp	S	F	W
Southeastern	-	-	-	R
Southcoastal	R	-	-	R
Southwestern	U	-	U	C
Central ★	C	R	U	C
Western ★	C	C	C	C
Northern ★	C	C	C	-

Hoary Redpoll

Pine Siskin
Carduelis pinus

Field marks. 5". Heavy to light streaking on underparts; streaking on upperparts; touch of yellow on wings and tail base (sometimes difficult to see).

Similar species. Juvenile redpolls have thicker bill and lack any yellow on wings and tail base (not always visible on Pine Siskin). Adult redpolls have red cap, blackish chin, and less streaking on underparts.

Voice. Long, buzzy *schhrreeee*. In flight, utters a scratchy *shick-shick* and a thin *tseee*.

Habitat. Coniferous forests. Nests in conifers, usually well out on branches. During non-nesting season may be found in deciduous trees and on the ground.

Region	Sp	S	F	W
Southeastern ★	C	C	C	C
Southcoastal ★	C	C	C	U
Southwestern	+	+	+	-
Central ★	R	R	R	+
Western	+	+	-	-
Northern	-	+	-	-

Pine Siskin

CASUAL AND ACCIDENTAL SPECIES

The birds described in this section do not appear in Alaska regularly, and the probability of seeing one is quite small. They are known as casuals or accidentals. Those classed as casual are species that appear at irregular intervals, usually within certain seasons and regions, although Alaska is beyond the boundaries of their normal annual range. Those classed as accidental have been reported in Alaska only once, or at most a few times, and present no seasonal or regional pattern.

The following abbreviations are used in this section. The geographical areas refer to the Alaskan regions in which these birds have been found. The figures in inches refer to the length of the bird.

Rare* = Status changed according to Gibson (1999)
Cas   = Casual
Acc   = Accidental

SE   = Southeastern
SC   = Southcoastal
SW   − Southwestern
C   = Central
W   = Western
N   = Northern

GREBES
Eared Grebe *(Podiceps nigricollis)*. Acc. C. 12"-14". *Breeding:* Blackish crest, neck, breast and back. Golden ear tufts. *Winter:* Dark top and sides of head, whitish patch behind ear. Has more peaked crown, longer, thinner bill, rides higher in water than Horned Grebe.

FULMARS, PETRELS, SHEARWATERS
Cook's Petrel *(Pterodroma cookii)*. Acc. SW. 10"-11". Uniformly gray above, dark M across wings and back; mostly white wing linings; whitish outer tail feathers.

PELICANS
American White Pelican *(Pelecanus erythrorhynchos)*. Acc. SE. 54"-70". Long flat bill; mostly white; black wing tips.

FRIGATEBIRDS
Magnificent Frigatebird *(Fregata magnificens)*. Acc. SC, SW. 37"-45". Long, narrow wings, crook at wrist; long, deeply forked tail. *Male:* Mostly black. *Female:* White breast. *Immature:* White head and breast.

BITTERNS, HERONS
Yellow Bittern *(Ixobrychus sinensis)*. Acc. SW. 14½". Brown above, pale yellow below; greenish yellow legs. *In flight:* Distinct pattern of black flight feathers contrasts with buff-colored wing coverts and brown back. *Male:* Black crown. *Female:* Brown crown; buff-colored stripes on underparts.

Great Egret *(Ardea alba)*. Cas. SE, SC. 39". Large white heron. Yellow bill; black legs and feet.

Chinese Egret *(Egretta eulophotes)*. Acc. SW. 27". All-white plumage, black legs, yellow feet. *Breeding:* Bright blue forehead, short crest, yellow bill.

Chinese Pond Heron *(Ardeola bacchus)*. Acc. SW. 18". Rich reddish-brown head and neck, slaty back and white wings.

Cattle Egret *(Bubulcus ibis)*. Cas. SE, SC, SW. 20". *Nonbreeding:* Yellow bill; yellow or greenish legs, though some with black legs.

Green Heron *(Butorides virescens)*. Acc. SE. 18". *Adult:* Black crown, dark grayish-green back, chestnut-colored neck; crow-sized.

Black-crowned Night-Heron *(Nycticorax nycticorax)*. Cas. SE, SC, SW. 23"-28". *Adult:* Black cap and back; whitish underneath; gray wings. Call is a loud, barking *kwok!*

SWANS, GEESE, DUCKS

Lesser White-fronted Goose *(Anser erythropus)*. Acc. SW. 21"-26". Resembles small Greater White-fronted Goose but has a much smaller bill and white on forehead extends higher onto crown. Yellow eye ring visible at close range.

Ross's Goose *(Chen rossii)*. Cas. SE, SC, N. 24". Like a petite Snow Goose, but has smaller bill and lacks black "lips."

Wood Duck *(Aix sponsa)*. Cas. SE, SC. 18". *Male:* Striped, crested head; red at base of bill, around eye, and on breast; iridescent blue wings. *Female:* Similar but shorter crest; white around eye; some blue on wings; generally drab brown.

Baikal Teal *(Anas formosa)*. Cas. SW, W, N. 18". *Male:* Striking face pattern of yellow and green; white vertical shoulder stripe. *Female:* Like Green-winged Teal, but has distinctive white spot at base of bill.

Falcated Teal *(Anas falcata)*. Cas. SW. 19". *Male:* Gray body; crested dark green and purple head; white spot on forehead. *Female:* Dark speculum, gray bill.

American Black Duck *(Anas rubripes)*. Acc. SE, SC, C. 22". Like Mallard, but very dark body; head very pale.

Spot-billed Duck *(Anas poecilorhyncha)*. Cas. SW. 23"-24". Dark bill with yellow tip; black stripe running backward from base of bill.

AMERICAN VULTURES

Turkey Vulture *(Cathartes aura)*. Cas. SE, C, W. 27". In flight, shows 2 tones from underneath: light gray flight feathers, black wing linings.

HAWKS, EAGLES

White-tailed Eagle *(Haliaeetus albicilla)*. Cas. SW. 27"-35". Similar to Bald Eagle, but with short, wedge-shaped tail; head usually pale but not white. *Immature:* Mostly dark brown with whitish lines and patches in underwing.

Steller's Sea-Eagle *(Haliaeetus pelagicus)*. Cas. SE, SW. 27"-36". *Adult:* Dark head, massive bill, white shoulders; white, wedge-shaped tail.

FALCONS

Eurasian Kestrel *(Falco tinnunculus)*. Cas. SW. 12"-15". Similar to American Kestrel but larger, with 1 dark vertical bar on face. *Male:* Rust-colored wings and gray tail. *Female:* Rust-colored tail.

Eurasian Hobby *(Falco subbuteo)*. Cas. SW. 12". Similar to Peregrine Falcon but smaller, with narrower dark patch on each cheek; breast and belly heavily streaked, not barred.

RAILS, COOTS

Virginia Rail *(Rallus limicola)*. Cas. SE. 8½"-10½". Long-billed; gray face, white throat. Calls are a loud, grunting, descending *wak-wak-wak* or *kick, kick, kid-ick, kid-ick, kid-ick.*

Eurasian Coot *(Fulica atra)*. Acc. SW. 16". Resembles American Coot, but entire forehead and bill are white; undertail feathers black.

CRANES

Common Crane *(Grus grus)*. Acc. C. 45". Adult distinguished from Sandhill Crane by different head pattern; black throat and neck; white stripe that curves from eye to base of neck. *In flight:* All plumages show black primary and secondary feathers.

PLOVERS

Snowy Plover *(Charadrius alexandrinus)*. Acc. W. 6¼". *Adult:* Very pale; thin, dark bill; partial breast band; dark ear patch.

Little Ringed Plover *(Charadrius dubius)*. Cas. SW. 7". Resembles Semi-palmated and Common Ringed plovers, but smaller and has yellow eye ring (when breeding), mostly dark bill, and no white wing stripe.

STILTS, AVOCETS

Black-winged Stilt *(Himantopus himantopus)*. Acc. SW. 14¾". Very long, pink legs; long, slender neck; thin, black, almost straight bill; black wings; white underparts. *Male:* Upper head and neck dark gray to blackish, but never sharply black as in Black-necked Stilt (not seen in Alaska). *Female:* All-white neck and head. *Juvenile and adult:* Lack white spot above eye found in Black-necked.

American Avocet *(Recurvirostra americana)*. Acc. SC. 17"-18½". Thin, upturned bill; long, bluish legs; black-and-white pattern on wings.

PRATINCOLES
Oriental Pratincole *(Glareola maldivarum)*. Acc. SW, W. 9¼". Ternlike aerial feeder with short forked tail; chestnut underwing coverts. Adult has cream throat outlined in black. *In flight:* White rump contrasts with all-brown upperwings and back. *Juvenile:* Upper feathers fringed with buff color.

SANDPIPERS
Marsh Sandpiper *(Tringa stagnatilis)*. Acc. SW. 10". Long, very thin bill; long, dull green legs. *In flight:* White extends up back, like a dowitcher. See Common Greenshank.

Spotted Redshank *(Tringa erythropus)*. Rare*. SW. 12". Like Greater Yellowlegs, but with bright red or red-orange legs; base of lower bill red, unlike yellowlegs. *In flight:* White on rump up back to point, like a dowitcher. *Breeding adult:* Blackish plumage. *Juvenile:* Barring (often heavy) on flanks, belly, and undertail.

Green Sandpiper *(Tringa ochropus)*. Cas. SW, W. 9½". Like Solitairy Sandpiper, but larger, with white rump and darker underwings. Wood Sandpiper has paler underwings, smaller white rump, and more bars on tail. Teeters like Spotted Sandpiper.

Terek Sandpiper *(Xenus cinereus)*. Rare*. SC, SW, W. 9". Conspicuous long, upturned bill; short, orange-yellow legs. *Breeding:* 2 black stripes down back (also often present on juveniles, but less distinct).

Little Curlew *(Numenius minutus)*. Acc. W. 12". Tiny curlew with bold buff-and-brown head pattern. Like Eskimo Curlew, but has pale buff wing linings, finely streaked breast (Eskimo has strong chevrons); wing tips extend to tail tip (Eskimo's wing tips extend well beyond).

Eskimo Curlew *(Numenius borealis)*. Acc. W, N (not seen in Alaska since 1886). 14". Like Whimbrel, but much smaller, darker above, thinner bill, less patterned on crown, cinnamon-colored wing linings.

Far Eastern Curlew *(Numenius madagascariensis)*. Cas. SW, W. 20"-26". Much larger than Whimbrel and Bristle-thighed Curlew. Boldly streaked beige underparts; head finely streaked, without conspicuous stripes of other curlews found in Alaska.

Black-tailed Godwit *(Limosa limosa)*. Cas. SW, W, N. 16". Only godwit with straight bill. Like Hudsonian Godwit but straighter bill, and in breeding plumage has immaculate cinnamon-colored head and breast, and paler flanks barred with bold black bars. *In flight:* White wing linings (black in Hudsonian) and bold white wing stripe.

Great Knot *(Calidris tenuirostris)*. Cas. SW, W. 11½". Shaped like Red Knot, but larger and more heavily marked. *Breeding:* Colored like breeding Surfbird, but with much longer bill; back marked with rufous color, breast heavily blotched with black, and sides covered with bold black heart-shaped or arrowhead-shaped spots.

Little Stint *(Calidris minuta)*. Cas. SW, W, N. 5". Unwebbed toes. Like Red-necked Stint, but in breeding plumage has orange feather edges on back, dull rusty-orange crown, and face that contrasts with white throat and breast. *Nonbreeding and juvenile:* Nearly identical to similar-plumaged Semipalmated Sandpiper and Red-necked Stint.

Temminck's Stint *(Calidris temminckii)*. Cas. SW, W, N. 5½". Outer tail feathers pure white rather than the gray of similar-sized sandpipers. Only stint with brown rump; others have black rump, darker than back.

Purple Sandpiper *(Calidris maritima)*. Acc. N. 9". Like Rock Sandpiper, but lacks black patch on lower breast when breeding. *Nonbreeding and juvenile:* Very difficult to distinguish from Rock Sandpiper; some authors consider Purple and Rock sandpipers to be the same species.

Curlew Sandpiper *(Calidris ferruginea)*. Cas. SE, SC, SW, W, N. 8½". *All plumages:* Long, evenly downcurved bill; longer neck, legs, and wings than other sandpipers of similar size (such as the Dunlin and Rock). *Breeding:* Bright rufous color above and below. *Nonbreeding:* Gray, rather clear-breasted; shows clear white rump and conspicuous white wing stripes in flight.

Spoonbill Sandpiper *(Eurynorhynchus pygmeus)*. Cas. SW, N. 6". Broad, spoon-shaped bill tip; otherwise like Rufous-necked Stint.

Broad-billed Sandpiper *(Limicola falcinellus)*. Cas. SW. 6¾". Thick, longish black bill that is slightly drooped at the tip; 2 white lines over eye and conspicuous white V on back.

Jack Snipe *(Lymnocryptes minimus)*. Acc. SW. 8". Short bill unlike other snipes; unmarked, wedge-shaped tail. Lacks pale central stripe on dark crown (found in Common Snipe).

Pin-tailed Snipe *(Gallinago stenura)*. Acc. SW. 10¼". Very similar to Common Snipe, but fainter white lines on back; narrow, fainter white along trailing edge of wing; darker under wing. Call is *jeht, jeht,* different from Common.

Wilson's Phalarope *(Phalaropus tricolor)*. Cas. SE, SC, C. W, N. 9". Only phalarope that lacks white wing stripe and has white rump and tail. Thin needlelike bill. Feeds on shore more than other phalaropes. *Breeding female:* Gray above; black and rust-colored neck stripe; cinnamon breast. *Breeding male:* Duller version of female.

JAEGERS, GULLS, TERNS

South Polar Skua *(Catharacta maccormicki)*. Cas. SE, SC, SW, N. 21". All dark at a distance; very broad, black wings with conspicuous white patch near tip.

Franklin's Gull *(Larus pipixcan)*. Cas. SE, SC, SW. 14½". Conspicuous white crescents around eye. Adults have white band just inside of black stripe near wing tip; rest of wing slate gray.

Heermann's Gull *(Larus heermanni)*. Cas. SE. 16½"-18½". *Adult:* Black tail with white tip; red bill; gray body with white head. *Juvenile:* Flesh-colored bill with dark tip; dark chocolate brown overall.

Black-tailed Gull *(Larus crassirostris)*. Cas. SE, SC, SW, W. 18". *Adult:* Blackish gray above, no white in primary feathers, prominent black tail band. *Juvenile:* Mostly brown above, white below; black tail.

Lesser Black-backed Gull *(Larus fuscus)*. Cas. SE, SC. 21"-22". Adult slightly smaller than Herring Gull, but has much darker mantle. Outer primary feathers black with single white spot; dark gray underwings; yellow legs.

Western Gull *(Larus occidentalis)*. Cas. SE, SC, W. 25". Like Glaucous-winged Gull, but dark gray above with black wing tips in adult; pink legs. Often hybridizes with Glaucous-winged.

Great Black-backed Gull *(Larus marinus)*. Acc. SC. 28"-31". Largest gull in Alaska *Adult:* Black mantle. *Immature:* Shows some black on back after first winter. First winter bird has checkered mantle.

Forster's Tern *(Sterna forsteri)*. Acc. W. 14"-16". *Breeding:* In flight shows white rump and a silvery white upper surface on the wing primaries. *Winter:* White crown and black from eye back.

Sooty Tern *(Sterna fuscata)*. Acc. SW. 15"-17". *Adult:* Black above, white forehead. *Immature:* Brownish-black.

White-winged Tern *(Chlidonias leucopterus)*. Cas. SC, SW. 8½"-9½". *Breeding:* Distinctive with blackish head and body, white rump and tail, upperwings mostly pale gray. *Other plumages:* Very similar to Black Tern, but bill and tail shorter and tail less deeply notched.

Black Tern *(Chlidonias niger)*. Cas. SE, SC, C, N. 9½". Gray tail. *Breeding:* Head and underparts black, mantle and tail gray. *Immature and winter adult:* Smaller, shorter-tailed, and much grayer above than other Alaskan terns.

ALCIDS
Long-billed Murrelet *(Brachyramphus perdix)*. Acc. C. 11½". *Breeding:* Similar to Marbled Murrelet but less rufous on back and head and has a paler throat. *Winter:* Like Marbled Murrelet but lacks a white collar.

PIGEONS, DOVES
Oriental Turtle-Dove *(Streptopelia orientalis)*. Cas. SW. 13". Head, neck, and underparts brownish to pinkish gray, with black and gray fine-striped patch on side of neck and rufous edgings on back feathers.

White-winged Dove *(Zenaida asiatica)*. Acc. SE. 10"-12½". Black wings with large white patch.

CUCKOOS

Common Cuckoo *(Cuculus canorus)*. Cas. SW, W. 13". Slender, long-tailed bird. Pointed wings somewhat like a falcon, but bill slender and not hawklike. *Brown phase:* Like Oriental Cuckoo, but has unbarred rump and upper tail coverts. *Gray phase:* Very difficult to separate from Oriental Cuckoo, but has pure white undertail coverts, slightly narrower, lighter barring and lighter underparts. Voice of Common Cuckoo, *cuc-coo;* Oriental Cuckoo, a monotone *po-po-po-po.*

Oriental Cuckoo *(Cuculus saturatus)*. Cas. SW, W. 13". See Common Cuckoo.

Yellow-billed Cuckoo *(Coccyzus americanus)*. Cas. SE. 11"-13". Lower bill yellow. *In flight:* Long black tail with 6 white spots can be seen from below.

TYPICAL OWLS

Oriental Scops-Owl *(Otus sunia)*. Acc. SW. 7"-8". Very small; streaked and barred brownish gray. Like Western Screech-Owl, but less streaked and barred on underparts.

Long-eared Owl *(Asio otus)*. Cas. SE. 15". Long ear tufts; rust-colored facial disk. Lacks white throat of larger Great Horned Owl and has vertical chest markings rather than horizontal. Voice is *hoooo,* repeated at intervals; also catlike calls.

GOATSUCKERS

Lesser Nighthawk *(Chordeiles acutipennis)*. Acc. N. 8"-9". Like Common Nighthawk, but outermost primary feather shorter, giving wing tip a slightly rounded appearance, and pale wing patch close to wing tip.

Whip-poor-will *(Caprimulgus vociferus)*. Acc. SE. 9"-10". Rounded wings (nighthawk wings are pointed). *Male:* White patches on tail; narrow white throat patch. *Female:* Buff-colored throat; lacks white tail patches.

Jungle Nightjar *(Caprimulgus indicus)*. Acc. SW. 11". Rounded wings. Much grayer than other nightjars or nighthawks in North America. *Male:* Conspicuous white patches in tail.

SWIFTS

Chimney Swift *(Chaetura pelagica)*. Acc. SW. 5½". Very much like Vaux's Swift, but slightly larger and usually more uniformly brown.

White-throated Needletail *(Hirundapus caudacutus)*. Cas. SW. 8¼". White throat, pale back, white V on undersides near square-cut tail.

Common Swift *(Apus apus)*. Acc. SW. 6½". Larger than Vaux's Swift, with much more deliberate flight. Short, slightly forked tail; diffuse whitish chin and throat.

Fork-tailed Swift *(Apus pacificus)*. Cas. SC, SW. 7". Like Black Swift, but much longer-winged and has conspicuous white rump and a much more deeply forked tail.

HUMMINGBIRDS

Ruby-throated Hummingbird *(Archilochus colubris)*. Acc. SW, N. 3¼"-3½". Like Rufous Hummingbird, but lacks rufous coloration.

Costa's Hummingbird *(Calypte costae)*. Cas. SE, SC. 3"-3¼". *Adult male:* Violet-blue gorget elongated at sides. *Female:* Like Anna's Hummingbird, but lacks red spotting on throat.

HOOPOES

Eurasian Hoopoe *(Upupa epops)*. Acc. W. 12". Erectile crest; long down-curved bill; striking upperparts, with pinkish head and upper back and black-and-white wings and tail.

WOODPECKERS

Eurasian Wryneck *(Jynx torquilla)*. Acc. W. 7½". Black stripe extends from head to rump; mottled soft gray and brown above.

Yellow-bellied Sapsucker *(Sphyrapicus varius)*. Rare*. SE, SC, C. 9". Red forehead, 2 white horizontal stripes across face, black bib across upper breast, straw yellow belly.

Great Spotted Woodpecker *(Dendrocopos major)*. Acc. SW. 9¼". Mostly black and white. Two large white patches on lower back visible in flight and at rest. Upper back solid black. Lower wings appear strongly barred black and white when at rest, but spotted white in flight.

TYRANT FLYCATCHERS

Yellow-bellied Flycatcher *(Empidonax flaviventris)*. Rare*. SE, C. 5½". Like Pacific-slope Flycatcher, but with slightly more yellowish underparts; tail longer; wings and back slightly browner; wing bars slightly less conspicuous. Voice is an abrupt *killik* or *chilink* and a whistled *chu-wee* rising in pitch.

Willow Flycatcher *(Empidonax traillii)*. Rare*. SE, SC, W. 5¼"-6½". Like Alder Flycatcher, with faint eye ring but slightly browner back. Best distinguished by voice, *weep a dee ar* or *fitz-bew,* uttered explosively. Call is a sharp *pwit.*

Dusky Flycatcher *(Empidonax oberholseri)*. Cas. SE, N. 5¼". Like Hammond's Flycatcher, with grayish olive back; pale yellow belly; white eye ring and wing bars. Bill and tail slightly longer than Hammond's; paler edges on outer tail feathers. Voice also similar to Hammond's, but less hoarse and emphatic; sounds like a staccato series of chirps, like *se-lip, churp, treep.* Call is a sharp *wit,* less sharp than the peck of Hammond's.

Eastern Phoebe *(Sayornis phoebe)*. Cas. SE, N. 6½"-7". *Adult:* Dark head and upperparts, whitish underparts; no eye ring or wing bars. *Immature:* Like adult, but with 2 wing bars and pale yellowish tinge to underparts. Voice is a *fee-bee, fee-bee* repeated.

Great Crested Flycatcher *(Myiarchus crinitus)*. Acc. SC. 7"-8". Bright yellow belly; wings and tail marked with rufous; gray throat.

Tropical Kingbird *(Tyrannus melancholicus)*. Cas. SE. 8"-9". Bright yellow from midbreast to tail; thick bill; brown tail with notched tip.

Western Kingbird *(Tyrannus verticalis)*. Cas. SE, SC, C. 8½". Olive gray above, light gray breast, yellow belly. Black square-cut tail with white edges. Call is a sharp *wit* or *wik*.

SWALLOWS
Purple Martin *(Progne subis)*. Cas. SC, SW, C, W, N. 8". *Male:* Entirely blue-black. *Female:* Brownish black above, gray below.

Common House-Martin *(Delichon urbica)*. Cas. SW, W. 5¼". Like Tree Swallow, with glossy bluish black upperparts and pure white underparts, but has large white rump patch.

JAYS, MAGPIES, CROWS
Clark's Nutcracker *(Nucifraga columbiana)*. Cas. SE, SW, C, W. 12½". Gray; wings and tail black with large white patches; bill much longer than Gray Jay's.

CHICKADEES
Mountain Chickadee *(Poecile gambeli)*. Cas. SE. 5½". Like Black-capped Chickadee, but has conspicuous white line over the eye.

OLD WORLD WARBLERS
Middendorff's Grasshopper-Warbler *(Locustella ochotensis)*. Cas. SW, W. 6". Chunky warbler with hefty bill. Whitish line over eye; long, white-tipped tail with black spots near base; olive brown above; whitish below with olive wash on sides (in breeding plumage) or yellowish brown below (in fall plumage). Ground skulker.

Lanceolated Warbler *(Locustella lanceolata)*. Acc. SW. 4¾". Heavily streaked brown upperparts; distinctive dark streaks in a band across breast and down flanks; whitish eyebrow and throat. Ground skulker.

Wood Warbler *(Phylloscopus sibilatrix)*. Acc. SW. 5". Yellow breast, throat, and eyebrow; white belly; olive green back.

Dusky Warbler *(Phylloscopus fuscatus)*. Cas. SW, C, W. 4½". Like Arctic Warbler, but darker and more brownish; also smaller, and lacks any greenish or yellowish color and has no wing bars. Fine bill; buff-colored line above eye. A skulker. Call is a harsh *tsack,* which it utters frequently.

OLD WORLD FLYCATCHERS
Narcissus Flycatcher *(Ficedula narcissina)*. Acc. SW. 5¼". *Male:* Striking combination of black upperparts, yellow-orange eyebrow, yellow rump, orange throat, and white patch on wing. *Female:* Olive brown upperparts, pale brownish gray underparts; pale throat; mottled brown on breast.

Red-breasted Flycatcher *(Ficedula parva)*. Cas. SW, W. 5¼". Black tail with white patches at base of outer tail feathers. Often flicks up tail. *Adult male:* Dull rufous-orange throat. *Female:* Buff-white throat and breast.

Siberian Flycatcher *(Muscicapa sibirica)*. Cas. SW. 5½". Small and short-tailed; upperparts dull sooty-brown. *Adult:* White throat that extends onto neck as half-collar; sooty streaks and smudges across breast; pale wing bar. *Fall immature:* Spotted back and dingy, streaked underparts.

Gray-spotted Flycatcher *(Muscicapa griseisticta)*. Cas. SW. 6". Like Siberian Flycatcher but slightly larger, with longer tail and pale area in front of eyes; breast and flanks heavily streaked with dark grayish-brown.

Asian Brown Flycatcher *(Muscicapa dauurica)*. Acc. SW, W. 5". *Adult:* Upperparts grayish brown, underparts whitish or pale gray with faint brownish streaks on breast and flanks; narrow white eye ring. *Juvenile:* Brownish above with pale spots.

THRUSHES

Siberian Blue Robin *(Luscinia cyane)*. Acc. SW. 5½". *Male:* Upperparts dull blue, underparts clear white. *Female:* Upperparts olive brown, whitish underparts mottled with olive brown; bluish tail.

Red-flanked Bluetail *(Tarsiger cyanurus)*. Cas. SW, W. 5½". *Adult male:* Bright blue above; bright orange flanks. *Adult female:* Dull, bluish rump and tail; pale rufous flanks; olive brown upperparts.

Stonechat *(Saxicola torquatus)*. Cas. SC, C, W. 5". *Breeding male:* Black head, back, wings, and tail; white on neck, shoulders, rump, and belly; orange on breast. *Breeding female:* Brownish upperparts streaked with black; pale yellowish brown underparts and rump; pale eyebrow; white on shoulders and throat.

Veery *(Catharus fuscescens)*. Cas. SE. 7¾". Lightly spotted buff-colored breast unlike other similar-looking thrushes, which are more heavily spotted below. Distinctive song is a downward-spiraling series of trilling *veeer* notes. Call is a whistled *whee-ou*.

Dusky Thrush *(Turdus naumanni)*. Cas. SE, SW, W, N. 9". *Adult male:* Distinctive bird with bold white eye line and throat; 2 black breast bands and spotted sides; wings and base of tail washed with bright cinnamon. *Female:* Duller, with less black underneath.

Fieldfare *(Turdus pilaris)*. Cas. W, N. 10". Large thrush with gray head and rump that contrast with red-brown back and wings and blackish tail. Arrowheadlike spots adorn buff-colored breast and sides. Yellowish bill, black legs. *In flight:* Flashes white wing linings.

MIMIC THRUSHES

Gray Catbird *(Dumetella carolinensis)*. Acc. C, W. 8½". Dark gray with black cap and tail. Voice is a catlike mewing call.

Northern Mockingbird *(Mimus polyglottos)*. Cas. SE, SC, C. 10". Robin-sized bird; gray above, whitish below. *In flight:* Striking white borders of black tail and white wing patches.

Brown Thrasher *(Toxostoma rufum).* Cas. C, N. 11½". Bright reddish upper-parts; whitish underparts tinged with buff and with brown streaks; long tail; yellow eyes.

ACCENTORS
Siberian Accentor *(Prunella montanella).* Cas. SE, SC, C, W, N. 6". Ground-dwelling bird with thin bill. Distinct orange-buff stripe above eye; black mask and crown; buff-colored throat and breast; dark reddish brown above.

WAGTAILS, PIPITS
Gray Wagtail *(Motacilla cinerea).* Cas. SW, W. 7". Like Yellow Wagtail, but gray back (not olive). *Adult male:* Black throat. *Female:* White throat. *In flight:* Yellowish rump and white wing stripe visible.

Tree Pipit *(Anthus trivialis).* Acc. W. 6". Brown back with distinct dark streaks; buff-white below; yellowish wash on breast; flesh pink legs.

Olive-backed Pipit *(Anthus hodgsoni).* Cas. SW, W. 6½". Obscurely streaked back. Olive in breeding plumage; otherwise variably gray to dull brown. Strongly streaked breast and crown; prominent stripe above eye that extends around dark ear patch; pink legs.

Pechora Pipit *(Anthus gustavi).* Cas. SW, W. 5¾". Heavily striped breast and back; 2 distinctive whitish streaks on back; buff rather than white outer tail feathers. Call is a hard 1- or 2-noted *pwit,* given 2 to 3 times in series.

SHRIKES
Brown Shrike *(Lanius cristatus).* Cas. SC, SW, W. 8". Much smaller than Northern Shrike; reddish brown with black mask and buff-colored sides. *Female and immature:* Narrow, dark, wavy bars on sides and across breast.

VIREOS
Cassin's Vireo *(Vireo cassinii).* Cas. SE. 5"-6". White around and before eye creates a spectacled appearance. Gray head, greenish back, dull yellow sides, whitish wing bars. Voice consists of loud, rich, slurred notes, with pauses between notes usually longer than the duration of the notes themselves: *chu-wee, cheereo, bzurrp, chuweer.*

Philadelphia Vireo *(Vireo philadelphicus).* Cas. SC, C. 4¾". Like Warbling Vireo, but with yellowish throat and breast and black line through eye. Song is a series of 2- or 3-syllable whistles, like the Red-eyed Vireo but higher pitched and slower.

WOOD WARBLERS
Chestnut-sided Warbler *(Dendroica pensylvanica).* Acc. SE, SC. 5". *Breeding male:* Yellow crown, black eye line, chestnut on sides. Breeding female: Greenish crown with some chestnut on sides. *Fall adults and immatures:* Lime green above, whitish underparts, yellowish wing bars. Song resembles Yellow Warbler but with next to last note accented and ending in a downward slur. Has been described as *please please pleased to meet'cha.*

Cape May Warbler *(Dendroica tigrina)*. Cas. SE, SC, C, N. 5". *Breeding male:* Chestnut cheek patch; yellow on face and sides of neck and rump; underparts heavily striped with black. *Female and fall birds:* Very dull, but show yellow side of neck; vague yellowish rump patch; lightly but extensively streaked below, olive above.

Black-throated Green Warbler *(Dendroica virens)*. Acc. SE. 5". Yellow face with greenish patch in center; black streaks on side. *Male:* Black throat and upper breast. *Female:* Black across upper breast.

Prairie Warbler *(Dendroica discolor)*. Acc. SE, SC. 4¾". *Adult male:* Yellow face; yellow below, yellowish green above; black streaks on side; 2 black marks on face. *Female:* Similar but duller. *Immature:* Duller yet; gray face, yellow underparts. Prairie Warbler has a habit of bobbing tail.

Palm Warbler *(Dendroica palmarum)*. Cas. SE, SC, C, W, N. 5½". Ground-dwelling; constantly wags tail when feeding. *Adult:* Rufous-colored cap; yellow eyebrow; grayish below, with yellow throat. *Immature:* White eyebrow; yellow only on undertail coverts. Song is a trill given on 1 pitch.

Black-and-white Warbler *(Mniotilta varia)*. Cas. SE, N. 4½"-5½". Noticeably streaked with black and white; white eyebrow. *Male:* Black throat. *Female:* White throat. Crawls on sides of trees.

Ovenbird *(Seiurus aurocapillus)*. Cas. SE, C, N. 5½"-6½". Behaves and looks like a Northern Waterthrush, but lacks eyebrow stripe. Has white eye ring, olive green upperparts, heavily streaked underparts, and orange stripe on head bordered with brown. Voice is a loud ringing series: *cher-tea, cher-tea, cher-tea, cher-tea, cher-tea.*

Mourning Warbler *(Oporornis philadelphia)*. Acc. SC. 5"-5¾". Like MacGillivray's Warbler, but lacks white eye ring (male) or eye ring much fainter (female), and has lighter gray hood.

Canada Warbler *(Wilsonia canadensis)*. Acc. N. 5"-5¾". Yellowish color around and in front of eye gives a spectacled appearance. Yellow underparts, with black spots across upper breast (faint in female); bluish gray upperparts. *Adult male:* Side of head has black. *Female:* Side of head has gray.

TANAGERS

Scarlet Tanager *(Piranga olivacea)*. Acc. N. 6½"-7½". *Breeding male:* Brilliant red and black plumage. *Adult female:* Greenish above, yellowish below; dark wings without wing bars.

GROSBEAKS

Rose-breasted Grosbeak *(Pheucticus ludovicianus)*. Cas. SE, C. 7"-8½". *Breeding male:* Black head and upperparts, red breast, white patches in black wings. *Female:* Pale eyebrow, dark crown with whitish center stripe, streaked breast. Song similar to American Robin, but softer and more melodious.

Black-headed Grosbeak (*Pheucticus melanocephalus*). Cas. SE. 7"-8½". *Breeding male:* Black head, orange-brown breast. *Female:* similar to Rose-breasted Grosbeak but with less and finer streaking on breast and flanks. Song is a rich warble similar to that of a robin but softer, sweeter, and faster.

Blue Grosbeak (*Guiraca caerulea*). Acc. SE. 6"-7½". *Adult male:* Unmistakable with its deep blue plumage, rust-colored wing bars, and stout bill. *Adult female:* Rump tinged with blue; otherwise mostly brown, darker above, with rust-colored or buff wing bars.

Indigo Bunting (*Passerina cyanea*). Cas. SC, N. 5½". *Adult male:* Like Blue Grosbeak, but much smaller, lacks wing bars, and has short conical beak; deep blue overall with darker wings and tail. *Female:* Buff-gray breast with faint streaks; faint buff-colored wing bars. *Immature:* Like female, but with more streaks on breast.

SPARROWS, BUNTINGS

Spotted Towhee (*Pipilo maculatus*). Cas. SE. 7¼"-8¼". Blackish head, breast, and upperparts; reddish sides and flanks; white spots on wings.

Clay-colored Sparrow (*Spizella pallida*). Cas. SE, C, N. 4¾"-5¼". *Adult:* Head pattern distinct with contrasting buff-gray central stripe, whitish eyebrow, brown ear patch, gray on side and back of neck. Obvious blackish streaks on buff-brown upperparts; unstreaked underparts. *Immature:* Similar to adult but duller, with more buff coloring.

Brewer's Sparrow (*Spizella breweri*). Rare*. SE, C. 5½". Like Clay-colored Sparrow, but has fine black streaks on brown crown and lacks buff-gray central head stripe and has a prominent eye ring.

Lark Sparrow (*Chondestes grammacus*). Acc. C. 6½". *Adult:* Distinctive head pattern with white center stripe bordered by chestnut band, white line above eye, chestnut ear patch, black line down side of white throat; underparts are whitish with dark spot in breast. *Juvenile:* Much duller, with streaks on breast and sides. *All plumages:* Tail has white corners that are conspicuous in flight.

Swamp Sparrow (*Melospiza georgiana*). Cas. SE, SC. 5¾". *Adult:* Chestnut crown, gray face, white throat; reddish wings (without wing bars) and tail. *Immature:* Blackish stripes on head, gray central stripe, reddish wings.

White-throated Sparrow (*Zonotrichia albicollis*). Cas. SE, SC, C, N. 6½". Like White-crowned Sparrow, but in all plumages has white throat, sharply distinct from gray breast; also has darker bill and rounder head (not as angular-looking).

Pine Bunting (*Emberiza leucocephalos*). Acc. SW. 6½". *Breeding male:* White crown, cheek, collar, and patch on breast; chestnut above eye, on throat, across breast, and on rump. *Female:* Chestnut rump; brown breast band.

Little Bunting (*Emberiza pusilla*). Cas. SW, W, N. 4¾". *Breeding male:* Rufous medium stripe on crown; rufous eyebrow and cheek outlined with black. *Female and immature:* Also have rufous coloration, but head pattern is duller.

Yellow-throated Bunting *(Emberiza elegans).* Acc. SW. 6". Short dark crest and face mask on yellow head.

Yellow-breasted Bunting *(Emberiza aureola).* Cas. SW, W. 5½". *Breeding male:* Chestnut crown, nape, back, and band across breast; black face and throat; yellow underparts. *Female:* Yellow underparts, brown upperparts with darker brown streaks; creamy white stripe above eye, pale stripe on crown.

Gray Bunting *(Emberiza variabilis).* Acc. SW. 6". *Breeding male:* Distinct dark slate-gray. *Female:* Dark brown above, paler below; similar to other female buntings, but lacks the white in the tail of other species; in flight, female can be distinguished by chestnut rump.

Pallas's Bunting *(Emberiza pallasi).* Cas. W, N. 5½". Like Reed Bunting, but different in the following respects: smaller; paler back; more grayish brown; lacks rusty coloration; bill is more slender and pointed.

Reed Bunting *(Emberiza schoeniclus).* Cas. SW. 6". Warm rust-colored above; lacks grayish coloration of Pallas's Bunting. *Breeding male:* Entire head and throat are black except for a white line extending back and down from the bill, and a white hindneck. Female and winter male are heavily streaked. Call is loud *tseek,* somewhat like that of the Yellow Wagtail.

BLACKBIRDS
Bobolink *(Dolichonyx oryzivorus).* Acc. SE, N. 6"-8". *Breeding male:* Mostly black, with golden buff on hindneck; whitish rump and scapulars. *Female:* Mostly buff-colored, with dark streaks on back, rump, and sides; brown stripes on head. *All plumages:* Sharply pointed tail feathers.

Western Meadowlark *(Sturnella neglecta).* Cas. SE, SC, C, N. 10". Shaped like a starling. Streaked brown and white above; short tail with conspicuous white edges; mostly yellow below, with a conspicuous black V on breast.

Yellow-headed Blackbird *(Xanthocephalus xanthocephalus).* Cas. SE, SC, C, W, N. 10½". *Male:* Entirely yellow head and neck; white wing patch conspicuous in flight. *Female:* Considerably smaller; brown with yellow throat and breast.

Brewer's Blackbird *(Euphagus cyanocephalus).* Cas. SE, N. 9". *Male:* Black with whitish eye, purplish reflection on head. *Female:* Dark eyes; gray-brown plumage.

Common Grackle *(Quiscalus quiscula).* Cas. SE, SC, C, W, N. 12". Yellow eyes. Iridescent like male Brewer's Blackbird, but larger in size, with much longer and heavier bill and long, wedge-shaped tail (which is longer in males).

FINCHES
Common Rosefinch *(Carpodacus erythrinus).* Cas. SW, W. 5¾". *Male:* Rich red on head and breast that may extend to back and rump; lacks distinct eyebrow and head streaking. *Female:* Brown above, obscurely streaked with brown below; pale throat; 2 obscure wing bars. Call is soft and 2-syllabled, rising at the end to a squeak.

Purple Finch *(Carpodacus purpureus).* Cas. SE, SC, SW, W, C. 6". *Male:* Reddish head, throat, breast, and back. *Female:* Distinctive face pattern of dark brown streak behind eye with whitish streak above (eyebrow) and below; heavily streaked underparts.

Cassin's Finch *(Carpodacus cassinii).* Cas. SC. 5¾"-6". *Male:* Like male Purple Finch, but back is paler with little red. *Female:* Like female Purple Finch, but has a less distinct face pattern and narrower streaks on breast.

House Finch *(Carpodacus mexicanus).* Cas. SE. 6". *Adult male:* Red forehead and throat, streaked underparts. *Female and Juveniles:* Streaked with brown overall, lacks distinct ear patch and eyebrow of Purple and Cassin's Finch.

Eurasian Siskin *(Carduelis spinus).* Acc. SW. 4¾". *Breeding male:* Black crown and chin; yellow face, chest, and rump and sides of tail; black-and-yellow wing. *Female and juvenile:* Less yellow and more streaked than male; no black on head.

American Goldfinch *(Carduelis tristis).* Acc. SE, W. 4½"-5½". *Breeding male:* Very striking, with black crown, bright yellow back and underparts, black wings and tail. *Female:* Lacks black crown; has dull olive-yellow upperparts, black wings and tail.

Oriental Greenfinch *(Carduelis sinica).* Cas. SW. 6". Greenish brown body, dull greenish head, bright yellow patches on wings and tail.

Eurasian Bullfinch *(Pyrrhula pyrrhula).* Cas. SE, SC, SW, C, W. 5¾". Black cap; white rump and wing bars. *Male:* Gray above, rosy below. *Female:* Dull brownish above, more buff-colored below. Movements of the Eurasian Bullfinch are slow and deliberate. Call is a soft, piping whistle.

Evening Grosbeak *(Coccothraustes vespertinus).* Cas. SE, SC, C. 7½". Large, pale greenish to ivory bill. *Male:* Striking, with brown and yellow; conspicuous yellow eye line; black wings with large white bases. *Female:* Duller gray-brown with less white in wings. Loud, ringing call is often a clue to the presence of these nomadic birds.

Hawfinch *(Coccothraustes coccothraustes).* Cas. SW, W. 7". Stocky, short-tailed, with huge gray bill. Brown with black wings and conspicuous white patches. Brown tail with white tip. Call is a loud, metallic *tik.*

OLD WORLD SPARROWS
House Sparrow *(Passer domesticus).* Cas. SE, W. 6¼". *Breeding male:* Black throat and upper breast, gray crown, whitish cheek, chestnut hindneck, white wing bar. *Female:* Streaked above, plain below; pale eyebrow.

FURTHER READING

Andrew, J., et al. *Birds of Seward Alaska*. Seward Chamber of Commerce, 1988.

Armstrong, R. H. *Alaska's Birds*. Seattle: Alaska Northwest Books, 1994.

Armstrong, R., and R. Gordon. *Finding Birds in Juneau*. U.S. Forest Service, Alaska Region. Juneau, 1995.

Clark, W. S., and B. K. Wheeler. *A Field Guide to Hawks of North America*. Peterson Field Guide Series 35. Boston: Houghton Mifflin, 1987.

Clement, P. *Finches and Sparrows: An Identification Guide*. Boston: Houghton Mifflin, 1993.

Delap, D., R. L. Scher, D. Sonneborn, and T. Tobish. *Birds of Anchorage Alaska: A Checklist*. Anchorage Audubon Society, 1993.

Farrand, J., Jr., ed. *The Audubon Society Master Guide to Birding*. New York: Alfred A. Knopf, 1983.

Gabrielson, I. N., and F. C. Lincoln. *The Birds of Alaska*. Harrisburg, Pa.: The Stackpole Company; Washington, D. C.: Wildlife Management Institute, 1959.

Gibson, D. D. *Alaska Region, American Birds* (for the years 1978-1986). New York: National Audubon Society.

————. *Checklist of Alaska Birds*, 9th ed. Fairbanks: University of Alaska Museum, 1999.

Gibson, D. D., and B. Kessel. "Seventy-Four New Avian Taxa Documented in Alaska 1976-1991." *The Condor* 94 (2): 454-467 (1992).

Gibson, D. D., T. G. Tobish, Jr., and M. E. Isleib. *Alaska Region, American Birds* (for the years 1987-1989). New York: National Audubon Society.

Godfrey, W. E. *The Birds of Canada*. National Museum of Canada Bulletin no. 203, Biological Series no. 73, 1986.

Grant, P. J. *Gulls: A Guide to Identification*. Calton, England: T and AD Poyser Ltd., 1982.

Harrison, H. H. *A Field Guide to Western Birds' Nests*. Boston: Houghton Mifflin, 1979.

Harrison, P. *Seabirds: An Identification Guide*. Boston: Houghton Mifflin, 1983.

Hayman, P., J. Marchant, and T. Prater. *Shorebirds: An Identification Guide*. Boston: Houghton Mifflin, 1986.

Isleib, M. E. *Birds of the Chugach National Forest, Alaska: A Checklist*. U.S. Forest Service, U.S. Department of Agriculture. Anchorage, n.d.

Isleib, M. E., and B. Kessel. *Birds of the North Gulf Coast—Prince William Sound Region, Alaska*. Biological Papers no. 14. Fairbanks: University of Alaska Fairbanks, 1973.

Isleib, P., R. Armstrong, R. Gordon, and F. Glass. *Birds of Southeast Alaska: A Checklist*. Alaska Natural History Association, U.S. Forest Service Alaska Region, Audubon Society Juneau Chapter, and the State of Alaska Department of Fish and Game. Juneau, 1987.

Johnson, S. R., and D. R. Herter. *The Birds of the Beaufort Sea*. Anchorage: BP Exploration (Alaska), 1989.

Kaufman, K. *Advanced Birding*. The Peterson Field Guide Series. Boston: Houghton Mifflin, 1990.

Kertell, K. *Bird Checklist for Denali National Park*. Alaska Natural History Association in cooperation with the National Park Service, 1985.

Kertell, K., and A. Seegert, *Bird-Finding Guide to Denali National Park*. Alaska Natural History Association in cooperation with the National Park Service, 1985.

Kessel, B. *Birds of Interior Alaska*. Fairbanks: University of Alaska Museum, 1980.

————. *Birds of the Seward Peninsula, Alaska*. Fairbanks: University of Alaska Press, 1989.

Kessel, B., and D. D. Gibson. *Status and Distribution of Alaska Birds*. Studies in Avian Biology no. 1. Los Angeles: Cooper Ornithological Society, 1978.

King, J. G., and D. V. Derksen. "Alaska Goose Populations: Past, Present, and Future." Transactions, North American Wildlife and Natural Resource Conference, 51: 464–479 (1986).

Lethaby, N. *A Bird Finding Guide to Alaska*. Self-published, 1994.

MacIntosh, R. *Kodiak National Wildlife Refuge and Kodiak Island Archipelago: Birdlist*. Kodiak National Wildlife Refuge. Kodiak, 1986.

Madge, S., and H. Burn. *Waterfowl: An Identification Guide to the Ducks, Geese, and Swans of the World*. Boston: Houghton Mifflin, 1988.

————. *Crows and Jays: A Guide to the Crows, Jays, and Magpies of the World*. Boston: Houghton Mifflin, 1994.

National Geographic Society. *Field Guide to the Birds of North America*. Washington, D.C.: National Geographic Society, 1999.

Paige, B. *Birds of Glacier Bay National Park and Preserve*. Alaska Natural History Association and National Park Service, 1986.

Paulson, D. *Shorebirds of the Pacific Northwest*. Seattle: University of Washington Press, 1993.

Petersen, M. R., D. N. Weir, and M. H. Dick. *Birds of the Kilbuck and Ahklun Mountain Region, Alaska*. U.S. Fish and Wildlife Service, North American Fauna 76, 1991.

Peterson, R. T. *A Field Guide to Western Birds*. Boston: Houghton Mifflin, 1990.

Prater, A. J., J. H. Marchant, and J. Vuorinen. *Guide to the Identification and Ageing of Holarctic Waders*. British Trust for Ornithology, Field Guide 17. Beech Grove, Tring, Herts, 1977.

Quinlan, S. E., N. Tankersley, and P. D. Arneson. *A Guide to Wildlife Viewing in Alaska*. Alaska Department of Fish and Game, 1983.

Robbins, C. S., B. Bruun, and H. S. Zim. *A Guide to Field Identification, Birds of North America*. New York: Golden Press, 1983.

Roberson, D. *Rare Birds of the West Coast of North America*. Pacific Grove, Calif.: Woodstock Publications, 1980.

Scher, R. L. *Field Guide to Birding in Anchorage*. Self-published, 1993.

Springer, M. I. *Bird Watching in Eastcentral Alaska*. Fairbanks: A Falco Publication, 1993.

Stromsem, N. E. *A Guide to Alaskan Seabirds*. Alaska Natural History Association in cooperation with the U.S. Fish and Wildlife Service, 1982.

Terres, J. K. *The Audubon Society Encyclopedia of North American Birds.* New York: Alfred A. Knopf, 1980.

Tobish, T. G., Jr. *Alaska Region, American Birds* (for 1993). New York: National Audubon Society.

————. *Alaska Region, National Audubon Society Field Notes* (for 1994–1999). New York: National Audubon Society.

Tobish, T. G., Jr., and M. E. Isleib. *Alaska Region, American Birds* (for the years 1989-1992). New York: National Audubon Society.

Udvardy, Miklos D. F. *The Audubon Society Field Guide to North American Birds— Western Region.* New York: Alfred A. Knopf, 1977.

Vliet, G. v., M. Schwan, R. Gordon, and S. Zimmerman. *Birds of Juneau, Alaska Checklist.* Juneau Audubon Society, 1993.

Walsh, P. J. *Checklist of the Birds of Mitkof Island.* Petersburg, Alaska, 1993.

Walsh, T. "Identifying Pacific Loons: Some Old and New Problems." *Birding* 20 (1): 12-28 (1988).

Watson, C. *A Bibliography of Bird Identification Articles in Five Journals, with Cross-References to a List of over 650 Species.* Oregon Field Ornithologists, Special Publication No. 4. P.O. Box 10373, Eugene, OR 97440, 1990.

West, G. C. *A Birder's Guide to the Kenai Peninsula, Alaska.* Homer: Pratt Museum and Birchside Studios, 1994.

Whitney, B., and K. Kaufman. "The *Empidonax* Challenge: Looking at *Empidonax,* Part II." *Birding* 17 (6): 277-287 (1985).

Zimmerman, S. T., and I. L. Jones. "Birding the Pribilof Islands, Alaska." *Birding* 23 (5): (1991).

INDEX

PHOTO CREDITS

Photos were provided by the author and other photographers and agencies. Photo position on pages is indicated after page number by t (top), b (bottom), m (middle), l (left), r (right).

R. H. Armstrong: Front Cover, 1, 5, 6, 10, 20t, 26b, 42, 48t, 49, 50, 51m, 52t, 55t, 56t, 57t, 57b, 60t, 60b, 63, 64t, 66t, 66b, 71, 72t, 72r, 73t, 73b, 74t, 74b, 75, 76t, 76b, 79, 81t, 82, 83t, 83b, 84t, 84b, 88b, 91, 95t, 96t, 96b, 97t, 97m, 98b, 99b, 100, 103, 104, 105t, 105b, 106t, 106b, 110b, 111t, 112, 114t, 114b, 115t, 115b, 117, 118t, 120t, 120b, 121, 122, 127t, 127m, 127b, 128t, 128b, 129t, 129b, 130b, 131t, 132b, 133t, 133b, 136t, 136b, 138t, 139t, 139b, 141t, 142t, 142m, 142b, 144, 146t, 146b, 147t, 147b, 148, 149t, 149b, 150b, 151, 156t, 156b, 157t, 157m, 157l, 157r, 160b, 161b, 163t, 163b, 165b, 172b, 175b, 178b, 179t, 179b, 188, 189b, 190, 191, 192b, 194, 195l, 196, 198t, 199b, 203r, 204l, 204r, 205, 206, 208, 210, 211, 212, 213b, 215, 216, 217t, 217b, 219, 220, 221t, 222t, 222b, 223, 224r, 224l, 225, 226t, 227, 228, 229, 230b, 231, 232, 233, 234, 235, 236, 237b, 240t, 241t, 241b, 242, 243, 245b, 251b, 252, 254t, 254b, 255t, 255b, 258, 261t, 261b, 263t, 265t, 267, 273b, 274, 275, 276, 277b, 278t, 278b, 279t, 280t, 280b, 281t, 282b, 284b, 286r, 287t, 287b, 290, 291t, 291b, 294, 295, 296, Back Cover (m) and (b).

S. Bahrt, VIREO: 124t, 124b.

R. Behrstock, VIREO: 72l.

T. Bomford, OXFORD SCIENTIFIC FILMS: 171.

R. & N. Bowers, VIREO: 34t, 45t, 46t, 58t, 77t, 125t.

A. Brady, VIREO: 199t.

K. Brink, VIREO: 284t.

J. D. Bulger, PHOTO RESEARCHERS, INC.: 198b.

G. V. Byrd, VIREO: 184t.

J. Cancalosi, VIREO: 101.

R. J. Chandler, VIREO: 111r, 145l, 145r, 240b.

B. Chudleigh, VIREO: 119b, 134, 218.

H. Clarke, VIREO: 80t, 244b, 256.

W. S. Clark, VIREO: 162.

P. G. Connors, VIREO: 140, 149m, 150t.

A. Cruickshank, VIREO: 67m.

H. Cruickshank, VIREO: 170.

R. Curtis, VIREO: 22t, 81b, 169t.

S. Dalton, PHOTO RESEARCHERS, INC.: 113t.

P. Davey, VIREO: 54t.

T. Davis, VIREO: 130t, 158r.

R. H. Day: 51b, 172t, 181.

B. de Lange, VIREO: 247.

N. Dennis, PHOTO RESEARCHERS INC.: 113b.

G. Dremeaux, VIREO: 126t.

J. L. Dunn: 135.

J. Dunning, VIREO: 259t, 266b.

L. Farr, VIREO: 62b.

K. W. Fink, PHOTO RESEARCHERS, INC: 54b.

S. Finnigan, VIREO: 116, 119t.

S. Fried, VIREO: 214, 250.

B. Gadsby, VIREO: 45b, 61b, 81m.

G. S. Grant, PHOTO RESEARCHERS, INC.: 29t.

W. Greene, VIREO: 78b, 85b, 192t, 195r, 262b, 293b.

C. H. Greenwalt, VIREO: 21, 239t, 239b, 262t, 289.

V. Hasselblad, VIREO: 209.

J. Helle: 197t.

B. Henry, VIREO: 193, 292t, 292b, 293t.

D. R. Herr, VIREO: 86l, 86r, 92t.

D. Hill, VIREO: 24t.

S. Holt, VIREO: 67t, 87r, 270, 288b.

M. P. Kahl, VIREO: 69b, 155t.

K. T. Karlson, VIREO: 22b.

A. Kraynik: 109.

S. LaFrance, VIREO: 26t, 32t, 174b.

S. J. Lang, VIREO: 23b, 52b, 273t, 286l.

G. Lasley, VIREO: 23t, 24b.

P. La Tourrette, VIREO: 168b, 264t.

C. Lensink: 285.

S. Lipschutz, VIREO: 61t.

M. Marin, VIREO: 201r.

Now enjoy these other beautiful bird books
from Alaska Northwest Books®.

Alaska's Birds
By Robert H. Armstrong
A convenient pocket guide including in-depth portraits of sixty-one representative species, including information on unusual behaviors, habitats, and seasonal adaptations. Softbound, 128 pages, $14.95, ISBN 0-88240-455-5

One Wing's Gift: Rescuing Alaska's Wild Birds
by Joan Harris
This extraordinary illustrated book tells the heartwarming stories of rescued wild birds from eagles to owls to chickadees. Marvel at the fascinating relationships that develop between birds and their caregivers. Softbound, 64 pages, $16.95, ISBN 0-88240-560-8

The Least of These: Wild Baby Bird Rescue Stories
By Joan Harris
Harris brings these gangly, delicate babies and their stories of rescue and rehabilitation to life on the page in meticulously detailed, Audobon-like drawings. Softbound, 64 pages, $16.95, ISBN 1-55868-860-9

Also, look for Alaska Northwest Books' Alaska Pocket Guide series, which includes *Alaska's Bears, Alaska's Fish, Alaska's History, Alaska's Mammals, Alaska's Mushrooms, Alaska's Seashore Creatures,* and *Alaska's Wild Plants,* with other titles to come.

Ask for these books at your favorite bookstore, or contact Alaska Northwest Books®.

Alaska Northwest Books®
An imprint of Graphic Arts Center Publishing Company
P.O. Box 10306, Portland, OR 97296-0306
503-226-2402

ABOUT THE AUTHOR

Robert H. Armstrong
(Homo sapiens)

Field marks. 69".

Behavior. Bob Armstrong has pursued a career in Alaska as a biologist, naturalist, and nature photographer since 1960. From 1960 to 1984, he was a fishery biologist and research supervisor for the Alaska Department of Fish and Game, an assistant leader for the Alaska Cooperative Fishery Research Unit, and associate professor of fisheries at the University of Alaska Fairbanks. He retired from the state of Alaska in 1984 to pursue broader interests in the natural history of Alaska and nature photography.

Voice. Bob Armstrong has led bird walks in Denali National Park and Preserve and for the Juneau Audubon Society, and has given numerous lectures and workshops throughout Alaska on bird identification and photographing birds. Besides the classic *Guide to the Birds of Alaska,* he has also written *Alaska's Birds,* a popular pocket guide to selected species, and coauthored *The Nature of Southeast Alaska,* an illustrated guide to the natural history of his home region. He has authored and coauthored more than 100 scientific and popular articles on fish, birds, mammals, plants, and insects in Alaska.

Habitat. Armstrong lives in Juneau, where he continues to photograph and write about the natural history of Alaska.

Notes. In recognition of his contributions to Alaska, he received an honorary doctorate of science from the University of Alaska in Juneau and the Wallace H. Noerenberg award for fishery excellence from the Alaska chapter of the American Fisheries Society.

Bob Armstrong with Black Currawong in Australia